Beyond Desire

Beyond Desire

Sexuality in Modern Tamil Literature

Kiran Keshavamurthy

OXFORD
UNIVERSITY PRESS

OXFORD
UNIVERSITY PRESS

Oxford University Press is a department of the University of Oxford. It furthers the University's objective of excellence in research, scholarship, and education by publishing worldwide. Oxford is a registered trademark of Oxford University Press in the UK and in certain other countries.

Published in India by
Oxford University Press
YMCA Library Building, 1 Jai Singh Road, New Delhi 110001, India

First Edition published in 2016

ISBN-13: 978-0-19-946745-7
ISBN-10: 0-19-946745-5

Typeset in Scala Pro 10/13
by Tranistics Data Technologies, Kolkata 700091
Printed in India by Replika Press Pvt. Ltd

To Amma, Appa, and Prashant
for their loving support

To Nikhil, Aniruddhan, and Veena
for always being with me

And to all those literary scholars who believe
that they are at the mercy of social scientists

Contents

Acknowledgements

Unlike most acknowledgements that begin by thanking friends and colleagues and then close friends and family, I choose to begin with the latter. After all, one cannot isolate the intellectual production from one's emotional life. I cannot be more grateful to my parents for not forcing me or my brother to study commerce or engineering, and for supporting our passion for literature and the humanities. Although I never studied Tamil formally in school (which probably explains my current interest in Tamil literature), I have my grandmother and great-aunt to thank for helping me learn the language from newspapers and popular magazines. Thier limitless warmth and generosity over the three bleak years I spent in Bengaluru studying commerce were a blessing. I thank them for their limitless warmth and kindness.

I am very lucky to have a literary scholar for a brother. My sincere thanks to Prashant for inspiring my interest in literature, for helping and guiding me at critical junctures of my life, and for all his invaluable comments and suggestions. I owe my professional success to you. Words cannot express my love. Heartfelt thanks to my sister Veena Rathnam for the years of love and support that have made the miles that separate us bearable. I also wish to thank my other sister,

Divya Saravanabhavan, whose spontaneous love and generosity have always warmed my heart.

I would like to thank Nikhil Govind and Aniruddhan Vasudevan, two of my closest friends, for their love and companionship. I am grateful to Nikhil for his patient willingness to listen to me talk about my work, and for his insightful comments that are a reflection of his literary sensibility. I cherish our stimulating conversations about modern Indian literature. Your companionship during those long lonely years of PhD at the University of California, Berkeley, was a tremendous source of comfort. As for Aniruddhan, I cannot thank you enough for loving me and for reassuring my intellectual and emotional insecurities. I will always treasure your cooking and the times we read Tamil poetry to each other or listened to Carnatic music. Watching you dance has been and will always be a great source of pride and admiration. I thank you for inspiring me with your ability to write in lucid and elegant Tamil.

A special thanks to Ryan Nelson Parker for her warmth and generosity, and for giving me a sense of home in Berkeley.

I am thankful to Bhavani Raman and Aparna Balachandran for helping me get around Chennai when I first began studying Tamil. I will fondly remember our times together.

I am very grateful to M. Kannan for introducing me to some of the finest modern writers in Tamil. This book would not have been possible without your help and support. I thank you and your wife for your generosity and hospitality during my visits to the French Institute of Pondicherry and your lovely home.

I am really thankful to A. Mangai and V. Arasu for their valuable suggestions and for introducing me to an excellent Tamil writer like Tanjai Prakash.

My heartfelt thanks to my PhD advisor George L. Hart for his kindness, and for inspiring me with his sheer love for Tamil literature. I will always cherish your translations of Caṅkam literature and Kamban's *Irāmāvatāram*, which are truly a reflection of your creativity and literary genius. I thank you for encouraging me to study modern Tamil literature at a time when everyone else was working on older Tamil literature. I would also like to thank Kausalya Hart for her dedication as a teacher and for sharing her knowledge of older Tamil literary and grammatical texts.

I will always be grateful to Dorothy Hale for showing interest in my work and for her kindness and intellectual support. I also wish to thank Catherine Mary Gallagher and Lawrence Cohen for their invaluable suggestions and comments.

A special thanks to Dilip Kumar for our conversations on modern Tamil literature and for promptly supplying me with all the books I needed.

I wish to thank all my friends at Berkeley, Gowri Vijayakumar and Joshua Williams for their love and for introducing me to fine theatre, Jennifer S. Clare for her sense of humour and for making San Francisco special, Preeti Shekar for her caring presence and generosity and for introducing me to wonderful friends, Zachary Burt for the caring friend that he is, Soham Mehta for his earnest affection and for inspiring me to workout, Richard Bacon for his kindness and pleasant company, Royce Conner for being a wonderfully caring man, Rooben Morgan for his generosity and cooking, Rebekah Collins for the gentle, loving woman that she is, Rebecca Whittington for being a wonderful flatmate and for her remarkable linguistic skills, Abhijeet Paul for his warmth and generosity, and Sanjay Barbora and Dolly Kikon for making Berkeley feel like home.

I wish to thank my friends and colleagues at the Centre for Studies in Social Sciences, Calcutta, Partha Chatterjee, Rimli Bhattacharya, Sibaji Bandyopadhyay, and Zaid Al Baset for enriching the book with their comments and insights.

A special thanks to my friends from Jaipur, Anthony Savari Raj, V. Rajesh, and Sanchit Mehta, for their love and warm company.

My love to Niyoti Aunty and Shanto Uncle for their infinite warmth and support.

My love and gratitude to Kadambari Misra for being a genuine friend.

And lastly, I am grateful to Oxford University Press India, for sheer professionalism and for sending this manuscript to fine reviewers.

Barring Janakiraman's *Ammā Vantāḷ* and Mauni's short stories, all other works quoted in this book have been translated by me.

Introduction

This book offers an interpretation of shifting scenarios of (largely) male desire in modern Tamil literature across the twentieth century. In exploring modern literary discourses of desire in the Tamil context, my aim is twofold—first, to trace shifting notions of the sexual, and, second, to complicate and unsettle normative structures of understanding the body, gender, and sexuality. The early precursors of the Tamil novel and short story, informed by anti-colonial, nationalist debates, reformed certain sexual bodies like those of the (upper-caste) widow, the prostitute, and even the promiscuous man through a socially arranged marriage.[1] The writings that concern me suggest an anxiety with the institution of marriage itself, where desire, no longer contained by marriage, threatens the normative form of the joint and conjugal family. This may not imply a consummation of desire in the sexual act, but is evident in the very admission of desire without marriage, where the mind or imagination rather than the body becomes the site where sexual norms are both established and transgressed. This, then, contradicts and complicates legal or even scholarly reductions of infidelity to an embodied sexual act. I thus foreground an uneasy correlation between desire and the body, where desire may not end in intercourse, but evokes bodily presence through senses of proximity like touch and senses of distance like sight, smell, and sound. Even in scenarios where desire is consummated in the body, it only results in disillusionment and the redirection of desire in spirituality or artistic creativity. This book thus resists the reduction of desire to intercourse and explores the sensual possibilities that include a whole range of intimacies not reducible to the sexual act. What emerges from a reading of these texts is a set of conflicted and fragile protagonists whose eroticism interpenetrates other modes of sensuality like spirituality, altruism, and creativity. Through a literary understanding of the sensual, I hope to show that the desiring subject is not reducible to her sexual body or even to her desire. The sensual, I argue, is a larger category with an existential and ontological significance, which constantly reconfigures the relationality between the embodied self and the other.

In this book, I trace a shift from early articulations of desire in the novelists of the late nineteenth and early twentieth centuries, where desire is reformed and operates within the confines of an arranged marriage, to a later scenario of desire where illicit desire becomes inseparable from its potential as a social force that reconfigures and binds marginalized subjects. The book analyses the writings of seven writers that are mostly focalized through men and their sexuality. My choice of these writers is determined by the fact that most of these writers formed part of a literary group that was partly influenced by one of the earliest writers of sexuality in Tamil, K.P. Rajagopalan (1902–1944). These writers shared thematic concerns and were also affected by one another's writings, as can be seen in their fiction and essays. Additionally, a reading of their texts reveals the productive possibilities of desire that undercuts the notion of a stable self to reconfigure male subjectivity. The men in these texts are embattled and vulnerable as they oscillate between longing and an unsuccessful transmutation of their desires in spirituality, altruism, or creativity. Although these texts fail to undo sexual difference, they imagine certain non-dominant forms of masculinity that are characterized by vulnerability and empathy. There is an attempt to consider the possibility of a form of masculinity and male sexuality that is not reducible to violence and oppression. Some of these literary thinkers also explore the role men could play in the everyday lives of women to enable them to participate in the project of female empowerment.

There is an emphasis, for instance, on the mostly empowering bonds of intimacy between men and women and among men that cannot be equated to violence and misogyny. I highlight sensitive and affirmative portrayals of women in the writers under consideration, and where necessary, critique the gendered limitations of their texts.

The women in these works are by no means insignificant objects; on the contrary, there is a significant shift in the representation of female sexuality not just among these writers but also within the oeuvre of a specific writer.[2] The female characters in many early male and female writers in Tamil are embodiments of chaste sexuality who conform to the dictates of arranged marriage and motherhood. As Tamil writer C.S. Lakshmi notes in her survey of female writers in Tamil, most of the early (dominant-caste) female writers were preoccupied with questions of female chastity and marriage. It is only in the 1960s and the 1970s that women writers, beginning with Rajam Krishnan, shifted their attention to other concerns like caste and female labour (see C.S. Lakshmi). This book partly reflects this transition from the sexual to the labouring body. The women characters in the earlier writers I discuss, such as K.P. Rajagopalan, T. Janakiraman (1921–1983), Karichan Kunju (1919–1992), M.V. Venkatram (1920–2000), and Mauni (1908–1985), are subjects and objects of desire and beauty that often undermine and remake male subjectivity. But the women in Dandapani Jeyakantan (1934–2015) and Tanjai Prakash (1943–2000) either resist and forswear desire to forge reformative friendships with men or transmute desire in the rhythms of labour to reconfigure and transcend their own sense of the self. The latter scenario also includes the possibility of exclusive intimacies among working-class women that render men vulnerable and increasingly redundant.

The ambiguous perception of the (dominant-caste) woman as an object of fear, desire, and devotion in the early writers of this book—by no means unique to modern Tamil literature—can be traced back to an important figure, in the early nationalist debates on the social and political emancipation of women, Tamil writer and poet Subramania Barati (1882–1921). Considered the forerunner of modern Tamil literature, Barati's creative and journalistic works present different perspectives, mostly on the question of gender and partly on sexuality. His three-part series of essays on the liberation of women and the long lecture he delivered at Pondicherry in 1918 argued for equal political rights and access to education. Barati exhorted women to realize their own potential and campaign for their rights. However, in some of his poetry, particularly his long poem '*Pāñcāli Capatam*' (Panchali's Vow: 1912) based on the game of dice and Draupadi's disrobing scene in Vyasa's Mahabharata, there emerges a distinctly different imagination of gender. This imagination inspired by his devotion to Shakti, the divine symbol of feminine power, perceived the masculine and feminine as equal and complementary domains of the self. The feminine was figured as Parashakti, the supreme goddess, resonating with the worship of Shakti where the feminine is equated with sacred and creative power. In '*Pāñcāli Capatam*', which Barati dedicated to Parashakti, Draupadi is represented both as a goddess embodying Bharat Mata or Mother India who invigorates the effete, colonized male subject along the path of nationalist struggle and as a vulnerable woman whose humiliation is an allegory of the colonized nation and of the subjugation of its women (Srinivasan 2014: 24). Woman as feminine is at once equal to and superior to man in the way she mediates the access to phallic power (Srinivasan 2014: 24). Most of the writers discussed in this book similarly imagine women as both a fallible and sacred power that alternately constitutes, redeems, seduces, and often emasculates or fragments the male protagonist. This moment of the loss of self-ownership conditions the possibility of reconfiguring male subjectivity to potentially enable more meaningful ways of being in the world. The relationships between men and women in these texts by no means dismantle sexual difference, but are nonetheless characterized by unusual, often gestural forms of intimacy that constantly negotiate with sexual difference.

By the 1930s, with the emergence of a writer like K.P. Rajagopalan, there emerges the possibility of women, or men for that matter, transgressing the social segregation of the sexes or choosing their own partners based on love. What is noteworthy is that these transgressions take place within the space of the house, upsetting the structural understanding of it as a private space that secures women and their sexualities from the public world of men. Here, I turn to feminist critiques of gender and kinship that have exposed the structural and functionalist distinction between the politico-juridical and the domestic domains of kinship. These critiques have argued against much scholarship on kinship for upholding essentialist binaries of male and female and production and reproduction. They have shown the correlation between the 'public' realm of male power and politics and the 'private' realm of the domestic, including sexuality and motherhood. These critiques have opened up the possibility of male contributions to domestic care and child-rearing and of female engagement in other forms of labour outside the domain of the house.[3] This book engages with the possibility of alternative masculinities that do not conform to what R.W. Connell (2005 [1995]) has called 'hegemonic masculinity', an ideal model of patriarchal masculinity that is characterized by autonomy, authority (political) power, wealth, sexual domination and monogamy, and juridical rights. The male characters in this book are not only undermined by women and their own desires for them, they also, in some instances, practice abstinence (without being able to altogether renounce worldly life or the dividends to be had from a patriarchal system) as they are transformed into vulnerable embodiments of care and responsibility.[4] There is thus a sexual hierarchy that is retained even in the most caring and sensual relationships between men and women.

The sexual transgressions within the space of the household in Rajagopalan, or even in a later writer like T. Janakiraman, often take the form of sensual exchanges that undermine a stable sense of the self. Thus, male subjectivity in these works is undercut and reconfigured by (female) desire. The male protagonists in these works are conflicted by a perceived opposition between desire or love and their own autonomy and integrity as pious aesthetes and householders. If masculinity has been conventionally equated with autonomy, authority, and integrity, these men represent masculinities compromised by an imagined conflict between desire and duty or abstinence. Many of these men try to sublimate their desires, albeit mostly unsuccessfully, in asceticism and spirituality or acts of creativity, which strengthens their resolve to potentially transcend their sense of finitude. In the process of undermining conventional notions of masculinity, these texts produce wounded and tortured men who have to embrace their insecurities and even reorient their relationship to religion, family, and to the world at large to potentially arrive at more meaningful and liberating ways of being. That they only partially sublimate their desires enables an ongoing process of change and self-transformation. In complicating and historicizing masculinity and male sexuality, I draw attention to the fundamental instability of and disjunction between gender and sexuality.

While there have been edited anthologies of multidisciplinary enquiries of gender and sexuality, there have been very few book-length literary models of gender and sexuality in the modern and postcolonial South Asian context. Although these anthologies have addressed the sexual in various fields ranging from law to popular culture, they have not adequately addressed literary articulations of the sensual, which includes, but also goes beyond, the sexual act. While there are many social histories of modern literature in Hindi, Urdu, and Bengali, literary analyses of premodern literature in Sanskrit and of Indian writing in English, little has been produced in terms of monographs on modern Indian literature in the vernacular. This book attempts to fill that gap. It is also the first sustained meditation in English on genders and sexuality in modern Tamil prose or, for that matter, in modern south-Indian literatures, and thus contributes to the existing scholarship on these topics. I refer in particular to earlier literary critiques of gender and sexuality in the precolonial, colonial, and postcolonial contexts by Ruth Vanita and Salim Kidwai's anthology *Same-Sex Love in India: A Literary History* (2000), Ruth Vanita's *Gandhi's Tiger and Sita's Smile: Essays on Gender, Sexuality and Culture* (2005), and a few historical and literary works on the predominant model of South Asian masculinity—the colonial and its construction of the Hindu male ascetic—which include Mrinalini Sinha's *Colonial Masculinity: The 'Manly' Englishmen and the 'Effeminate Bengali' in the Late Nineteenth Century* (1995), Indira Chowdhury's *The Frail Hero and Virile History: Gender and the Politics of Culture in Colonial Bengal* (1998), Priyamvada Gopal's *Literary Radicalism in India: Gender, Nation and the Transition to Independence* (2005), and Anjali Arondekar's *For the Record: On Sexuality and the Colonial Archive* in India (2009). Though Vanita and Kidwai's anthology has focused more on a broad historical spectrum of sexual intimacies, there has not been a consistent engagement with sexuality in any particular literature(s) in the Indian context. Further, there seems to be at least an implicit assumption that same-sex sexual relations are inherently unconventional or emancipated and those between men and women are necessarily conventional. This book reveals the possibility of sensual bonds between men and women that often resist sexual definition and are perceived as transgressive in different historical moments of modern Tamil literature. These bonds possess an ontological significance for the characters as they negotiate their relationship with the world and its norms. Vanita's *Gandhi's Tiger and Sita's Smile* is a more detailed intertextual analysis of various premodern and modern Indian-language texts that historicizes sexual personhood and reveals the enmeshments and divergences of gender and sexuality in the pre-colonial, colonial, and postcolonial Indian context.

The scholarship on colonial masculinity by Sinha and Gopal is closer to the scholarship of some of the early writers whom I have discussed and are more pertinent to its focus. In *Colonial Masculinity*, Mrinalini Sinha traces the mutual implication of modern Western and traditional Indian conceptions of masculinity in imperial politics. She exposes the inconsistencies in colonial rule and its professed ideals of masculinity and discusses the way notions of effeminacy were introduced to justify racial exclusions from colonial institutions like courts of law, the public service commission, and the Indian volunteer corps. Her book, though a purely historical study, is useful in analysing gender in its intersections with class, caste, and national categories.

Indira Chowdhury's *The Frail Hero and Virile History* and the more recent *Masculinity, Asceticism, Hinduism: Past and Present Imaginings of India* (2011) by Chandrima Chakraborty, which extends the scope of Sinha's work, examine nationalist discourses of masculinity and Hindu asceticism. Chowdhury's book focuses on the contrasting imagery of the figure of the heroic goddess Durga as Mother India and Indian woman and the spiritual recuperation of the seemingly effeminate Bengali man's masculinity by Swami Vivekananda. Chakraborty's readings of Bankim Chandra Chattopadhyay, Rabindranath Tagore, Mahatma Gandhi, Raja Rao, V.D. Savarkar, M.S. Golwalkar, and others reveal how ideas of masculinity and Hindu asceticism came to be reworked for cultural and political purposes. Over the colonial period she observes that Indian leaders and the literati were impelled to contest colonialist views of Hindu effeminacy. In the process, asceticism, she argues, became a critical site for notions of masculinity, especially for the Hindu right.

I depart from these works by drawing attention to men who are conflicted by a perceived opposition between desire and a spiritualized sense of autonomy and self-control. Their attempt to sublimate desire in piety or asceticism is mostly unsuccessful, thus undermining and reconfiguring male subjectivity. In *Literary Radicalism in India*, Gopal explores the representation of masculinity as a lived experience and as a social category in the writings of Urdu writer Saadat Hasan Manto (1912–1955). Masculinity in these writings, Gopal observes, is undercut by female sexual indifference, particularly in the mercenary figure of the prostitute and the refusal of the woman to return or reassure male desire and autonomy. What reflects the argument in my own work is that, according to Gopal, Manto's depictions of male sexuality—unlike female sexuality—is characterized by what Gopal calls a 'lyrical metonymy' and does not provide metaphors for social exploitation or function as the point of departure for social critique (2005: 93). Manto, like the writers mentioned in this book, develops an aesthetic to describe the sensuality of nature and male desire. Male sexuality in Manto, Gopal argues, becomes an occasion to observe sexuality as an object in itself, with an emphasis on pleasure and innocence rather than a means through which social criticism is effected (2005: 93). Though it is broadly true that most literary representations of female sexuality, particularly those by women writers, emphasize the structural inequities or violence that produces female desire and subjectivity, it obviously does not imply that masculinity or male desire is outside the realm of ethics and politics. In fact, one of the concerns of the writers I discuss is to precisely address the greater constraints around female choice and agency while also revealing the power of a woman to desire and simulate desire to the point of blurring the very boundaries that are necessary for sexual identity and meaning. This becomes clearer in my later chapters on Dandapani Jeyakantan and Tanjai Prakash where I gesture at models of fallen masculinity and the way sensuality opens up other possible ways of being in the world. Thus, desire in Jeyakantan is channelized in cross-gender bonds of asexual companionship and altruism, and in Prakash, the betrayed desires of women for the male protagonist are redirected to form the basis of a labouring collective of women belonging to different castes.

Significant later accounts of masculinity and male sexuality include more recent literary criticism like Nikhil Govind's *Between Love and*

Freedom: The Revolutionary in the Hindi Novel (2014). Govind traces the moral genealogy of primarily the male revolutionary in Bengali and Hindi novels of the interwar period. While Bengali novelists construct a moral revolutionary who eschews the use of violence, the later revolutionaries in the Hindi novels are morally ambiguous as they introspect the ethical use of violence as a means to political, social, and individual freedom. What interests me is the way in which anti-colonial revolutionary politics and male sexuality are intermeshed, so that by the 1930s, as Govind argues, the revolutionary becomes an interruption in the apathetic middle-class household opening up a space for political and sexual desire. His book directly speaks to my own in important ways. Like Govind's book, desire in my book operates across the porous realms of the private and the public in Tamil society. Although the male subjects in my work are not driven by political desires, their sexual desires are catalysts that enable them to reconfigure their relationship with the world and their own subjectivities. Like Govind's revolutionaries, male subjectivities in my work are undercut by (female) desire, which renders the protagonists vulnerable and subject to change. Desire becomes a productive agent that compels men to partially reorient their desires in spirituality, altruism, and reform, or in acts of creativity.

Scholarship on the Tamil-speaking regions has largely been historical in nature (see Eugene F. Irschick, V. Geetha and S.V. Rajadurai, Sumathi Ramaswamy, and A.R. Venkatachalapathy). The bulk of literary scholarship in English and Tamil has essentially focused on premodern Tamil, starting from the Caṅkam period during the turn of the first millennium to poetic genres composed in the fourteenth and fifteenth centuries. This book thus emerges in the absence of any sustained form of literary criticism in Tamil or English on modern Tamil literature. Literary criticism, understood as an evaluation of modern prose literary texts, is itself a relatively recent phenomenon that emerged in the first decades of the twentieth century with writers and critics like V.V.S. Iyer (1881–1925), but in a more sustained fashion after the 1930s. Even as later critics like K.N. Subramaniam (1912–1988) drew from various strands of western European and Russian literary criticism and Sanskrit aesthetics to formulate a modern category of Tamil literary criticism, there remained a gap between their formulations and their actual practice of reading texts.

The form that these exercises of literary evaluation took were brief and rather prescriptive, and summary book reviews that expressed like or dislike for a writer by comparing the writer to a list of other writers. What was missing, were the protocols of textual interpretation that went beyond personal likes and dislikes based on selective surveys. It is only since the mid-1980s and the 1990s that literary critics like K. Kailasapathy, Kartikesu Sivathambi, T.M.C. Ragunatan, and, more recently, Jeyamokan, have attempted to offer more comprehensive readings of the Tamil novel and short-story drawing from various strands of romanticism, new historicism, and post-structuralism.

This book also makes an intervention in the field of gender and sexuality studies both in the Western and Indian contexts. It aims to contribute to a relatively new field of masculinity studies in the South Asian context. I refer to two recent anthologies that pluralize culturally specific forms of masculinity and the networks of care that men forge with women and other men: *Reframing Masculinities: Narrating the Supportive Practices of Men* (2007) edited by Radhika Chopra and *South Asian Masculinities: Contexts of Change, Sites of Continuity* (2004), edited by Radhika Chopra, Caroline Osella, and Filippo Osella. Another recent publication that has been particularly pertinent to my work has been Filippo and Caroline Osella's ethnographic study *Men and Masculinities in South India* (2006) where they explore the tensions between men's roles as husbands and householders and their intimate bonds with other men in Kerala. Both these volumes have been crucial in opening up other understandings of masculinity that are not already tainted by power and violence but, on the contrary, are characterized by care and responsibility. This, of course, does not preclude the possibility of power and sexual hierarchies between and among men and women. This becomes pertinent to my discussion of cross-gender relations in Chapters 2 'T. Janakiraman: Male Sexuality and the De-Idealized Woman', Chapter 3 'Karichan Kunju and M.V. Venkatram: Between Desire and Disease', and Chapter 5 'Dandapani Jeyakantan: Loving Outcastes, Spirituality, and Reformation', on Janakiraman, Karichan Kunju, and Dandapani Jeyakantan, respectively, where the mutual recognition of lack and abjection becomes the basis for an empowering bond that forswears desire to finally end either in asceticism and death or in the reformation of desire and the world. Even as these narratives depict unconventional relationships between men and women outside the fold of marriage and family, there is no denial of sexual difference or hierarchy.

K.P. Rajagopalan: His Literary Milieu and Legacy

In this section, I briefly outline the literary linkages between K.P. Rajagopalan and the writers I discuss in the following chapters. However, before outlining the literary cartography of the book, it is important to note the literary and political milieu of the concerned writers. Tamil prose had for the longest time taken the form of commentaries on premodern Tamil grammars and literary texts. In his history of print in colonial south India, Stuart Blackburn (2003) traces the rise of commercial printing and publishing in the nineteenth century, although the seventeenth century had already witnessed the arrival of Jesuit and Lutheran missionaries who set up printing presses along either coast of south India. Some of the earliest texts to be printed in Tamil and other Indian languages were translations of the Bible and other religious catechisms, grammars, and interlingual dictionaries between south Indian and European languages and folklore. Blackburn goes on to underline the role of several Jesuit missionaries in creating Tamil discursive prose. The most significant among these was the Italian Jesuit missionary and Tamil scholar Constanzo Beschi's (1680–1742) *Paramārttakuruviṉ Kataikaḷ* (The Stories of Paramarthaguru: 1822), a satirical piece on a religious leader and his equally obtuse disciples. By 1800, Madras (now Chennai) had become the centre of printing and publishing where pundits and munshis, who were earlier involved in printing, became publishers in their own right. Blackburn shows how Tamil, like other South Asian languages, became an object of new kinds of knowledge production and the focus of new kinds of social and political mobilization. Thus, the printing of the Tamil classics that were 'rediscovered' by the pre-eminent Tamil scholar and lexicographer U.V. Saminathaiyer (1855–1942) were considered a mark of the antiquity of Dravidian civilization, which was constructed by Dravidian nationalists in the early twentieth century in opposition to Europeans and Sanskrit Brahmanism.[5]

Journalism, with the advent of printing presses and commercial publishing in the nineteenth century, produced a modern idiom of Tamil prose that some early writers drew from, even as it was considered inferior to fictional writing. In his literary history of the Tamil novel *Tamil̲ Nāval Ilakkiyam* (Tamil Novel Literature: 1968), the Sri Lankan Tamil Marxist literary critic K. Kailasapathy dwells on the proliferation of hundreds of Tamil news journals from 1830 onwards. He reveals the overlapping of journalistic and narrative styles in some of the early novels and the rising popularity of the novel as a 'worldly', 'spoken', and realist idiom that (awkwardly) encapsulated earlier literary genres and invited the reader to identify with its characters and their everyday experiences. Early examples of the Tamil novel most famously included Samuel Vedanayagam Pillai's (1826–1889) *Piratāpa Mutaliyār Carittiram* (1879), A. Madhavaiya's (1872–1925) *Patmāvati Carittiram* (1898), and Rajam Iyer's (1872–1898) *Kamalāmpāḷ Carittiram* (1897).[6] Vedanayagam Pillai, B.R. Rajam Iyer, and A. Madhavaiya had either directly or indirectly contributed to the nationalist freedom struggle through their writings. Vedanayagam Pillai, a judge, for instance, had written the first Tamil novel *Piratāpa Mutaliyār Carittiram* that through its ideal characters valorized feminine virtues of chastity and domesticity. He also wrote *Nītinūl* (1859) and *Peṇ Mati Mālai Peṇ Kalvi Peṇ Man̲am* (1978), a book of poetry and aphorisms, respectively, aimed at educating and training young women to become good mothers of future citizens in a soon-to-be-independent India. A. Madhavaiya, a student of Madras Christian College and an officer in the salt department of the colonial government, wrote in both English and Tamil. He campaigned for female education and widow remarriages and even argued for raising the age of consent for women.[7] His first novel *Patmāvati Carittiram* (1898), like some of his other novels, used largely stereotypical notions of gender and reinforced marriage as the solution to male sexual waywardness and female prostitution. Rajam Iyer, another bilingual lawyer, wrote his only novel *Kamalāmpāḷ Carittiram*, which again advocated chastity and marriage for men and women. What is salient to all these early novels is that they took the form of *carittirams* or fictional biographies of virtuous female characters. Many of the novels by these writers included traditional poetic forms, spoken idioms and proverbs, and historical allusions and references to earlier periods and texts. The rambling plots of these novels often took the shape of a romantic fantasy full of incredible and melodramatic twists only to end with a happy reinforcement of virtue, religiosity, love, and marriage. Such reinforcement, as Kailasapathy argues, could be a partial defence against the estranging impact of Western education and the dissolution of the social fabric of the village and the extended family with urban migrations to the colonial urban centre of Madras.

There were some significant and prolific women novelists of Rajagopalan's time, including Ammani Ammal, the Gandhian V.M. Kodainayagiammal (1901–1960) who was known for writing scores of reformist novels that ranged from communal harmony, widow remarriage, patriotism, the evils of liquor, and the need for women particularly to adopt Gandhism to reform their violent and drunken husbands, and the doctor and writer S. Thiripurasundari or Lakshmi (1921–1987), who like the others, was invested in marriage and described the sufferings of middle-class and upper-caste/Brahman wives in their families.[8] Another woman novelist Mathuram Bhoothalingam or Krithika (1915–2009) most well known for her novel *Vāsavēcvaram* (1966) was a bilingual writer who addressed social issues faced by women of her time besides producing a significant corpus of children's literature. Another important woman writer was Rajam Krishnan (1925–2014) whose social-realist novels, inspired by Gandhi, dealt initially with the plight of middle-class Brahman women in the nationalist and postcolonial period, but later focused largely on the fraught intersections of gender and class.[9] So many of her later novels particularly *Rōjā Itaḻkaḷ* (Rose Petals: 1973), *Karippu Maṇikaḷ* (Grains of Salt: 1979), *Cēṟṟil Maṉitarkaḷ* (People in the Mud: 1982), and *Maṇṇakattu Pūntuḷikaḷ* (The Fine Drops under the Earth: 1988) address a number of issues, from the economic and sexual exploitation of working-class women and working-class revolutions that bring exploited men and women together, to female foeticide and infanticide, and the plight of marginalized communities in the face of modernization. Unlike some of the other women writers like C.S. Lakshmi (b. 1944), Sivasankari (b. 1942), or even Vasanthi (b. 1938), Krishnan's oeuvre spanned a wide social spectrum of female characters. Also noteworthy is the fact that Krishnan sometimes suggests the possibility of collaborations between men and women instead of simply positing the sexes as polar opposites.

All these writers are Brahman or dominant-caste non-Brahman writers, and the political concerns of their fictional works, if any, were at least initially, restricted to the nationalist movement and Gandhi's ideologies of non-violence and spiritual abstinence rather than more immediate local and political events.[10] Neither Rajagopalan nor any of the other writers discussed in this book seem to be concerned with the emergence of the non-Brahman Dravidian movement or its radical phase, the self-respect movement, headed by the anti-caste iconoclast E.V. Ramasami Naiker (1879–1973) or Periyar (The Great One), as he was known. Most of the authors I discuss occasionally thematize the problem of caste, and in certain instances, caste is subsumed by the seemingly more amorphous or generic category of class. Rajagopalan, like many other serious writers of his time, reserved his non-fictional essays for his explicit political concerns and his fiction for his romantic imagination. Thus, in his essays he wrote admiringly of the Bengali revolutionary Aurobindo Ghose, who by the late 1930s had taken refuge from colonial persecution in Pondicherry, a French political haven in British India.[11] He also wrote the earliest biography of Subramania Barati who was also directly involved in nationalist political debates. However, his stories only make oblique references to the nationalist movement and give primacy to love and intimacy, particularly in the lonely and itinerant lives of freedom fighters and political revolutionaries. One of the purposes of this book is to tentatively explore the reasons and implications of the conspicuous absence of the non-Brahman movement in these writers.[12] One apparent reason seems to be the fact that all these writers were Brahman, and many enjoyed the privileges of a government office. The concentration of bureaucratic power in the hands of the Brahmans who constituted a small fraction of the population of the then Madras Presidency was one of the primary reasons for dominant-caste non-Brahman resentment. That the loyalties of most of the Brahmans lay with the Congress and Mohandas Karamchand Gandhi, further alienated them from the elite non-Brahman leadership. The support by some Brahman political leaders for the imposition of Hindi as a national language at different points in the 1930s and the 1960s, that lead to many violent protests, reinforced the general perception of Brahmans as Aryan outsiders out to vanquish Tamils. Another reason for the absence of a direct engagement with the local political context also has to do with the refusal of these writers to mix the literary with the political. Many of these writers believed engaging with politics in their fiction or instrumentalizing their fiction for a social purpose would compromise the aesthetic quality of their work. Of the earlier group of writers, the upper-caste non-Brahman short-story writer Pudumaippittan was a prominent exception to most of his contemporaries in his explicit and consistent engagement with social issues such as (urban) poverty and disease. A third reason suggests the importance of religion and spirituality in partially reorienting desire in some of these writers, which ran counter to the rationalist principles of the non-Brahman, particularly the self-respect movement. In fact, Periyar had alienated many of his supporters with his spectacular crusade against idolatry and religious texts.

In fact, V.V.S. Iyer wrote what is considered the earliest collection of modern short stories, *Maṅkaiyarkkariciyiṉ Kātal* (Mankairkkarici's Love) before K.P. Rajagopalan's time.[13] These stories, full of magic and romantic intrigue, appeared more than 30 years after Vedanayagam Pillai's *Piratāpa Mutaliyār Carittiram*. After 1930, all well-known short-story writers of the time were exposed to English education and many of them did not betray any knowledge of traditional poetic forms even when they wrote free-verse poetry (*vacana kavitai*). The most well known of the early short-story writers of the 1930s and the 1940s, including Rajagopalan, wrote for the literary journal *Maṇikkoṭi* (1933–9); many of them believed in not instrumentalizing literature for social purposes, although this is belied by some of their writings where many of them elaborated the social and psychological estrangement of the modern individual.[14]

Rajagopalan was one of the earliest short-story writers of modern Tamil literature to write about sexual and romantic themes. Like some of his contemporaries, his writings made oblique references to the nationalist struggle and romanticized the figure of the nationalist freedom fighter. However, his stories were more focused on questions of love and companionate marriage, which were not devoid of politics understood in a broader sense. The social and political potential of Rajagopalan and the writers who were to follow him lay in subtly transgressing, or even radicalizing, relationships between and among men and women, within and without the boundaries of marriage and family. Although Rajagopalan was one of the much criticized writers of the *Maṇikkoṭi* group of writers, he became an aesthetic model to be admired and emulated by younger writers including S. Mani or 'Mauni', T. Janakiraman, D. Narayanasami or 'Karichan Kunju', M.V. Venkatram, and Saminatha Athreya to mention a few. The literary lineage that was established between Rajagopalan and some of these writers will be elaborated in the following chapters. For now, I briefly explore the literary linkages between Rajagopalan and his successors.

As noted earlier, one of the strands that ties Rajagopalan to the later writers is their sensual ideal of love and intimacy. Rajagopalan, like Subramania Barati, based this on the ideals espoused by the English romantic poets John Keats and Percy Bysshe Shelley. For Rajagopalan, the true value of love could only be experienced when it was unfulfilled and immortalized in the lover's heart. The emphasis of his stories was on the sensual purity of romantic longing that was often evoked through nature or music. The brief intensity of the romantic encounters in his stories was characterized by a heightened awareness of the beloved's presence, captured by fleeting moments of sight, sound, or touch.

If desire can be affirmed with certainty in Rajagopalan's stories, it is conflicted, and even simulated, in the later writers. The pious male protagonists of Janakiraman's novels, for instance, try to practice abstinence even though they are unable to forswear desire altogether. In many instances, they are compelled to partially reorient their desires in altruism, music, or spirituality. Their imagined conflict with their own sexuality determines their perception of women, who are objects of both desire and veneration. Janakiraman delineates an ambiguous moral bifurcation of women, attempting to desexualize or sacralize and sympathize with them and their desires. Janakiraman's narratives are constituted by an irresolvable tension between sexual transgression and an eroticized prohibition that results in the acknowledgement of male (and female) desire and the partial reorientation of desire in social reform and creative activity.

In the novels of Karichan Kunju and M.V. Venkatram, there is a similar engagement with the pious Brahman man, who is torn by a conflict between desire and spirituality. However, the difference lies in the fact that this conflict is embodied in both the writers by the diseased male body. In Kunju's novel *Pacittamāṉiṭam* (Hungry Humanity: 1978), disease and disability assume a visible form that compels the itinerant protagonist to search for sexual recognition in the pretext of an apparent longing for spiritual transcendence. It discusses a case of failed narcissism, where the protagonist is unable to acquire a lasting sense of self-identity through the other, which ultimately compels him to reconfigure his sense of the self by channelizing his desire in ethical acts of compassion and altruism.

In M.V. Venkatram's *Kātukaḷ* (Ears: 1992), disease takes the invisible form of psychological disorder. The protagonist's visual and aural hallucinations of gods and women dramatize the desire for sexual self-recognition. Like some of the other writers of this book, the trope of the woman as goddess and seductress who alternately undercuts and assures male subjectivity is seen in Venkatram's novel. Again, there is no resolution to a psychic oscillation between imaginary signs of self-estrangement and self-ownership that dramatize the quest for identity.

One of the primary concerns of this book has been to explore desire as a creative force that enables real or imaginary possibilities of reconfiguring meaning and subjectivity. In Mauni's short stories, romantic separation and loss produce dreamlike scenarios that foreground the fluidity of the self. Characters seem to magically substitute or overlap with one another to the extent of blurring temporalities and the distinction between perception and reality. The woman is again an inscrutable object of desire and awe, although the female characters in some of Mauni's later stories are invested with greater inner complexity. The triangular scenarios of desire in Mauni's stories resonate with those of Rajagopalan or Janakiraman, and like Rajagopalan, there is a return to older tropes of love as waiting and separation that can be traced back to Sanskrit playwrights like Kalidasa and the ancient corpus of Tamil Caṅkam poetry. But the difference in Mauni's triangles lies in the fact that there is not such a sharp moral bifurcation of women, or even men. Mauni's stories suggest that the temporality of romantic loss and agony is characterized by the blurring of the boundaries between the self and other, which dissolves moral oppositions and suggests universal states of self-alienation.

Jeyakantan's works share the spiritual preoccupations of the earlier writers and gesture at the possibility of reorienting desire in altruism. A common theme is the desire and mutually redemptive love between male and female outcastes. Desire, in Jeyakantan, is renounced and transmuted into an abstinent or even ascetic form of companionship that purports to redeem the stigma of being an outcaste. Another way of addressing sexual stigma, for Jeyakantan, is the transmutation of desire in asexual forms of male–female friendships that aim to reform the world.

For the last writer in this book, Tanjai Prakash, the insatiability of desire makes it a creative agent that forms the basis for self-remodelling. Here, desire possesses a deceptive impetus whose true object is not the body but the desire of and recognition by the other. Prakash's novels share a particular scenario of desire where its repeated evocation and betrayal by the male protagonist compels the working-class female characters to redirect their betrayed desires for him, and consequentially for each other, in labour. Through acts of labour, these working-class women are able to reconfigure their own sense of the self. Desire and labour thus reinforce each other in an ongoing process of becoming that is enabled only when the women internalize the male protagonist. Thus, the female body, by internalizing the unattainable male protagonist, is activated to become a labouring body. It is in this way that the act of creation through labour is couched in a masculinist and heterosexist axis even as it focuses on the (self) transformative abilities of the female body.

Chapter Organization

This book looks at the sensual possibilities of desire in the porous realms of the domestic and public spaces of Tamil society, where desire does not necessarily coincide with the sexual act. Sensuality, I argue, becomes the lens through which the ontological possibilities of the embodied sexual subject in Tamil literature are explored. Chapter 1, 'K.P. Rajagopalan: Desire and Ideal Love', discusses Rajagopalan's stories, where illicit desire moves between the domestic and public spaces, and may not be consummated in the body. And if desire is consummated, it has to be legitimized by love and marriage. I also look at instances where love cannot lead to marriage, but persists as a sensuous memory and ideal in the lover's heart. I also note a paradigm of triangular desire in these stories, where one of the characters mediates the relationship between the other two, and the gendered implications of having a male or a female mediator.

Chapter 2, 'T. Janakiraman: Male Sexuality and the De-Idealized Woman', extends the idea of the sexually fraught space of the domestic in the novels of one of Rajagopalan's literary disciples,

T. Janakiraman. The Brahman male protagonists of these novels are torn between their sexual desires and their religious integrity. To offset the danger of desire, they idealize the beauty of the women they desire. This idealization is couched in the apparently contradictory impulses of desire and devotion or duty. The crisis in the novels occurs when the woman asserts her desiring self, thus compelling the de-idealization of the woman and the acknowledgement of male sexuality. Like Rajagopalan, triangular desire is a motif in Janakiraman's novels as well, where the male protagonist's conflicting desires for two contrasting women precipitates a crisis that compels the partial sublimation of desire in artistic creativity or social reformation.

Chapter 3, 'Karichan Kunju and M.V. Venkatram: Between Desire and Disease', is a comparative study of Karichan Kunju and M.V. Venkatram, who also display the contradiction between desire and devotion in the diseased body. The experience of disease, I argue, is at once interpreted as an expiatory sign of sexual excess and as enabling certain modes of sensuality. The diseased body embodies an ascetic Brahman masculinity that becomes the site of sexual transgression, but also a marker of a stigmatized existence that has to be endured in the longing for spiritual freedom. By embracing abjection and negotiating their desires, the protagonists are able to remake their selves.

Chapter 4, 'Mauni: Desire as Dream and Fantasy', a comparative study, examines the works of Mauni, a short-story writer, who reflects some of Rajagopalan's thematic concerns with the sensuality of romantic loss and longing. Mauni produced some of the most experimental short stories in the history of modern Tamil literature. Like his predecessor, Mauni sensuously evoked illicit desire and love through dreams and fantasies, without allowing a physical consummation. He was invested in the question of romantic longing, loss, and the power of the imagination to produce oneiric scenarios of sensual desire that miraculously substitute or replicate the loss of a loved one. In many ways, his stories foreground the metonymic slippage that characterizes the movement of desire from one part-object to another. His characters dramatize and narrativize desire that can be neither completely satisfied nor extinguished, giving his stories an open-ended quality. Mauni's fantastical sequences were similar to Janakiraman's in the way they invoked the female body as an unsettling object of desire and devotion. Like in the works of the earlier writers, here, too, male integrity is constantly threatened and reconfigured by (female) desire.

Chapter 5, 'Dandapani Jeyakantan: Loving Outcastes, Spirituality, and Reformation', spells a shift from the earlier emphasis on the intersections between desire and spirituality. This chapter and the next analyse the social and transformative potential of desire to bind and reconfigure marginalized individuals and communities. A recurring motif in Jeyakantan's novels is the empowering love between outcastes, which cuts across hierarchies. Such a love reforms desire to a non-sexual companionship between men and women that may lead to asceticism or social reformation. If the earlier writers were engaged with the fraught relationship between desire and love, in Jeyakantan's novels, asexual love between the marginalized represents the idealized possibility of an egalitarian society.

Chapter 6, 'Tanjai Prakash: Between Desire and Labour', extends the social potential of desire in the novels of Tanjai Prakash. In Prakash's novels, the repeated disappointments of desire by the body suggest that the true object of desire is not the body but the other's desire and recognition. If the ultimate aim of desire is to overcome the ontological disparity between the self and the other, this is never fulfilled. In striving to attain identity, however, betrayed desire is sublimated in creative labour, thus enabling individual and collective forms of self-realization. The social potential of desire to negotiate between the individual and the social; between identity and difference becomes crucial when it comes to establishing and transforming labouring communities of women belonging to different castes.

Notes

1. It is important to distinguish the promiscuous man from the polygamous man. There was nothing in Brahmanical law that prohibited Hindu men from marrying more than one woman or having a mistress. While the desire of the polygamous man was directed at a particular few women, the promiscuous man's lust was, in principle, at least, indiscriminate. The ideal, of course, with the nationalist debates on female education and marriage, was an emphasis on chastity and monogamy for both sexes. See J. Derrett and M. Duncan (1973).
2. Some of the writers I discuss, like Mauni and Tanjai Prakash, invest their women characters with greater aesthetic complexity. Mauni's male and

female characters possess a psychological depth that complicates the question of desire and sexual difference through a humanistic understanding of existence. Prakash's female characters, on the other hand, may not be distinct characters invested with an equal degree of psychological complexity as their individuality is subordinated to their function as self-transformative, labouring bodies.

3. For a discussion of feminist critiques of gender and kinship as a site for the reproduction of gender and class inequalities, see Jane Fishburne Collier, and Sylvia Junko Yanagisako (1987).
4. For an analysis of masculinity, the male role, hegemonic masculinity, and its variants, see R.W. Connell (2005 [1995]: 1–25). Here, Connell maps out a hierarchy of masculinities that draw from a hegemonic model of masculinity. He uses hegemonic masculinity as a purely analytical category that is reinforced by other 'lesser' masculinities and what he calls a hierarchy of emphatic femininities that draw dividends from it.
5. For a critical understanding of the nineteenth-century reception and circulation of the Tamil classics, see V. Rajesh (2014).
6. In a revealing essay entitled 'The First Six Novels in Tamil', the Czech scholar of Tamil Kamil V. Zvelebil (1986: 1–14) points out four other novels that were published between *Piratāpa Mutaliyār Carittiram* and *Kamalāmpāḷ Carittiram*—the Sri Lankan Muslim writer Mukammatu Kacim Sitilevai Marikkar's *Ācāṉ Pī Carittiram* (1885), Vedanayagam Pillai's *Cukuṇā Cuntari* (1887), C.V. Gurusami Sarma's *Pirēmakalāvatyam* (1893), which had a definite influence on Rajam Iyer's novel, and Saravanmuthu Pillai's *Mōkaṉāṅki* (1895). Zvelebil also identifies a text written as early as 1775, but published in 1895 as narrative prose called *Vacaṉa Campiratāya Katai* by an unknown writer.
7. The legal age of sexual consent was equated in practice to the marriageable age for women. The explicit introduction of a marriageable age in law is only a recent phenomenon. For a biography of Madhavaiah, see Sita Anantha Raman (2005).
8. V.M. Kodainayagiammal was also the first woman to be on the editorial board of the literary journal *Jakaṉmōkiṉi* that published her contemporaries and was managed by her husband when she was imprisoned for participating in Gandhi's agitations against toddy, foreign liquor, and cloth, along with other women social workers and writers like Ambujam Ammal, Rukmany Lakshmipathy, and Vasumathi Ramaswamy. She continued to write prolifically in prison.
9. Many Tamil and Indian writers and poets writing from the 1920s to the 1940s were influenced by Gandhi and his ideas of non-violence

and abstinence. In the Tamil context, these included Chidambara Subramanian, *Maṇikkoṭi* writer C.S. Chellappa, N. Parthasarathi, M.S. Kalyanasundaram, and Subramania Barati.

10. In *Tamil̲ Ci̲rukatai Pi̲rakki̲ratu* (The Birth of the Tamil Short Story: 1974), a survey of the Tamil short story from 1920 to 1939, literary critic C.S. Chellappa mentions four major journals from the 1930s founded by four ardent nationalist agitators—R. Krishnamurthy's *Kalki*, T.S. Chokkalingam's *Gandhi*, V. Ramasami's *Maṇikkoṭi*, and Sangu Subramanian's *Cuntantira Caṅku*. Later, Chokkalingam along with K. Srinavasan co-edited *Maṇikkoṭi*. Chellappa identifies Krishnamurthy with the moderate faction of the Congress while B.S. Ramiah, co-editor of *Maṇikkoṭi* and the poet and writer N. Pichamurthy are identified as radical revolutionaries. This was reflected in their stories and the kinds of stories that were published in *Maṇikkoṭi*. See C.S. Chellappa (2002).
11. It is important to remember that the nationalist poet and writer Subramania Barati, and V.V.S. Iyer, another revolutionary writer who wrote the first short story in Tamil, met the Bengali revolutionary Aurobindo Ghose during their stay in Pondicherry (1908–18). Here, they—and subsequently Rajagopalan—were introduced to and influenced by the writings of Rabindranath Tagore and Bankim Chandra Chattopadhyay.
12. For a history of the non-Brahman movement and Tamil politics, see Irschick (1969, 1986), V. Geetha and S.V. Rajadurai (1998), Marguerite Ross Barnett (1976), Narendra Subramanian (1999), and Thomas R. Trautmann (2006). Trautmann traces the polarization between the Dravidian and the Aryan to the idea postulated by the missionaries F.W. Ellis and Caldwell of a Dravidian language family, of which Tamil was the oldest, as separate from that of the Aryan-Sanskritic posited by the philologist William Jones. Their theories of a distinct Dravidian language family and the 'discovery' and printing of the Tamil classics in the late nineteenth century partly fuelled the cultural nationalism of the non-Brahman movement. There was also the emergence of certain Dalit voices, most famously that of the anti-caste leader Ayoti Thass (1845–1914), and the activist and freedom fighter Rettaimalai Srinivasan (1860–1945) who were critical of caste privilege and Brahmanism during this period.
13. There is a difference of opinion on when the first short story was written. The literary writer and critic Jeyamokan believes that A. Madhavaiya wrote the first modern short story, possibly in the 1900s or in the 1910s.
14. For a history of *Maṇikkoṭi*, see B.S. Ramiah (1980).

1

K.P. Rajagopalan

Desire and Ideal Love

K.P. Rajagopalan was born in the temple town of Kumbakonam in 1902 to a modest Telugu Brahman family from the Karanakamma community. Soon after his birth, Rajagopalan's father, a railway clerk, shifted with his family from Kumbakonam to Tiruchirapalli. Rajagopalan completed his matriculation from the National College before moving back to Kumbakonam to complete his bachelor of arts at the Government Arts College. It is here that Rajagopalan studied English and Sanskrit literatures, particularly the English romantics Percy Bysshe Shelley (1792–1822) and John Keats (1795–1821), and the pre-eminent Sanskrit playwright Kalidasa (*c.* fifth century AD). His readings of the pre-eminent Bengali writers Bankim Chandra Chattopadhyay (1838–1894) and Rabindranath Tagore (1861–1941), inspired him to translate several of their works into Tamil later. Of the Russian writers, the writings of Leo Tolstoy won his admiration, which later prompted him to write a vivid biography of the writer.

His admiration for Tagore and Tolstoy was by no means an isolated phenomenon, but true of many other Indian writers of his generation. As the Tamil literary critic and writer B. Jeyamokan opines, Rajagopalan derived his idea of European modernism and aesthetics through his readings of Shelley and Keats, but more importantly Bankim and Tagore, of whom the latter had a definite impact on the generation of Tamil and Malayalam writers after the Bengal partition. This is suggested by the romanticism and idealism of his stories and his female characters that appeared to imitate their Bengali counterparts' exposure to European culture, education, and individualism. While the earliest prose writers in Tamil, particularly A. Madhavaiya and Vedanayakam Pillai, rooted their novels in the Tamil-speaking country, Rajagopalan was emblematic of a generation of Brahman writers whose works were set in an indefinite and universalizable location. As Jeyamokan suggests, Rajagopalan's female characters are educated, open-minded, and beautiful, and deliver dialogues in stage Tamil that betray their resemblance to Tagore's Brahmo women (see Jeyamokan 2003b and Kunju 1990).

Following his move to Madras, Rajagopalan became a full-time writer, publishing his works in several major albeit short-lived journals of the time including *Cutantira Caṅku*, *Maṇikkoṭi*, *Kalaimakaḷ*, *Cūrāvaḷi*, *Haṉumāṉ*, and *Hintustāṉ*. In his decade-long writing career, Rajagopalan produced around 94 short stories, a collection of essays and reviews, eight one-act plays, and translations of Bengali, Russian, and English literatures into Tamil. He also co-authored with P.G. Sundararajan (1910–2006) the first book of criticism on arguably the greatest figure of Tamil modernism, the poet and writer Subramania Barati. Like some of his contemporaries, the most well known of whom was Pudumaippittan (1906–1948), Rajagopalan led a life of hardship because of his inability to hold a permanent job and his rather idealistic insistence on relying solely on writing as a source of sustenance. This partly explains his prolific output in the span of a decade and the compromised quality of some of his short stories. However, unlike Pudumaippittan, who was admired by progressive Marxist writers like T.M.C. Ragunatan and Ponneelan for his depictions of poverty and discrimination, poverty and social injustice were never the chief subjects of K.P. Rajagopalan's fiction. Furthermore, Rajagopalan was criticized by the progressive writers, most famously by a fellow writer Chidambara Subramaniam, for what they believed were unjust and pornographic portrayals of women. He was accused, as were some of the other *Maṇikkoṭi* writers including Mauni, L.S. Ramamirtham, and B.S. Ramaiya, of producing formally innovative fiction that was unrelated to the everyday struggles of the poor and the disenfranchised.

The *Maṇikkoṭi* writers, dubbed as the creators of art for art's sake, defended their principle to revolutionize literature and aesthetics at a time when Tamil academics and readers were obsessed with older literature and refused to uncritically embrace every aspect of the old. Rajagopalan clearly supports this in his essay '*Putu Eḻuttu*' (New Writing, 1943) where he identifies trends set by three literary journals, *Āṉanta Vikaṭaṉ*, *Kalaimakaḷ*, and *Maṇikkoṭi*. Of these, Rajagopalan saw *Maṇikkoṭi* as the most radical, as it acknowledged the ultimate truth of poverty, disease, and sorrow, and promoted the struggle to enable change. In fact, many of the *Maṇikkoṭi* writers held conflict as the core of their revolutionary aesthetic spirit and were as political and progressive as some Marxist writers in their engagement with social inequality. Their writings suggest that their preoccupation with the sensual possesses a social potential of its own in the way it radicalizes man–woman relations. In his own defence, Rajagopalan believed his explorations of intimacy were a fraught but fundamental aspect of human subjectivity that could not be subordinated or opposed to a narrow idiom of political writing about poverty and disease.

> I remember someone who critiqued my collection of stories writing that I only write about broken aspirations, disappointed desires and extinguished loves. If this is an accusation I am a culprit. As far as I have observed, that is what I see in my experience and life. You may ask if a story is writing about what can be seen. When a story is being formed, what can and cannot be seen mix like copper mixes with gold. That experience attracts events and states of mind like a magnet attracts many bits of iron. Principles collide with the writer's experience to form many stories. (Rajagopalan quoted in Kunju 1990: 4)

His friends and fellow writers P.G. Sundararajan, N. Pichamurthy (Pichamurthy and Rajagopalan's parallel careers led to their identification as the 'Kumbakonam Twins'), and his literary disciple Karichan Kunju, who wrote the only full-length analysis of his oeuvre, defended his fine and sensitive portrayals of love and intimacy against charges of obscenity. Pichamurthy, in his evaluation of Rajagopalan's writings, suggested his portrayal of man–woman intimacy is not obscene, unlike the way in which men and women actually interact. Here he, like Rajagopalan does in one of his essays, is probably referring to the rising number of elopements and the use of contraceptives.[1]

> Most of his writings are fundamentally about man-woman relations. He has not written any story or poem on any other theme. He is incomparable in his effortless and subtle capturing of the emotions that like clouds envelop and darken the woman's mind and her disappointed desires. He is an expert in describing the woman's mind.... They say there is something obscene in his writings because he deals with man-woman relations. These are the words of those who don't want to think of—or are scared to see the truth or speak of—what a woman's heart can be. That they deny is a testimony of his writings. If it is vulgar it is not his fault, it is the fault of the way in which man and woman relate today. Hiding the truth is not art; scratching and cooling [the wound] is the best medicine. (Rajagopalan quoted in Kunju 1990: 2)

P.G. Sundararajan and K.N. Subramanian, another literary critic and writer, were also careful to distinguish Rajagopalan's treatment of intimacy from those who actually produced erotic literature. Karichan Kunju believed Rajagopalan's conceptions of love and desire were not invested in the physicality of the woman; rather, they aestheticized the female body and the intimate encounters between men and women that went beyond the body. Many of his essays and stories sympathized with female enslavement and the need for equal opportunities. Another disciple, T. Janakiraman suggested that some critics charged Rajagopalan with perversity as though, '[he] was [like] a woman who having lost her chastity, moved to a rented house in "that" street (of prostitutes)' (Rajagopalan quoted in Kunju 1990: 280). In response, Rajagopalan accused his critics of being hypocrites who were worried he was writing about their wives (quoted in Kunju 1990: 280). Janakiraman also agreed with the other writers over the minimalism and emotional intensity of Rajagopalan's stories:

> Emotions in KP Rajagopalan's stories are given central importance.... What Barati [*sic*] said about *Putumai Peṇ* in his stories, Rajagopalan has said from a different angle in his stories.... Even simple unostentatious words attain a new meaning and intensity with an emotional initiative and a collective force.... That's why his stories, with the coalescing of silent

swiftness and brevity shine as sculptural victories that harmonize density and compactness.... Only he has truly written stories that are full of silences. (Rajagopalan quoted in Kunju 1990: 48)

Rajagopalan's long, open-ended essay entitled '*Marumalarcci*' (Renaissance: 1938), dramatizes the debates on the modern literary renaissance in Tamil through a dialogue between two friends, Rajam and Mani. While Mani represents those who are critical of the inaccessibility and solipsism of modern Tamil literature, Rajam reflects Rajagopalan's own defence of the modern. The modern for Rajam is both continuous with, and a break from, the premodern in terms of 'form, literary devices and principle' (Rajagopalan quoted in Murugan 2013: 348). The modern tracks the development of prose, which until then had been restricted to grammatical commentaries, and focuses on shorter prose genres like the short story, the one-act play, and literary criticism, rather than the *kavya* or the novel. This was true for Rajagopalan's time and even later, when writers excelled more at the short story, which was a more popular form than the novel. Rajam echoes Rajagopalan's opinion in his essay '*Putu Eluttu*' (New Writing: 1943), where the first goal of modern renaissance literature is to emulate the psychological complexity of ancient Caṅkam literature, while erasing the authority of classical Tamil to bring the literary closer to the spoken idiom. For Rajam, both the premodern and the modern emphasize in varying degrees individual subjective experiences, but the modern sensibility is a broader category that includes not just the possibility of transforming Tamil from its borrowings from other languages, but the transformation of gender relations and the emergence of the modern working woman as well. Here Rajagopalan alludes to Subramania Barati as '*putumaippeṇ*' (the modern/new woman) who stands for freedom from illiteracy and patriarchal enslavement.[2] He also suggests, echoing Keats, that in terms of principle, modern literature captures the beauty and nobility of an otherwise mundane life. The enslaved female body becomes a preoccupation not only in his essays, but also in some of his stories where the woman as the subject and object of desire breaks down the binary opposition between private and public. I return to this point later in the chapter.

Rajagopalan was known for his rather minimalist and suggestive depictions of desire and romantic love. A reading of his short stories yields at least two overlapping scenarios of desire: in the first, desire is either secretly or openly acknowledged but never consummated. The focus in these stories is more on the acknowledgement of desire and the sensual moment of transgression that, however, cannot end in a sexual act. Considering the conservative social and literary climate of Rajagopalan's time, even the secret acknowledgement of desire, without marriage, was itself a controversial move that elicited his critics' and fellow writers' disapproval. In the second scenario, desire is ennobled or even legitimized in an ideal of love that may or may not end in marriage. In instances where love does not lead to marriage, it persists in sensuous memories of young love. Love in these stories is precious and undying precisely because it takes the form of a memory or fantasy that substitutes an actual relationship. As Rajagopalan discusses in his essay '*Mutaṟkātal*' (First Love: 1944), love as an undying sense of longing is only revealed in separation, while there can only be bliss or joy in union. Thus, the (female) body in both scenarios harbours desire or love as a haunting image of sensual intimacy. In both these scenarios, Rajagopalan, like some of the other writers discussed in this book, falls back on the classical tropes of love in separation, as seen in the Sanskrit plays of Kalidasa or in the ancient corpus of Tamil Caṅkam poetry.[3] To begin with, let us look at some of Rajagopalan's stories that depict the first scenario of desire.

The Transgressive Potential of Desire

Rajagopalan's stories are largely set in domestic spaces in and around the house where sensual encounters—not necessarily resulting in the sexual—are possible. What interests me are the ways in which the distinction between the public and the private worlds in Rajagopalan's stories are blurred by gender and sexual relations. The domestic, which has traditionally been conceptualized as a space that secures women and their desires from the public world of men, ironically becomes a fraught space of transgression. In a world where the sexes are segregated to the point of making any exchange between them suspect, the house and its surrounding area is the only space where unrelated men and women can have unexpectedly intimate encounters. The domestic sphere is thus ironically the space where marriage and structures of gender and sexuality are both established and challenged.

The public–private binary has been rooted in Western political philosophy, law, popular discourse, and recurrent spatial structuring practices. These practices have isolated a private sphere of the domestic from an allegedly disembodied political world located in the public sphere. The public–private construct has been regulated and maintained to control and construct, confine, exclude, and suppress sexual differences and reinforce patriarchal and heterosexist power structures. The public–private distinction is undoubtedly gendered in the way it has been used to produce identities and regulate sexuality. The private as an ideal has been associated with the domain of domesticity, the embodied, the family, including motherhood and childrearing, unwaged labour, intimacy and sexuality, and immanence; the public as an ideal has been associated with the domain of the disembodied, the cultural and political, civil society, citizenship, production, waged labour, the state and transcendence, and so on. With the rise of the European nation state (and this is evident even in Indian nationalist discourse), the political authority of the state became limited over the reproductive family unit. This is significant because the home was considered the microcosm of the political order, with the male as the head of the household.[4] Even in liberal discourses, individual autonomy has been in practice equated with the autonomy of the family. Women have been treated as private, embodied, and apolitical subjects who, unlike men, cannot traverse private and public spaces with the same degree of legitimacy or security. Men have been less burdened with responsibilities as caregivers of children, and women have not had the same opportunities or rights to waged labour outside the home. Feminist critiques of kinship have been crucial in questioning the construction of the domestic and private realm of women and reproduction as one that is subordinated to and encapsulated by the public world of male production and politics.

Another important feature of Rajagopalan's stories is that they have no more than three major characters. The third character mediates the potential relationship between the other two while precluding the possibility of erotic rivalry. The nature of mediation, which may be either a distraction from or facilitation of the relationship, differs depending on whether the mediator is male or female. Generally, where there are two men and a woman involved, the men share either an amicable or hostile affinity that is mediated by the woman. The woman may be reduced to a projection of their cultural values even as she subtly resists them. Where there are two women and a man, the women are bound by kinship or friendship and their mutual desire for the man does not concede the possibility of rivalry. The possibility of rivalry among women over a man would not be socially permissible in Rajagopalan's time, when women were meant to be chaste and had arranged marriages at an early age. What also emerges from some of these triangular scenarios of desire is an implicit moral opposition between men, where the good man is chaste and respectful of women and their bodies, while the bad man, often a husband, is representative of the double standards of a dominant model of masculinity.[5]

An early example of the sexually fraught space of the domestic is Rajagopalan's controversial story '*Kaṉakāmparam*' (Crossandra: 1938). The story locates the upper-caste Brahman woman or wife at the centre of an ideological contradiction between perceived notions of tradition and modernity. The female character has to embody two conflicting ideals—on the one hand, she is posited as the chaste wife bound by rural tradition, and on the other, has to conform to male ideals of urbane modernity. The story describes the husband Mani's suspicion of his wife Sarada's loyalty, when, in his absence, she innocently welcomes his friend Ramu. Ramu is taken aback when Sarada tells him Mani is out and leaves hastily in embarrassment without telling her his name. Mani is upset by Sarada's carelessness and what he perceives to be her lack of urban refinement.[6] When Ramu later encounters Mani, he feels awkward and fears the possibility of ruining Mani's relationship with Sarada by confessing what transpired between him and Sarada. In the next scene, Mani mocks Sarada's attempt to conform to his notion of female urbanity when he sees her wearing *kaṉakāmparam* flowers in her hair like some of the other women in Madras. He insinuates her social hypocrisy when he insults her apparent suavity for inviting a stranger into the house. When Mani discovers Ramu was the one who visited him in his absence, he feels guilty for suspecting Sarada's loyalty and tries to apologize to her. Sarada dismisses him by dismissing the kaṉakāmparam flowers—a symbol of female urbanity and indirectly male elitism—and reclaims her rural identity, 'I don't like kaṉakāmparam! What's wrong in what you said?' (Rajagopalan 2013: 159).[7]

Mani and Ramu represent the structural contradiction of an androcentric world where the feminine is posited as a lack that paradoxically has to reflect and reassure male autonomy. The power of woman, as Jacques Lacan would argue in his essay 'The Significance of the Phallus', lies in exposing the inherent contradiction and illusory autonomy of masculinity (2002). Sarada, on the one hand, reassures Mani and Ramu's elite self-perception by retaining her own lack of sophistication, which, on the other hand, threatens their social capital as westernized urban men. Mani and Ramu are progressive, college-educated men who believe in gender equality and reforming the condition of women. They have in the past openly interacted with their modern female classmates. However, their ideological principles are contradicted by their actual relationship with Sarada, the illiterate daughter of a wealthy mirasdar in a village. Ramu is shocked by the contrast between Sarada's forthrightness and her traditional appearance that for him betrays her rural ignorance and modesty. He later admires Sarada's transparency and innocent trust when she welcomes him and asks him to wait for Mani. For someone who is unaware of the social mores of urban life in Madras, Mani reads her bold response either as a sign of her stupidity or her insolence. When she tries to conform to his notion of female urbanity by wearing kaṉakāmparam flowers, Mani interprets her act as a pretence that is continuous with her unrefined invitation to a stranger. Finally, Sarada refuses to reassure Mani's urbanity by rejecting the flowers and reclaiming her rural femininity.

A similar story, '*Etiroli*' (Echo: 1939), again has three characters, a woman, her husband, and his married friend. The unexpected moment of sensuality between the friend and the woman, and the psychological conflict that follows, is explored from both their perspectives in different segments of the story. The elaboration of this conflict that arises from a mere moment of touch only suggests the highly regulated social world of the characters that makes it impossible, even for the characters themselves, to distinguish real from perceived intimacy. Perhaps this distinction is, beyond a point, immaterial in a world where the forbiddance of any form of social interaction between unrelated men and women renders even an accidental touch a source of great conflict and guilt. The two characters find themselves in a situation that is particularly conducive to the possibility of intimacy, even if this intimacy is not decidedly sexual or romantic. The man is sick, and in his wife's absence the woman attends to his health. The internal crisis occurs when the delirious man touches the woman's hand and she brushes away his hand in an impulse. In the impossibility of any verbal communication between the sexes, what follows is the psychological dramatization of uncertainty and guilt. The inner turmoil of the woman and the man nearly mirrors each other, except that the woman cannot even acknowledge her feelings for another man, while the man insinuates his fondness for her. The woman, Kamalam, is unsure about the innocence of his touch—she wonders if he desires her or accidentally touched her in his delirious state. When she thinks of the respectful distance he has maintained in the past, she feels guilty for insinuating his sexual intentions. Then she begins to doubt her own purity—her impulsive reaction to his touch becomes an occasion to suspect her own fidelity. She feels ashamed for apparently losing his esteem for her even as she chides him for testing her fidelity. She finally frees him of blame and accuses herself for distracting him. She realizes he only wanted to share his writings with her.

The next segment of the story dramatizes the man's guilt and anguish over the loss of his reputation and her esteem for him. He initially accuses her of testing his self-control by transgressing sexual boundaries. He then detracts his accusation and admires her for her sympathy and generosity. He suspects his sexual intentions and blames himself for trying to touch her 'just when he was close to her heart' (2013: 241). He feels guilty for taking advantage of her innocent concern in a moment of vulnerability. Even if his intentions of 'seating her afar on the throne of his heart' (2013: 242) are not enacted, the very thought of intimacy with a married woman is clearly forbidden. In the last segment of the story, Kamalam and her husband have moved to a new house. During a quarrel between the two, Kamalam's husband suggests that his suspicion of her relationship with his friend prompted him to move to a new house. Kamalam, confident of her innocence, believes that the move was her husband's attempt to conceal his affair with the 'sweeper' in their previous house. In the end, owing to their greater mobility and freedom, the men are held responsible for their sexual indiscretions, an idea that is seen throughout Rajagopalan's work. '*Etiroli*' raises and partly blurs an implicit opposition between the good man and the bad man; the good man, the friend, believes he has lost Kamalam's esteem in a moment of carelessness, and the bad man, the suspicious husband, represents a hypocritical model of patriarchal masculinity.

A similar story, '*Yār Mēl Picaku?*' (Whose Mistake Is It?: 1943), again erects a tacit moral opposition between the good man and the bad man. The bad man is the husband who incarnates insecure masculinity, while the good man is his friend who respects the wife. Pattu believes he is a liberal husband, and so gives his wife Rajam and his friend Natesan (who has come to stay with him), the liberty to get to know each other. Yet Pattu is unable to suppress his jealousy, which reaches its peak when he thinks he sees Natesan's hand touch Rajam as he gives her medicine for her illness. He imagines Natesan abruptly withdrawing as he enters the house. That is when he decides to test their relationship by suddenly leaving town on pretext of work. Rajam casually spends the night sitting with Natesan in the drawing room. Natesan, on the other hand, is uncomfortable and tries to avoid Rajam, fully aware of Pattu's plan. Unable to sleep alone, Rajam brings her mattress and pillow and places them next to Natesan's. Just as she removes her necklace and flowers and places them on the floor, Pattu knocks on the door without his customary call to Rajam. Natesan implores Rajam to take her mattress and pillow back into her room but she stubbornly refuses. She tries to open the door convinced it is somebody else but the now-panic-stricken Natesan grabs her arm and begs her. When Natesan touches her, Rajam grows indignant but reluctantly does his bidding, all the while feeling insulted for having to conceal an innocent relationship. The sight of Rajam's necklace and flowers are for Pattu a sign of their illicit intimacy. When he openly accuses and insults Rajam, she attributes his suspicion to a lack of faith in his own status as a husband. Pattu grows contrite and asks Natesan to stay but Rajam asks him to leave now that their relationship has been tainted. She regrets having befriended Natesan, 'It is my mistake, I should have known. Born a woman, I should not have freely mixed with another man' (2013: 407). Thus, in the sexually segregated world of the story, any form of interaction between the sexes is suspect. Considering the conservative social climate of the times, the informality of the wife's innocent relationship with her husband's friend must have been controversial.

Tirai (Veil: 1939) forecloses the potential of illicit desire to completely break down marital boundaries. This story, unlike the earlier ones has two women and a man, but the women are neither opposed to each other nor do they compete for the man. *Tirai* begins with a man visiting his wife Rajam at his in-laws' place for the first time after their marriage. He has never spoken to her before, but has fallen in love with her through their exchange of letters. In this story, as in some of Rajagopalan's other fiction, the letter becomes the only available means of expressing female desire and love. However, the man is surprised and angry when Rajam does not come to see him even after a day. When he hears a plaintive Telugu love song being played on the veena alluding to the player's secret longing, 'Your (female) lover waits for you ...' (2013: 261), he assumes that Rajam is the player and the writer of the letter. In his impatient longing, he calls out to Rajam and chides her for making him wait. But when he descends the stairs, he discovers that the player is not Rajam but her older sister Sarasvathi, a young widow. He concludes, from the meaningful beauty of her song, that it was she who wrote the beautiful letters for her sister. He then confronts Sarasvathi in his wife's absence, but she is unable to accept that she wrote the letters instead of her sister. From their brief conversation, it becomes clear that Sarasvathi has been deprived of love and intimacy and leads a vicarious existence through her sister, 'She spoke I wrote.... Her heart spoke I sensed it and wrote.... Where do I have a hand to write? Where do I have a mouth to sing? She is my hand, my life is through her. I live through her ...' (2013: 263–4).

One of Rajagopalan's better-known stories is *Ciṟitu Veḷiccam* (A Little Light: 1943). Like '*Tirai*', it is a poignant portrayal of a woman's longing for intimacy and her inability to escape a violent marriage. The story is perhaps Rajagopalan's most candid affirmation of female sexuality and the sexual dissatisfaction women experience in violent marriages. The story features three characters, a husband, his wife, and the narrator, their tenant, and begins with the wife Savitri's death. We learn from the narrator that Savitri was the daughter of a wealthy mirasdar. Why a beautiful daughter of a wealthy mirasdar is married to a simple banker who does not desire her is not explained. The narrator himself remains an anonymous character who is cautious to preserve his reputation by avoiding the possibility of having an affair with a married woman. In any case, Savitri is trapped in a violent marriage and her brief intimacy with the narrator enables her to unburden her bitterness. She does not, however, take sexual advantage of this opportunity.

The narrator initially resists the impulse to intervene in the violent altercations between the couple when the husband returns home late. Unable to bear Savitri's plight, he steps in. The husband suddenly leaves the house in a huff, leaving Savitri and the narrator alone. The narrator is surprised when Savitri enters his room and sits beside him. She tries to dissolve the formality of their relationship by addressing him as if he is older and asks him to use the informal singular pronoun '*nī*' with her. For a woman of the time, expected to be chaste even if she was married to an unfaithful husband, Savitri is rather bold when she asks the narrator if he is married. When he replies that he is unmarried, she feels comfortable and secure in his presence, but when he urges her to leave her husband she responds, 'Society has laid down the time I have to spend with him. Now where is there place for me in my parents' house? Whether it is parents or husband, it's all nonsense! Humans are like crows and sparrows. Will a bird welcome a chick that can fly back into the nest?' (2013: 390).

Savitri is disillusioned not just with her own husband but with all men, including the unmarried narrator, for their innate desire for sexual variety. 'The wife is new for the husband for a few months. Then she is like an empty container that once contained fresh juice.... A few months after your wife arrives, you will understand what I am saying ...' (2013: 391).

She seems to have accepted her fate, for she is unable to lie about her marriage and she fails in her attempt to kill herself. The narrator proposes that she go away with him, but Savitri refuses, convinced he will soon be bored of her beauty. She also insinuates that she has never experienced sexual pleasure with her husband. When the narrator offers to pleasure her, she suspects his sexual intentions. The story ends with their brief embrace that for Savitri is enough to redeem her lonely life. She abruptly interrupts their intimacy and, before leaving, turns off the light and asks him to leave soon, 'Turn off the light and sleep. This little light is enough' (2013: 394). Like '*Etiroli*', '*Ciṟitu Veḷiccam*' sets up and partially blurs a tacit opposition between the good man and the bad man in the eyes of the woman. The good man, the narrator, is initially concerned about his reputation, but later gives in to his desire for the woman. He even offers to pleasure her but the woman believes all men are essentially driven by their sexual urges. The bad man, the husband, like the husband in '*Etiroli*', would in all probability, not have tolerated the intimate exchange between his wife and the narrator had he discovered it. Both these men embody the paradox of androcentrism that require woman to represent lack and reassure its apparent integrity.

Love as Transcendent Ideal

The body in Rajagopalan's short stories is imagined to bear the sensuous memory of young love. Again like the previous scenario, love is never realized in the sexual act and survives as an idealized memory or fantasy, unless it is legitimized through a companionate marriage. Unlike the earlier set of stories on desire, these focus on the binary structure of love that makes the presence of a third character redundant. Rajagopalan's first short story, '*Nūruṉṉicā*' (1934), sets the tone for many of his subsequent ones on the powerful impact of love on memory. As discussed previously, in Rajagopalan's stories, the true nature of love is revealed only when it is not sexually consummated, and retained as an ideal in the lover's heart. Like some of his other stories, '*Nūruṉṉicā*' explores childhood and adolescent love, and its rekindling when the lovers meet again years later. '*Nūruṉṉicā*', as Rajagopalan claims in one of his essays '*Kataiyiṉ Mūlam*' (The Essence of the Story), is an autobiographical tale that captures his undying fascination with the beauty of the eponymous female character Nurunnisa:

> 'Nūruṉṉicā' is my first short story. When I was studying third standard at Trichy one of my classmates was a Muslim friend named Muhammad Ali. On Saturdays I would go his house to help him with his Math homework. Once I happened to see the idol like figure of Nurunnisa. I have never seen such a beautiful girl. At first sight the charming beauty of her face remained forever imprinted in my heart. Having remained in my heart, she came out twenty years later in the description of Nurunnisa. (2013: 63–4)

Rajagopalan sets some of his stories against the historical backdrop of the nationalist movement, and this can be seen in the brief, but significant details in his narratives. Some of his protagonists are young agitators who reflect the prevailing mood of disillusionment with the waning nationalist movement of the late 1920s. The story is set in 1930 when there is 'a stagnation in the nationalist movement and the Congress construction plan lay ruined' (2013: 62). Following his release from jail, the narrator, a young Gandhian, receives a letter from his old classmate Gulam Mohammed inviting him to his wedding. He can sense the letter has been written on behalf of his sister, who recognizes his initials and photograph in the newspaper. The letter triggers his sensuous memory of her rather idealized and indelible beauty. He suddenly recognizes the seductive beauty that has haunted his dreams for years, as hers. 'A young girl's innocent veiled face; two accusatory eyes that trembled between kohl lined eyes; her teeth slightly emerged biting her lower lip like jasmine among roses—such a Mohini like form has settled and possessed my heart ...' (2013: 65).

Love is experienced as the perfect union of two identical and indiscrete individuals. It is an inexplicable and involuntary force that transcends not just religiously marked bodies but space and time. To receive a letter by a young love after many years of loneliness and anonymity is perceived as a sign of luck, where love is equated with coincidence and destiny. He wonders if 'their states of being have matched ...' (2013: 65). Like Rajagopalan's other stories about young love, the protagonists' first experience of love is a tactile one that cannot be expressed in words. This is not merely because of the child's lack of access to romantic ideas but because of the inherent inexplicability of the experience of love. Any retrospective attempt to describe this experience fails. In his attempt to describe his first memory of Nurunnisa, language fails the protagonist; he realizes all the metaphors he employs to describe her beauty are conventional and fall short of capturing her incomparable beauty. He remembers the indescribable joy of feeling her 'soft rose like' (2013: 67) hands covering his eyes to surprise him. The memory of childhood love is vivid and innocent, and free of the social prohibitions that set in later.

His first—and momentary—glimpse of Nurunnisa's beauty is sufficient to create an indelible impact in his heart, and when he later goes to his friend's house on the full moon night before the wedding, he senses her spectral presence. As in some of Rajagopalan's other stories, the full moon here symbolizes the lack that characterizes love. The moonlit night here creates a mood of romantic longing. He longs for Nurunnisa's presence during the night, when she suddenly emerges from the darkness and hands him a letter, before asking him to leave the next day in what appears to be a dreamlike sequence. When he opens the letter, he is back in his house looking at the moon from his window 'with a different mental frame' (2013: 70). As noted earlier, the letter is the only means of confessing love in a world where any interaction between unrelated men and women is considered immoral. Nurunnisa calls her letter 'her promise and identity' (2013: 70). In the letter, she fantasizes them playing together like young children. She is glad he is not married and firmly believes in her heart that he will remain single for her. She has no wish to consummate her desire for him and taint the moon-like purity of their relationship. She promises to live tirelessly on her faith in his loyalty. The narrator enshrines her 'golden lotus like image' in his heart, which continues to inspire his arduous and itinerant life as an anti-colonial agitator (2013: 70). This story best exemplifies Rajagopalan's understanding of love as an ideal and eternal source of longing.

Love as Literary Ideal

The next three stories represent love either as a literary ideal that cannot be realized, or as an experience that will be immortalized for all time through literature. Unlike '*Nūruṉṉicā*', '*Puṉarjaṉmam*' (Rebirth: 1935) describes a man's transformative love and marriage to a young disillusioned agitator who has just been released from jail. This story is again set in a house and has three characters, one of whom facilitates the potential relationship between the man and the woman. The absence of the family, or any character in the story to regulate the interaction between the sexes, further enables the possibility of love and companionate marriage. By the end of the story, both man and woman are renewed by their experience of love. Sarada, the male protagonist Visvesaran's sister, shows him a photograph of her friend Annapurna. Visvesvaran learns of Annapurna's past from Sarada—that she lost her parents when she was young and the uncle who raised her is now dead. He also discovers she was convinced to live with a painter who claimed to love her, but later turned violent when she does not have any more money to give him. The experience colours Annapurna's judgement of men, who she believes are incapable of selfless love. Annapurna who has nowhere to go, lives with Sarada and Visvesvaran. Although she is moved by Visvesvaran's respect and loving concern, she suspects her own beauty will ruin him.

Visvesvaran's growing love for Annapurna transforms and redeems his hitherto lonely life. He is initially struck by Annapurna's extraordinary beauty, which for him matches literary ideals of beauty like Cleopatra. From his reading of literature, Visvesvaran he had thought that such extravagant/extreme beauty was mere show, and believed that it could only possess a destructive power. He is aroused by 'the pride of her beauty that seemed excessive to him. The bloom in her body parts and the energetic luster of her face ...' (2013: 115). He is drawn to her mature appearance; she is 20, way past the marriageable age for women of the time. But the disturbing sight of her seductive beauty transforms his lust into a sense of responsibility: 'Only someone with the nature of Shakuntala can occupy a devotee's heart; Urvasi can never comfort the human heart' (2013: 115). Note the invocation of Shakuntala, the eponymous heroine of Kalidasa's play, whose chaste beauty is an idealized object of love and devotion. When he actually sees her, Visvesvaran notices how contrary Annapurna is to her photograph and realizes he has been inexplicably transformed by her beauty. The narrative suggests that Annapurna's appeal no longer lies in her beauty but in her dedication to the nation's freedom as 'a servant of the nation ... in a saffron sari and chocolate colored blouse' (2013: 116). She is sobered and matured by her experience of jail, 'The arrogance of her body had slightly subdued. Sorrow underlined the gravity of her face. Her energetic appearance had disappeared and a very new calm had spread over. Her courage suppressed, a dullness could be seen. The indifferent look had given way to modesty' (2013: 116).

The crucial part of the story lies in the transformative conversation between Visvesvaran and Annapurna, incidentally the longest conversation between any male and female character in Rajagopalan's stories. Their conversation takes the form of a debate about the nature of truth in relation to the body and emotions. What is striking in the conversation is the reversal of the conventional association of man with the mind and rationality, and woman with the body and emotion. While Annapurna equates truth with permanence and prefers death to 'enslaving one's body to emotions' (2013: 120), Visvesvaran tries to convince Annapurna of the truth of the living body and love that is not based on any abstract notion of truth, but on feelings like kindness and affection. By the end of the conversation, Visvesvaran succeeds in mitigating her bitterness by convincing her of the sincerity of his sensual love that goes beyond his initial lust for her beauty. Many of Rajagopalan's early stories, as well as those of his literary disciples, display an ambiguous moral bifurcation of women characters, where the upper-caste woman embodies and upsets the binary opposition between the sacred and the profane. The seductress and the chaste wife thus share an uneasy correlation that is challenged in Rajagopalan's later stories and in the writings of many later writers.

The immortal love between Anarkali, a courtesan in Akbar's court, and his son Salim is the theme of Rajagopalan's 1938 story 'Aṉārkali'. Akbar disapproves of Salim's love for a courtesan, which comes in the way of his political responsibilities towards the state and its people. Akbar entreats his son to marry a Rajput princess to secure their relations with their Rajput compatriots and consolidate the power of the Mughal empire for generations to come. But the Salim's love for Anarkali is far greater than any promise of wealth, fame, and power. He tells his father, 'Anarkali doesn't have just beauty ... she has enslaved my heart. Now no one can rescue me from her ... [Akbar] In your love have you forgotten she is my slave? [Salim] She may be your slave but she is the queen of my heart' (2013: 188).

Salim's overpowering love for Anarkali makes him her slave in matters of the heart. The same rhetoric of love as absolute enslavement that frees the lover from all worldly desires, including the very desire to live, is perfectly reflected in Anarkali's love for him. When Akbar orders Anarkali to forget Salim, she is empowered by her selfless love for him, which releases her from the fear of her own mortality. She initially postures servitude in a semblance of powerlessness, but ends up asserting her immortal love for Salim that does not have to be acknowledged through intimacy or marriage to survive, but lives on as an idealized memory that will be celebrated by the people and the literature of the world. Akbar is humiliated at the thought of finally being defeated by a common woman.

[Anarkali] Who am I to forget or remember him? ... He hasn't given me any rights in that matter ... [Akbar] You are my slave! ... [Anarkali] My heart isn't your slave ... it is the prince's slave ... I will not let him go ... [Akbar] You're an innocent woman. You are depriving a prince of his throne to fulfill your desire for him. [Anarkali] No Shahanshah, it is he who has placed me on the great seat of affection [Akbar] You shall not see him from now on. [Anarkali] No loss! [Akbar] So you can't marry him! [Anarkali] I never asked for it; no marriage. His memory is enough. That will never go. Who can stop that Shahanshah? [Akbar] What if I get rid of your memory and you? [Anarkali] Is this all your cleverness! So what if I no longer am? As long as the pomegranate bud exists my memory will never disappear from Salim's heart or the heart of the world's literature! Even if you destroy me the story of the 'pomegranate bud' will never disappear! (2013: 190–1)

'*Kātal Nilai*' (The State of Love: 1939) reiterates a literary ideal of love that is seen in Rajagopalan's earlier stories. Love here is understood as a literary and artistic ideal that can never be realized in everyday life. The story explores the possibility of a romantic relationship between Navamani, a married woman and student of English literature, and her tutor Sundaram. They have a disagreement over the authenticity of Cleopatra's love for Anthony in Shakespeare's play *Anthony and Cleopatra*. While Navamani admires Cleopatra's self-sacrificial love for Anthony, Sundaram feels Cleopatra only loved herself. He perceives her as a clever and calculative queen who desired to defeat the warriors of the world to secure her own esteem. She kills herself when she finally realizes she cannot bear the insult. The irony of the story lies in the fact that although Navamani is trapped in a miserable marriage, she initially believes in the possibility of love in marriage, while Sundaram acknowledges his love for Navamani, even though he does not believe in realizing his love. There is thus a clash between the notions of love as self-sacrifice and love as a solipsistic or platonic ideal. Sundaram opines love and marriage are incompatible:

[Sundaram] Love ends the moment one gets married. Even those who try to establish love can only do so when they take refuge in death. Romeo and Juliet did that and so did Porphyria and her lover. All wonderful and superior love has been like that. [Navamani] If husband and wife agree why won't love develop? [Sundaram] What does it mean to agree? Two hearts uniting isn't it? One surrendering to the other isn't it? One nature surrendering to the other isn't it? ... What decides this? ... Doesn't it only end in a difference of opinion? ... (2013: 252)

When Navamani suggests the possibility of exploring their love, Sundaram refuses, defining love as an ideal that can survive as long as it is not realized in a relationship. Love can only be an imaginary ideal of wholeness that cannot be consummated in the body without resulting in isolation.

Love is what it is now. We should not go beyond this.... Love isn't just stainless and detached. It should not be stained by word or action.... It should survive in the heart without dying.... Only then will your beauty be ever youthful and my love will not die. Do you remember the great poet Keats' promise? What he said looking at two statues is the truth, O Youth! You will forever keep loving, she will remain a figure of beauty. [Navamani] ... I need support in life. [Sundaram] You don't need support in life. Let us remain like this ... this is the state of love! ... If love is always associated with the body it will appear like the distant greenery. Near and the beautiful dream dissolves. By trying to look for the illusory beauty by embracing each other it will only escape. There will only be bodies left. There will instantly be mutual hatred and betrayal. [Navamani] I feel what you say seems to be true. But I cannot be consoled by that emotional state. [Sundaram] Haven't you felt consoled by poetry and art? ... Love like truth and beauty is imaginary! [Navamani] Sexual pleasure? [Sundaram] That's different, it's not permanent.... It is nature but it will not on its own give continuous joy! [Navamani] Then what's life? [Sundaram] It is just a mix of joy and sorrow, nothing else! (2013: 255–6)

Desire, Love, and Kinship

Another set of stories by Rajagopalan focuses on the sensual possibilities of desire and love that are opened up through the intersections of marriage and kinship networks. '*Tai Mutal Tēti*' (The First of [the Tamil month of] Thai: 1940) is an example of this. The thematic focus of the narrative is the irony between marriage and intimacy, where a limited form of intimacy is enabled through kinship relations outside the social confines of marriage. The two characters of the story, Gopu and his niece Sellam, are initially promised in marriage. However, because of certain reasons, the elders cancel their wedding, and Sellam is married to another man. When they are engaged, Gopu and Sellam are distant and silent with each other, but once Sellam gets married they are inseparable. Unable to bear the possibility of never seeing Gopu again, she facilitates his marriage to a woman from her in-laws' family. She thus ensures his occasional presence in her life. Clearly, desire takes the form of longing for a proximate object that can never be exclusively possessed without violating the social and sexual boundaries of marriage. In this case, marriage is not equated with intimacy; in fact, a limited form of conversational intimacy that would otherwise be impossible becomes possible outside marriage precisely because the lovers are separated by the very structure of kinship that also enables their proximity. There is thus a fine balance between kinship and sexuality, where a limited form of intimacy is possible within kinship, but transgressing the boundary beyond the acknowledged limits of social propriety would be a violation. By getting married to individuals from the same family, their intimacy remains suspended between the strictures of marriage and family.

The title of the story alludes to the coincidences that separate and reunite the lovers, suggesting that their lives are inextricably entwined, even if they are not meant to be together. The first of the Tamil month of Tai marks Gopu's birthday, the day Sellam gets married to another man, and the day he meets her again. Gopu, thinking back on the number of occasions he accidentally meets Sellam, develops faith in their mutual destiny. On one such occasion towards the end of the story, they accidentally find themselves alone at Sellam's in-laws' house during a relative's wedding. In their solitary presence they are both tense and vulnerable. Their awkward conversation and the long silences implies their inexpressible longing for each other. But they realize the opportunity of physical intimacy is a threat to their future proximity. Sellam clearly fears the possibility of never seeing Gopu again if they succumb to each other.

[Gopu] 'Does the bride sing?' [Sellam] 'No. So what's so bad? It didn't help me.' [Gopu] 'Look at how life has rolled by Sellam!' [Sellam] 'What to do Gopu? What is destined will happen.' [Sellam] 'Why are they gone for so long? ... I am scared! ... Why did you come here so soon?' [Gopu] 'I didn't want to come on my own Sellam. I thought I would come and leave with the others ... why?' [Sellam] 'I know from the telegram. What would they know?' When Sellam said that, Gopu suddenly rose from the bed and sat up. [Sellam] 'Gopu!' Sellam warned him. But her heart was overflowing. Gopu blindly reached and bent to hold her hand. [Sellam] 'If you touch me I will never be able to see your face again!' ... [Gopu] 'No! Gopu came nearer.' [Sellam] 'Gopu! I cannot be without seeing your face once in a while! Don't touch me! Which is why, I found you a bride in this family. Don't touch me!' Gopu grew still. A shiver; then peace gradually took over.... [Gopu] 'Sellam, you are not to be touched!' In that clarity, they looked at each other carefully and achieved satisfaction. (2013: 340–1)

'*Mūṉṟu Uḷḷaṅkaḷ*' (Three Hearts: 1944) is similar to '*Tai Mutal Tēti*' in its focus on the uneasy negotiation between sexuality and kinship. Here the male character Sundaram is supposed to marry his cousin Meenakshi, but she is married to a lawyer, and Sundaram ends up marrying her younger sister Sunda. Although Sundaram and Meenakshi had a silent and awkward relationship when they were promised in marriage to each other, with their marriages to different people they start talking again. Their past relationship continues to haunt their present when Meenakshi visits Sunda to take care of her after an abortion. Sunda is secretly hurt by Sundaram's unchanged affection for Meenakshi and his constant concern and partiality towards her. Their love and concern for each other is mediated through Sunda. When Sunda expresses her visible displeasure with their relationship, Meenakshi withdraws and Sundaram senses the possibility of losing her forever:

Meenakshi was lying on her side on the floor.... There were tears running down her face. In the light of the lamp Sundaram could clearly see a longing that he had never seen before. Did the thought that the consolation of this small service would be interrupted evoke her disappointment and longing at that minute? ... [Sundaram] Through this hospitality, through the way she helps her sister, through the happiness she gets, she sweetens her emotions to an extent and to an extent she controls them. (2013: 510–11)

Love as Blindness

The last set of Rajagopalan's stories discussed employs a rather conventional trope of blindness to describe the ideal unconditionality of romantic love. '*Kāmuviṉ Katai*' (Kamu's Story: 1934) is again representative of Rajagopalan's idea of love as a metaphysical union that transcends the body. It literalizes the popular understanding of love as being blind to the limitations of the body.[8] Structured as a story within a story, the nested story thematizes the outer narrative frame. Kamu is a blind woman who, to her husband's pleasant surprise, masters the use of the typewriter. She types a story that alludes to the unconditional love she shares with her husband. In the inner story, the female character Moham is a blind orphan of impeccable beauty. She is raised by her aunt and uncle who fear the possibility of losing their reputation if she is not married. Her cousin Ramani resolves his parents' predicament by marrying her according to the norms of Dravidian kinship. Although Moham regrets ruining Ramani's life, Ramani considers himself fortunate to have a wife who will never judge him for his physical flaws. Moham regrets she will never be able to see her husband. Having read the story, Kamu's husband agrees with Ramani; blindness isn't limited to Kamu's physical blindness; it is a totalizing metaphor for the unconditionality of true love that unites both of them.

> Kamu! What Ramani says is right. If as the Vedantins say the state of not having the five senses is bliss, not having one of them is good too isn't it! Sound and light are two senses aren't they? The diminished night is so much more peaceful than the day! Your blind infatuation flows in me like a life giving breath! Kamu! In this world they say 'casting the [evil] eye', what is it? Everything that man sets his eyes on turns into ash like Shiva's third eye. Not having that eye isn't a flaw—for others ... tell me, how did you sense my heart? My heart is in this story. You are a 'magician'.... Come here, the dark veil of the night has also descended before me. (2013: 91–2)

'*Tiraikku Piṉ*' (Behind the Veil: 1942) explores the power of love to transcend socially erected barriers, including the body, to effect a spiritual fusion of two beings. It describes the blossoming love between Bilhana, an allusion to the blind eleventh-century Kashmiri poet, and a princess afflicted with leprosy. The king appoints the poet to teach the princess poetry and places a veil between them to ensure there is no contact. The veil is both significant and redundant. Its significance lies in its metaphorical function as an artificial barrier created by society that can only be overcome by true love. The screen becomes unnecessary for the same reason, not merely because the poet is blind, but because their love is an aesthetic ideal that is indifferent to their bodies and transcends their physical separation. Love is thus not directed to the body (which lacks any significance), for it is only an instrument that enables this authentic spiritual union.

The first segment of the story describes the poet's wonder at the princess' insights into his own poetry. In this segment, the poet is amazed at the princess' interpretive skills that seem to expand his own imagination. In a brief argument, the princess corrects his understanding of female nature, which is not a stable referent but a 'cloak' created by men to control women, and to which women conform to shield men from their true courage and intensity.

> [Princess] Do I truly believe female nature adorns woman with those ornaments [fear, modesty, innocence and chastity]? ... Aren't ornaments an artificial instrument to show something that does not exist? ... If that's the case, aren't fear, shyness and the other things that make up female nature adorn [a] woman to show she has what she does not really have? Female nature is thus a cloak, nothing else! ... Woman is scared and shy so that man can desire her and continuously pursue her. She knows he will not be able to bear her true courage and emotional intensity so she controls herself. (2013: 396)

The meaningless artifice of female nature is just another barrier that can only be overcome through the transcendental force of true love, which is beyond all divisions, including the body that constitutes meaning. The poet begins to believe the princess has revealed the secret of her own voice and beauty; a voice so unbearable she interprets his words, and a beauty so unbearable it has to be veiled. He longs to 'see' her in her perfect beauty.

In the second segment, the princess marvels at the power of the poet's imagination that seems to belie his inability to see. The authenticating force of their love enables her to shed her 'female nature' to be united with him. She realizes the mutual indifference to their bodies is precisely what enables them to experience a perfect fusion of hearts, where 'he is sound and she is meaning' (2013: 399). Note that a recurrent trope in Rajagopalan and in his literary successors is unveiling the masculine cloak of femininity to reveal the true and awesome power of woman. This, however, still equates woman with an essential notion of femininity that is characterized as a potential and inscrutable ideal of sacred power to redress, as it were, sexual inequality. As Rajagopalan mentions, 'Why does a man need to see? What will he look at besides a woman? He doesn't even have the strength to look at woman by day; his eyes hurt. And so he attracts a woman's heart like a thief in the cover of the night' (2013: 399).

Desire and love in Rajagopalan are valorized as ideals in the lover's heart that are irreducible to marriage or the sexual act. Although Rajagopalan was accused of being a pornographic writer, his stories, through subtle but significant gestures of sensuality, are powerful and provocative portrayals of intimacies between men and women. Even if these intimacies mostly do not end in sexual intercourse or illicit relationships, just the possibility of open and intimate conversations and situations becomes significant in the social context of the time, when any exchange between the sexes was considered transgressive. Although there is an impulse in Rajagopalan and his literary successors to essentialize women by equating them with an inscrutable sacred ideal of feminine power, some of Rajagopalan's female characters, I would argue, are more sexually assertive than the female characters in the later writers I discuss. One of these writers was T. Janakiraman, who drew on his repertoire of sensuality to interrupt, even if temporarily, conventional gender relations, although some of his works had socially conservative endings. As a novelist, Janakiraman also had the narrative latitude to elaborate the reorientation of disappointed desire in spirituality, music, or social reform to remake the self. This will be the premise of my next chapter.

Notes

1. E.V. Ramasami Naicker 'Periyar' had in the 1930s advocated the use of contraceptives by women, as he believed they should have claims over their own bodies and reproductive capacities.
2. In two other essays, '*Inta Peṇmai Pēccu*' (This Talk about Womanhood: 1939) and '*Avaḷ Iṣṭam*' (Her Wish: 1943), Rajagopalan believes that woman could never have been truly enslaved by man. She pretends to be entrapped, apparently willing to be the object of man's love and veneration. But the new woman sheds all pretence and refuses to be an idealized object of man's love. See Rajagopalan as quoted in Murugan (2013).
3. In an important essay on contemporary trends in Tamil literature '*Putu Eḻuttu*' (New Writing: 1943), Rajagopalan implicitly identifies his own writing with the poignancy of love and longing in Tamil Sangam poetry and with the devotional corpus of Vaishnava Bhakti poetry, which were,

for him, most intimately tied to human life. The literary critic and writer B. Jeyamokan, however, believes that Rajagopalan and his literary successors were not as familiar with these literary traditions as they were with Kalidasa's or Bhavabhuti's Sanskrit plays, or with Bengali and Russian literature. This is partly confirmed by Karichan Kunju's moving account of K.P. Rajagopalan's poor life and literary interests in *Ku.Pa.Ra.* 1990).

4. As Partha Chatterjee argues in his popular essay 'The Woman's Question', the (upper-caste) woman had to bear the burden of embodying and preserving the spiritual integrity of the home and a certain notion of Hindu tradition, which was a compensatory gesture for the compromises their men had to make in their exchanges with colonial authorities. See Partha Chatterjee (1990). For a critique of Jürgen Habermas's concept of the public sphere, see Nancy Fraser (1990).
5. For a discussion of the metaphysicality of triangular/mediated desire, see Rene Girard (1965) and Eve Sedgwick (1985) where what she calls male 'homosociality' is based on the mediation of male relationships by women.
6. Mani's perception of Sarada reflects the perception of Brahman women who married and moved to the city of Madras in the early twentieth century, unaware of the social mores of the city. Here, Sarada is expected by her husband to be modern in terms of being informal with men, and traditional in terms of being modest and chaste in her appearance.
7. In his book on Rajagopalan, Kunju suggests that in the 1930s, kaṉakāmparam flowers were normally worn by Christian or working women while domestic women wore jasmine flowers, among others. All subsequent quotes from Rajagopalan's stories given in this chapter are from K.P. Rajagopalan as has been quoted in Murugan's *Ku.Pa.Rā. Ciṟukataikaḷ* (2013).
8. Rajagopalan's preoccupation with blindness may also be attributed to the fact that he lost his eyesight for seven years before regaining it shortly before his death. During this period, he dictated his stories to his sister, Sethu Ammal.

2

T. Janakiraman

Male Sexuality and the De-Idealized Woman

In a collection of essays by 11 modern Tamil writers entitled *Etaṟkāka Eḻutukiṟēṉ?* (Why Do I Write?: 1962), T. Janakiraman (1921–1983) states that writing for oneself is the greatest and most honourable reason to write. While the writer can have different and separate relationships with his writing and his readers, for him, it is only when writing is a solipsistic exercise that one can experience 'the joy of making love, longing, expectation, union and sorrow' (Janakiraman 1962: 10). He describes the experience of writing for oneself as a source of illicit pleasure and compares it to the 'joy, longing and fulfilment' to be had in loving another man's wife (1962: 10). For Janakiraman, the illicit pleasure derived from writing for oneself is really a sign of the true and courageous writer who resists moral codes. It is the sign of an autonomous writer who, and here he alludes to contemporary literary debates on the moral function of literature, is not compelled to write on social problems. He adds, gently mocking those who believe that travelling is a necessary inspiration to write, that anything that piques the imagination of the writer without necessarily entailing the need to travel, is a subject worthy of writing: or, he says, '... it is better to make love' (1962: 12). Janakiraman believed that only in writing for oneself can one see one's true self in all its defects. Moreover, the artistic form of literature, which he differentiated from craftsmanship, emerges precisely when one is true to oneself in one's writings.

A reading of Janakiraman's novels confirms and extends the ideas in his essay. He clearly derives pleasure in defying the strand of socialist writing that places moral obligations on writers to address social issues. This pleasure is not an end in itself: it does not lie merely in transgressing prohibitions, but in exploring the spiritual and reformative possibilities of desire. This becomes pertinent when desire transcends the sexual act and enables individual and collective self-realization. In this chapter, I look at representations of dominant-caste masculinity and male sexuality, and its object of desire—the idealized dominant-caste woman woman—in Janakiraman's novels from the 1960s and the 1970s. Most of the male characters in these works are devout celibates or aesthetes who are debilitated by their sensuous desires for women that have to be suppressed because they are either (apparently) illicit or distractions from their seemingly spiritual or intellectual pursuits. A symptom of this suppressed desire is the idealization of female beauty, which can be interpreted as an aversion to the potential threat of (female) sexuality by rendering the woman inscrutable and desexualized. In other words, the idealization of women is couched in the contradictory impulses of desire and devotion/duty that can only be overcome through a crisis. In these novels, the moment of crisis that destabilizes a disciplined and religious self-perception of Brahman dominant-caste masculinity occurs when the women assert their sexuality resulting in their de-idealization and the acknowledgement of male sexuality. I also note a reversal in his later works, where the woman becomes a more central subject of desire.

Janakiraman, like his fellow writers Karichan Kunju and M.V. Venkatram, hailed from the most fertile—and perhaps the wealthiest—regions of what was the Madras Presidency, the Kaveri river basin. He was born in Vedakudi, a village in Mannarkudi, Tanjavur district (which is today in Tiruvarur district), to a landed Brahman family. Like his contemporaries, Janakiraman was raised in a religious, Brahman household tied to its rural, landed origins. His father was a Sanskrit scholar of the Puranas and a connoisseur of south-Indian classical music. Janakiraman often accompanied his father on singing tours and sang with him. The gradual urbanization of the rural landscape and the emergence of Madras as the urban centre of education and employment urged his family to move to more urban settlements, and some years after his birth, the family moved to Kumbakonam. Janakiraman completed his college education from here. His contemporaries, many of whom studied with him, included M.V. Venkatram, Karichan Kunju, Saminatha Athreya, and the modernist poet and writer N. Pichamurthy. According to Kunju, Janakiraman learnt Sanskrit and music from his father and developed an interest in English and Tamil literature and literary criticism from K.P. Rajagopalan. He set up a bookshop, close to where he worked as a teacher, and held literary discussions there with writers such as Rajagopalan, and Venkatram to name a few.

It is important not to read the novels discussed here as innocent representations of gender and sexuality isolated from their contemporary historical context. Janakiraman's novels are set in the rural landscape of Tanjavur district, where the joint or extended family becomes the site of transgression. Like in Rajagopalan's works, sensual transgressions in Janakiraman's novels threaten the presumed security of the domestic space and the apparent integrity of the family. The possibility of illicit desire is correlated to the threat of urbanization, which dissolves the joint family and the social fabric of rural society. This correlation may be formally represented either through an illicit love that crosses the rural–urban divide, or a motif of triangular desire, where the character is torn between his/her incompatible marriage to a traditional woman/man and his/her desire for a more liberal one. The dominant-caste Brahman man, and particularly the dominant-caste Brahman woman, embody the divide between the rural and the urban, which itself corresponds to an opposition between religiosity and secularity. Unlike the dominant-caste Brahman man who has greater power and freedom to traverse the rural–urban divide, the dominant-caste Brahman woman bears the burden of conforming to and preserving traditional norms. The traditional woman, who is embedded in the norms and practices of rural life, is idealized, while the modern woman often has to renounce the social and romantic freedom of urban capitalism to return to her rural roots. But there is an implicit acknowledgement of the futility of resisting the inevitable march of urbanization. The unsuccessful resolution of the conflict between the rural and the urban; love and arranged marriage is often sought in the sublimation of desire in asceticism, social reformation, or music.

Religion and family are two beleaguered institutions that represent the social order of an increasingly fragile rural world. Although Janakiraman's novels uphold these institutions, they also suggest their failure to counter the spread of urbanization. There is a certain anxiety over the loss of religiosity in an increasingly profane world. The impulse to cultivate a pious and spiritual disposition or reconstruct the village along modern lines proves to be an unsuccessful defence against the estranging and corrupting effects of urbanization. It is in this sense that Rajagopalan and his disciples both affirm and undermine a Gandhian impulse to spiritualize and sublimate desire in the service of reconstituting the village as a microcosm of the nation. If women are represented as victims trapped in rural institutions and practices, urbanization does not necessarily offer a way out; in fact, the newfound freedom of education and a professional lifestyle in the city often poses a threat to female security. Janakiraman's characters, like those of Rajagopalan, may not completely transgress social and sexual norms; many of them end up in arranged marriages even if their desires lie elsewhere. Janakiraman seems to endorse the preservation of rural society and traditional institutions like arranged marriage, which may be exploitative but promise security and preserve rural society. But this promise is untenable against the forces of industrial capitalism. The reformation of sexuality and the unsuccessful attempt to safeguard rural life from the onslaught of urbanization is evident across a range of themes in Janakiraman's novels: the modern reformation of the devadasi system through an inter-caste marriage (*Amirtam*: 1945); the inability of even educated and urbanized women to escape the arranged marriage system (*Malar Mañcam*: 1961); the urban commodification of art and the estrangement of the artist from his art and others (*Mōkamuḷ*: 1966); the dissolution of the joint family, and the dishonouring of motherhood (*Ammā Vantāḷ*: 1966); the attempts of Madras-based landowners to reconstruct villages with the help of local women (*Uyirttēṉ*: 1968); the inability to prevent the destruction of the joint family system, which ends on a socialist note (*Cemparutti*: 1968); and the cultivation of a spiritual disposition as the only means of resisting the erosion of rural life (*Naḷapākam*: 1983).

Ammā Vantāḷ (Mother Came: 1966)

Janakiraman's oeuvre has many male characters that are religious and have similar views on women and urbanization. Many of these men embody the contradictions of a modern world where religiosity shares an uneasy correlation with sexuality and an expanding urban culture. These men ostensibly typify Vedic religiosity and idealize women but later re-evaluate their relationship to both through their sexual experiences; they seem to reject city life and turn to the novelty and peace of the village, which, ironically, is unable to resist the impact of urbanization. Appu, the male protagonist of *Ammā Vantāḷ*, is in this sense a typical Janakiraman character. A young man in his early twenties, he is preparing to return home after 17 years in a Vedic school. Although the prospect of leaving the school upsets him, the thought of seeing his beautiful mother fills him with a sense of peace and joy. During his time at the Vedic school, Appu grows fond of Bhavaniammal, the Brahman widow who runs the school, and her widowed niece Indu; they become his surrogate family. In the secluded bucolic space of the school, Appu and Indu develop an unexpressed love for each other, which Indu finally acknowledges on the day of his departure. Appu's introspections suggest his ostensible preoccupation with his religious and spiritual pursuits, yet barely conceal his secret admiration for Indu's sensuous beauty. He struggles in vain to suppress his desire for her by finding fault with the apparent imperfection of her widowed beauty.

> That face ... it struck you like a blow. Fair, with hair that descended unusually low over the ears. A jet black cotton sari with a snow white blouse and strikingly fair feet and hands, their coloring accentuated by the fine down on the forearms and feet. Skin stretched tight over the bones, accentuating the pallor. Hair twisted into a neat, round bun. If only there had been a red dot on her forehead and bangles on her wrists.... Parasu had snatched those away long ago. (Janakiraman 1966: 12)

Janakiraman's sympathetic and rather controversial representation of widows comes through here. Many of his widowed characters resist the humiliating practices of Brahman widowhood, and some even affirm their sexual selves and dare to live unconventional lives. If the social reform movements of the late nineteenth and early twentieth century sought to reform and remarry young widows, it was to domesticate their sexuality and deny their sexual accessibility. And in most instances where widows could not be remarried, they were subject to the austerities of widowhood that regulated their modest appearance, their mobility, and their food habits. It is for this very reason that the young widow in Janakiraman becomes a transgressive subject and a tabooed, and, therefore, irresistible object of desire. For Appu, his desire for Indu is forbidden not only because she is a widow but because of their ostensibly filial ties. On the one hand, he is relieved that she is not shorn of her beauty owing to her husband's dying wish. But on the other, he realizes his relationship with Indu is the only significant relationship he has ever had, and he is unable to bear the thought of leaving her to be reunited with a family he barely remembers.

> These ties of family mean no more to him than the chirping of a cricket somewhere in the distance, audible only if he made a conscious effort to listen, that was all. The only thing close to him was Indu. Revolving around him at all times was this image alone, when the light broke at dawn, rose to a peak, faded to twilight and then to darkness ... it was Indu, this Indu. (1966: 17)

Like Rajagopalan's characters, Janakiraman's characters often develop childhood intimacies that are later perceived as incestuous and forbidden. However, this 'filialization' of cross-gender ties is unsuccessful in offsetting the threat of (female) desire to an already fragile and embattled masculinity. Appu couches his compromised feelings for Indu in the contradictory impulses of desire and devotion; a symptom of his desire for Indu is suggested by his idealized and detached descriptions of her beauty. He aestheticizes and fetishizes Indu's feet, one of the few visible parts of her sari-clad body. He identifies with Parasu's desire for Indu even as he contrasts Parasu's weak and fragile body to his own sturdy and well-built one. He feels he cannot betray Bhavaniammal, who he equates with his own mother, and taint the sanctity of the school. Even the memory of the delicious meals Indu cooked for him in a school that otherwise served poor food, makes him feel 'as though [he] had reached a world filled with fathers, mothers and siblings' (1966: 20).

Indu replicates the sympathetic figure of a sexually affirmative widow once trapped in an incompatible marriage, which can be seen in Janakiraman's other novels. This is a motif seen in Janakiraman's novels, and is contained within a rhetoric of moral purity that distinguishes the embodied sexual act from a moral core. When Indu demands a guarantee of their relationship, Appu's guilt about committing incest and desiring another man's wife prevents him from reciprocating her love. Indu invalidates her marriage to Parasu, which was not a consensual one. She refuses to believe she is a widow and claims that her body was married to and 'belonged' to her husband (1966: 27). When Indu swears her love on the Vedas, Appu is shocked by her blasphemy that degrades the Vedas, which 'are like his god, his mother' (1966: 36). The turning point in the novel occurs when Indu sullies Appu's exalted image of his mother Alankaram, accusing her of adultery and valorizing her own love for him. 'I at least am wasting away thinking only of you. Your mother's thinking of somebody else and she's thriving. I'm not like your mother, and I've never even thought of anyone else besides you, you wretch! Don't compare me with your amma. I don't know how to hoodwink everyone like her' (1966: 42).

If Appu's religious integrity is tied to his idealized mother, the discovery of her affair with a wealthy landlord and his identification with his emasculated father compels the loss of his integrity. In Freudian terms, this crisis can be read as the positive resolution of the Oedipus Complex in the normative psychosexual development of the male child, premised on the prohibition of homosexuality and maternal incest. Male heterosexual identity is a consolidation of the son's ambiguous identification with his more powerful father and the realization of the impossibility of competing with him for the affections of the mother, a tabooed object of desire. The mother's desire for the father (or father figure) forces the son to substitute other women for her, and it is only then that the son loosens his intimate ties to his mother and transfers his love to other women. In *Ammā Vantāḷ*, however, the separation of mother and son is not achieved when Appu extends his love for his mother to Bhavaniammal and Indu. However, his fixation with his mother, and consequently the other women, is lost when the mother, the very ideal of motherhood, is tainted by her unchaste sexuality. Her de-idealization in turn undoes Appu's religious integrity and compels him to acknowledge his vulnerability and desire for Indu. Clearly, gender identities are contingent (non-)positionalities that dramatize their mutual assurance and destabilization. As Lacan argues in his essay 'The Significance of the Phallus' (2002), the phallus is the irreducible signifier of sexual difference, relative to which man and woman occupy different symbolic positions of either having the phallus or being the phallus. The masculine position of having the phallus would imply perfect integrity and power while the feminine position of being the phallus would imply lack. But since these positions are symbolic correlates, the power of the feminine position lies in paradoxically being a lack that reassures and subverts male power.

In *Ammā Vantāḷ*, the mother's transgressive sexuality undermines the Tamil ideal of *kaṟpu* or female chastity, which is really an index of the woman's assurance of male integrity. Alankaram is initially perceived as a divine image of integrity, but her fallen stature undermines Appu's own integrity and frees him from his function as an instrument of her redemption. Through his older sister, Appu discovers that his mother's lover fathered their younger siblings, that 'only [his] last three [siblings] were born out of her heart ...' (1966: 34). The novel remains unclear whether Alankaram's affair had to do with an unhappy or sexually dissatisfying marriage, while her devout husband longs for her beauty so much that he is unable to punish her and ruin the family's reputation. There is a suggestion, however, that Alankaram may have been seduced by the city-based landlord's wealth, which mutually implicates the illicit affair with the incursion of the urban into the rural.

By the end of the novel, it becomes clear that Alankaram requires Appu to retain his ritual purity to attain her own spiritual redemption, and, therefore, refuses to get him married to a woman whose dead mother apparently had an affair with a Muslim man. Thus, Appu's caste integrity is retained by his final reunion with Indu when he is freed of the responsibility of redeeming his mother's sins. He inherits the Vedic school from Bhavaniammal, while his mother renounces her family to spend the rest of her life in the holy city of Varanasi.

Mōkamuḷ (The Thorn of Desire: 1964)

Mōkamuḷ features the motif of a devout man and his conflicted desire for an idealized woman. In *Ammā Vantāḷ*, desire is not sublimated in religion and eventually leads to marriage, in *Mōkamuḷ*, the desire of the male protagonist, Babu, is disillusioned by the sexual act and partly displaced in the pursuit of music. Although *Mōkamuḷ* received great critical acclaim, it is not a sensitive portrayal of women and their sexuality. *Mōkamuḷ* is focalized purely through Babu, and explores the vicissitudes of his desire for an older woman, Yamuna. Their relationship is perceived as a filial one not just by Babu and Yamuna but also by his parents and her mother. As in Janakiraman's other narratives, here too the male protagonist tries to disavow his quasi-incestuous desire for the woman and desexualizes their relationship by idealizing her beauty. Unlike Alankaram, who at least betrays her illicit desire for another man and seeks redemption, Yamuna lacks any inner complexity and is reduced to the stereotype of an unattainable and inscrutable ideal. Unlike Janakiraman's other female characters, Yamuna betrays no signs of desiring Babu or even being a sexual being. She ends up as a specular image that merely reflects and reassures Babu's desire. Even the perfunctory gratification of Babu's desire towards the end of the novel is an act of gratitude that serves the purpose of disillusioning and redirecting his desire towards music.

Babu, like many of Janakiraman's other male characters, is a sensitive young aesthete rendered vulnerable by his longing for a woman. The early chapters of the novel characterize Babu's sensitivity as a sign of effeminacy. He is praised by one of the characters for his role as a woman in a musical play. He remembers being so astounded by Babu's compelling performance of femininity in all its 'shyness, modesty and seductiveness' that he cannot believe Babu was actually a man (Janakiraman 1964: 5). Although the novel sustains the equation between his effeminacy and his later career as a Hindustani singer, there is an attempt to counter Babu's effeminacy through his relationships with other men in the novel. Relationships among men in the novel acquire significance in the way they constitute and reassure male sexual integrity. Babu's relationships with the three other male characters in the novel—his father Vaitti, his music teacher Ranganna, and his friend Rajam—consolidate his celibate masculinity. At various points, Babu promises to practice abstinence and deify women to ensure he is not distracted from the disciplined pursuit of music. Babu's poor father, a devotional singer and accountant, aspires to model his son in the revered image of his spiritual guru Raju, an ardent devotee of the goddess Devi. Vaitti teaches Babu a mantra he learnt from Raju to protect his spiritual interests from sexual indulgence and asks him to keep the mantra a secret to uphold its auspiciousness (1964: 159). He urges Babu to have faith in Raju's spiritual powers and his own moral strength to confront sensual pleasures. He reminds Babu to practice sensual and sexual abstinence and venerate women other than his wife, as 'lusting after other women is a loss of one's self-respect and reputation' (1964: 160).

There is little to distinguish Babu from the other men in the novel except for the fact that Babu eventually loses self-control and gives in to his desires. Unlike the other men who remain celibate ideals, Babu is humanized in the process of succumbing to Yamuna's beauty and exposing his vulnerability. Rajam, with whom he shares an intimate friendship, mirrors Babu's sexual struggles but retains his purity until his marriage. Rajam, like many of Janakiraman's male characters, is a sensitive young man who is easily unsettled by the mere sight of female beauty, but his attempts to resist temptation by deifying women apparently secure his relationship with god. However, the tension between the sexual and the sacred persists in Rajam's idealization of beautiful women. When Babu asks him to accompany him to the temple Rajam refuses, 'my mind wavers ... my attention is drawn to the women and even if my eyes turn to the deity my mind does not ...' (1964: 37). He remembers feeling betrayed by a woman he idealized when she eloped with her lover (1964: 200). Following Rajam's marriage and departure from Kumbakonam, Babu remembers him as a sensuous memory of slender beauty that he associates with Yamuna. Babu's inhibited desire for Rajam is couched in the same rhetoric of idealization that is used to tame the threat of female beauty. But the possibility of same-sex intimacy is averted with Rajam's departure.

Babu's pedagogical relationship with his devout father mirrors his relationship with his music teacher, Ranganna. For Babu, Ranganna is a model of spiritual discipline that he strives, but ultimately fails to attain. He internalizes Ranganna's spiritual imperative to maintain celibacy as a condition for the acquisition of musical knowledge; to achieve 'the satisfaction of the soul' (1964: 45). The goal for Ranganna is to attain spiritual satisfaction rather than commercial success, which would only cheapen the art and estrange the artist. Ranganna's character is consistent with the general distaste for urban capitalism that is implied in many of Janakiraman's novels. Art or music is posited as a pure and abstract form of spiritual expression that has to be protected from the corrupting effects of the modern monetary economy.

Babu's uncertain evaluation of Yamuna's beauty pre-empts the possibility of acknowledging his desire for a seemingly inaccessible ideal. Her beauty does not match her mother's, but her beauty is not limited to her physicality and indexes her essential nobility and grandeur. The suppression of his desire can be sensed in his apparent dissatisfaction with her beauty, which is apparently flawed by two related aspects of her identity—her unmarried status and her mixed-caste identity as the daughter of a Brahman father and Maratha mother. Her beauty is ostensibly incomplete when compared to her mother's perfect beauty, with the 'royal blood of the Marathas' (1964: 42). As Babu looks at old photographs of Parvatibai, he realizes her beauty eclipses that of Yamuna's:

> It is hard to compare Parvatibai's beauty. At this age even a child would say Parvatibai is more beautiful than Yamuna. One cannot say Yamuna is a favored beauty. Her facial features were like her father's. But besides her face, her height and her bodily frame, her hands and legs, her long fingers and curved nails were just like her mother's ... but she was slightly fairer than her mother. Still, if one glimpsed at their faces, Parvati's face and the curves of her parted hair along her forehead reminded one of a smiling statue with a blooming lotus bud sculpted on the pillar of a temple. Yamuna's face was not endowed with such a complete beauty. But, no one can hesitate in calling her a beauty. Yamuna's gait is more beautiful than Parvati's. When Parvati walks only a little bit of her right foot can be seen. Yamuna walks as though she is in a court. Although she is so beautiful.... (1964: 43)

In the absence of Yamuna's father, Babu performs the role of a surrogate son and brother, and assumes the responsibility of finding

Yamuna a husband. But her age and mixed caste prove to be impediments to her marriage. In the process of ending a marriage proposal from an older man who slanders Yamuna's birth and reputation, Babu admits his desire for her. But his desire for an ideal woman who does not return his love is doomed. Yamuna is not a desiring character; rather, she embodies an elusive sense of wholeness that desire strives to possess to complete the human subject. She resists interpretation and remains an inscrutable, aesthetic ideal that can never be possessed. If Yamuna is an unattainable ideal of wholeness that spurs Babu to transcend desire and the body, she is in stark contrast to Thangammal, a miserable young wife who seduces Babu. Babu interprets his sensual exchange with Thangammal as a betrayal to Yamuna, who remains indifferent to his desire. Thus, the final consummation of Babu's desire for Yamuna is disillusioning, which compels him to transfer his desire to the equally abstract plenitude of classical music. The true aim of desire seems to be the desire to keep desiring, so that desire can be neither satisfied nor eliminated.

Desire here has to be understood as an ideology that is constantly mediated by the ideal and the representational; the spiritual and the material. Yamuna and Thangammal are two ends of the ideology of desire: if Yamuna is an aesthetic ideal that goes beyond desire and the body, Thangammal's desires de-idealize her, and her desire for Babu reinforces his desire for Yamuna. The novel thus fixes Babu's position as an ever-desiring subject whose desire is to keep desiring an unattainable ideal. That his desire for Yamuna is neither exhausted by nor limited to their sexual encounter compels Babu to reconfigure his own sense of self.

Babu and Thangammal's encounter resembles the illicit encounters of Rajagopalan's oeuvre, where the traditional Tamil home ironically becomes the space of sensual transgressions. Thangammal is the neglected wife of a much older and sickly man who is insecure of her youthful beauty and incarcerates her at home on his way to work. The only space where Thangammal has limited access to the outer world is the backyard, which is open to the sky but is covered with iron bars and fortressed by tall walls. Babu's room overlooks Thangammal's backyard, but the two hardly exchange words. Yet, even when they are not exchanging glances, they are acutely aware of each other's presence. The sensuality with which Thangammal's presence is evoked and perceived by Babu is reminiscent of the sensual intimacy of Rajagopalan's lovers. Babu frequently observes Thangammal from his apartment window and comments that she 'does not have Yamuna's intelligent and lustrous face [although] her youth sparkles on her face' (1964: 231). When she stealthily seduces him at night, Babu is debilitated by his desire for her sensuous beauty. He notices

> her sparkling face. The beaming light from her diamond earring shone on her cheek. The loose tendril of hair above her ear had unusually descended on her face enhancing the luster of her face. Perhaps the beauty of her face was because of this tendril! The rose colored powder on her face was fragrant and cool. The flowers in her hair were white edged and particularly suitable. The turmeric and *kunkumam* on her forehead shone brilliantly. There was a diamond nose ring that shone on her nose. (1964: 350)

When Thangammal kisses Babu on his lips he is assaulted by

> her soft breath, the fragrance of the flowers, the beautiful and fragrant form of her youth ... the soft down hair on her cheek sparkles ... what a beautiful forehead! What gentleness in the strand of hair before her ears! She rubbed her cheeks against his neck.... But the next moment the wife's desire for Babu de-idealizes her and her beauty. He refuses to have a conversation with her and asks her to leave. (1964: 354)

Janakiraman's narratives betray sympathy for his sexually transgressive characters, many of whom are trapped in unhappy marriages. These transgressions exceed the limits of marriage without resulting in an open violation of social codes. Moral conflict is a purely internalized affair dramatized within the character rather than between the character and society. Neither Babu nor Thangammal is stigmatized for their illicit desire. Thangammal's solitary incarceration by a possessive, older husband initially evokes Babu's sympathy and indignation. When Thangammal is stung by a scorpion, Babu rushes to get medicines to assuage her pain. This act of compassion evokes Thangammal's awkward love and gratitude, which she expresses through a set of letters. The letter, like Rajagopalan's stories, is the only available means of expressing illicit love in a sexually segregated world. But the letters also become a source of fear and guilt for Thangammal and Babu, both of whom risk losing their reputation. Babu's guilt over the loss of his sexual purity, however, is far greater than the fear of discovery. He is haunted by the disembodied paternal voices of sexual prohibition—those of his father, Vaitti, his guru, Ranganna, and his friend, Rajam—shaming him for betraying their trust.

In Janakiraman's narratives, the conflict between desire and internalized paternal authority is depicted as a conflict between the profane and the sacred. The correlation between the two are mutually implicated in Babu's perception of the world, whether it is Thangammal, who is both deified and blamed for Babu's seduction, or the flowers his mother uses for her prayers, which connote auspiciousness and the profanity of illicit female desire. Babu interprets his contaminating encounter with Thangammal as a betrayal to Yamuna. In the conflict between desire and internalized paternal authority, there is a growing equation between Yamuna and music, both of which are at once physical and spiritual experiences. Babu's perception of Yamuna is mediated by her particular person and by her universal value as a divine ideal that transcends the body.

Yamuna is a special being. When I prepare to chant and shut my eyes she places her feet on my heart. She gives me faith and courage. She gives me fortitude from her undying eyes. But ... but ... why this ... can everyone receive her affection and kindness? Will they always receive it? Didn't anyone else receive it? Isn't this affection, this stubborn affection for me? Is this all this affection means? Why this dual form? When I meditate she is a goddess! Then ... a beautiful woman, a celebration of youth, removing the veil that covers her beauty, captures my thoughts, I lose my thoughts ... but she can be both at once! (1964: 380)

When Yamuna is shocked by his apparent confession of love for her, Babu replies:

You ask me how I dared to ask you something like this? Yamuna, why do you stubbornly refuse to understand anything? I never expected to ask you something like this. Over the past four months I feel as though I'm walking with a pair of slippers that took four months to find from several other pairs ... whenever I think of God your face appears before me. It's your feet that appear before me. I don't think of you as an ordinary woman. Bathing, eating, speaking ordinarily, getting married, running a family, becoming a mother—these are things ordinary women do. I think you are above all that. I can't understand the thought of you getting married. I got furious with that man who came from Coimbatore. His fear as he left made me relieved. [Yamuna] Because you don't have anyone to compete with? [Babu] That's what it must be. Now that you say it I understand. Only now do I feel it. Then, I felt angry without knowing why. I was upset that he was such a fool. [Yamuna] You mean you were jealous. [Babu] Maybe. It wasn't until last night that I was really clear. Even then I didn't have the courage to tell you. (1964: 390)

Babu's appreciation for Hindustani music is mediated by his idealization of Yamuna. His initial indifference to a performance by an itinerant Hindustani singer is retroactively transformed into admiration at the sight of Yamuna's absorbed engagement. The physiological signs of her otherwise inexpressible ecstasy determine Babu's relationship with music. Disillusioned by his sexual encounter with Yamuna, who no longer remains an alluring ideal of perfection, Babu partly sublimates his desire in music. He trains his voice under the tutelage of a Hindustani singer to capture the affective complexity of longing and loss. Thus, the narrative suggests a connection between the formal purity of Hindustani music and an idealized notion of femininity. In other words, Hindustani music, I argue, is characterized as a specifically feminine mode of expressing love and desire in separation, a traditional trope in many genres of Hindustani music and ancient Indian literature. Not only does Babu capture his longing for the ideal Yamuna, he also equates the aural purity of Hindustani music to the singing female voice while listening to the pitch-perfect voice of his female student. Early in the novel, Babu attributes the aesthetic superiority of instrumental and Hindustani music to their privileging of pure melody over words. To him it confirms, '... the superior taste of the listener and the expertise and aesthetics of the singer ... the singer needs to recognize the unique nature of a raga, a listener should be able to imagine and hear the form of the raga in his head ... music is not just for singing but also for meditation ...' (1964: 28).

Cemparutti (Hibiscus: 1968)

Cemparutti is representative of Janakiraman's larger oeuvre in its thematization of the conflict between desire and filial duty; a conflict that reconfigures subjectivity. The novel is largely focalized through its embattled male protagonist Sattanathan and traces the decline of the extended family in rural Tanjavur. Like in the earlier novels, *Ammā Vantāḷ* and *Mōkamuḷ*, in *Cemparutti*, ties among men constitute and reinforce male sexual integrity against the potential threat of (female) desire. However, here too the internalization of paternal authority fails to eliminate the power of illicit desire to destabilize and remake the self. It is the cultivation of an attitude of detachment and selfless love that finally enables the birth of a Sattanathan free of the ritual ties of religion and family.

The devout Sattanathan, due to a certain set of circumstances, ends up becoming the sole provider to a large extended family. But his reputation as a chaste and responsible householder is undermined by his fraught relationship with his sisters-in-law and his wife. These relationships—that constitute three narrative strands in the novel—are interlinked by the motif of sexual suspicion. Sattanathan's widowed sister-in-law Kunjammal bitterly resents him for privileging what she thinks is his reputation over his childhood love for her. His older sister-in-law Periyanni is an insecure and suspicious woman who discovers her husband Gopal's relationship with Andal, a virtuous devadasi.[1] Following Gopal's bankruptcy and disappearance, Periyanni and her children are compelled to depend on Sattanathan for their survival. Her financial insecurity and resentment for Sattanathan drives her to slander his relationship with Kunjammal. And towards the end of the novel, Sattanathan's wife Buvana, who accepted his past love for Kunjammal, imagines they are betraying her. Thus each woman at various points in the narrative suspects Sattanathan's integrity to the point that he begins to question his own loyalty to the family. The women's claims and accusations lead Sattanathan to challenge the moral strictures of marriage, family, and religion. He finally withdraws from the ritual ties of family and religion to potentially redirect his love towards the poor and disenfranchised during the Indian struggle for Independence.

The events in the story take place over a period of 40 years, from the early years of the twentieth century to the years after the Second World War and Indian Independence. Sattanathan is the youngest son of a landed upper-caste Veḷḷāḷar family who is generally immersed in religious texts when he is supposed to be helping his older brother Muthusami administer their land. Muthusami complains of his brother's irresponsibility, but secretly admires his piety and erudition. He arranges for him to receive religious instruction from Tandava Vattiyar, a teacher in the village. It is there that Sattanathan and Kunjammal, the teacher's daughter, secretly fall in love with each other without exchanging a word. But Sattanathan is betrayed when Kunjammal is married to Muthusami. Living with his brother and sister-in-law becomes a persistent source of remorseful longing and a reason for the ultimate estrangement of the extended family. This echoes a familiar trope in Janakiraman of the estranging effects of quasi-incestuous desire within the family even if this desire is never sexually consummated. Sattanathan and Kunjammal's sensual love persists despite or rather precisely because of the filialization of their relationship. Their sensual proximity is ironically ensured by the presumed sexual innocence of the relationship and the secured spaces of the traditional rural house like the veranda, the kitchen, and the backyard. They never openly look at each other and most of their conversations are mediated through Sattanathan's mother, who occupies the interstitial spaces between the kitchen and the front courtyard. During the occasional moments when they are alone in the backyard, Kunjammal upsets their formal relationship with memories of their childhood love. She holds him responsible for their separation, while Sattanathan accuses Kunjammal for her lack of loyalty. Their mutual resentment, however, suggests there is a greater impetus on men who have the freedom of voicing their desire to marry the women of their choice without being stigmatized. Their secret intimacy persists even as it is threatened by Muthusami's premature death by cholera. Before his death, Muthusami entrusts his wife and daughter to Sattanathan's care and arranges his marriage to Buvana, the daughter of a pious family. Sattanathan is trapped between his love for Kunjammal and his devotion to his brother. Following his death, Muthusami acquires the authority of an internalized father figure who forbids Sattanathan from realizing his desire for Kunjammal. Neither his devotion to his brother nor religious worship allow Sattanathan to sublimate his desire. Sattanathan's conflict is intensified by Kunjammal's widowed beauty and sexuality that resist the austerities of widowhood. Thus, like the other widowed characters in Janakiraman's works, the transgressive potential of the young widow lies in her ability to not conform to the abstinence prescribed for the widow.

Sattanathan's marriage to Buvana does not make a difference to his secret relationship with Kunjammal. The sensuality of their intimacy evokes bodily presence through sight, or even the sound, and odour of the beloved, a trope seen in depictions of illicit relationships in Janakiraman and Rajagopalan. There are several instances in the novel where Sattanathan betrays a heightened awareness of Kunjammal's seemingly spectral presence before he actually sees her appearing within the spatial limits of the veranda and kitchen. Even when he is fantasizing about Buvana's modest beauty, Sattanathan can sense Kunjammal's presence. As she comes to terms with the impossibility of having an actual relationship, the act of merely looking at him becomes a sufficient source of pleasure for Kunjammal.

> He turned and closed his eyes. Something like a form in between the two verandahs; he closed his eyes.... It was Kunjammal.... She stood looking at him without lifting her eyes. Even in the dark he could see her staring at him. If he couldn't see her his skin could feel it. That penetrating look must have woken him up.... [Kunjammal] 'Can I stay here after Buvana comes? ... I want to keep looking at you till I die.... I don't want to deceive anyone. If not my body, what will happen to what is within me? If I keep looking at you that's enough.' (Janakiraman 1968: 118)

Kunjammal's open endorsement of his marriage to Buvana suggests that her love for Sattanathan can survive in all its intensity only as a mediated sensual expression of longing. Kunjammal's longing for Sattanathan is displaced to an extent to Buvana. Sattanathan imagines Kunjammal's displaced affections when, to Buvana's discomfort, Kunjammal embraces and kisses her at the slightest pretext, 'Buvana's eye seemed to say, "It's because she can't hug you that she makes all this noise and fuss!"' (1968: 172). But over the course of the novel, Sattanathan becomes tied to his responsibilities as an impartial provider and caregiver for his extended family, and this checks the possibility of dedicating himself to Kunjammal. Sattanathan's status as a householder can only be legitimized by his moral integrity, which demands absolute fidelity to his wife, necessitating the filialization of all other ties. When Kunjammal accuses him of being cowardly and selfish for being more concerned about his moral reputation than his love for her, he encourages her to 'treat everyone like [her] child ...' (1968: 213). If Sattanathan's self-discipline conditions the possibility of selfless care and responsibility, Kunjammal represents the selfish exclusivity of romantic love that cannot be substituted for any other relationship. Their relationship ends when Kunjammal discovers to her shock and humiliation that Buvana knows of their past love. From the touch of Kunjammal's first and last embrace, Sattanathan realizes desire can never be destroyed even if it is illicit. He perceives Kunjammal's undying desire as a sign of her authenticity and exonerates her of blame and stigma. But for Sattanathan, desire has to be sublimated to realize its ethical and social potential. This first takes the form of religious worship but is later discarded for asceticism. Kunjammal believes that religious faith can never insure a person from pain and loss, and it is her rejection of religion that partly conditions Sattanathan's own rejection of religion and family later in the novel.

Cemparutti sets up a moral opposition between Periyanni, Sattanathan's older sister-in-law, and Andal, her husband Gopal's lover. Periyanni is held responsible for the fragmentation of the extended family and the crisis in Sattanathan's life. She is consistently represented as a formidable woman whose dominance barely conceals her financial and emotional insecurity. As the wife of a wealthy rice and ghee merchant, she resents Sattanathan's family for being given a part of their income. When her husband faces insolvency, she is unable to accept her poverty and the necessity of having to depend on Sattanathan. She is enraged but powerless to stop Gopal's secret relationship with Andal, a virtuous devadasi who redeems a part of his debts. Through Sattanathan, the narrator idealizes Andal's lustrous and auspicious beauty that corresponds to her benevolence. Her advice to the soon-to-be-married Sattanathan reflects Andal's own position as an ideal 'wife'. Her ideal of conjugality is premised not on physical beauty but on mutual tolerance and unity in the face of adversity. An ironic opposition is set up between Andal, the 'wifely' devadasi and Periyanni, the suspicious and undeserving wife. The novel further suggests that chastity is not a sufficient precondition for a good marriage. Andal mirrors some of Janakiraman's other women characters whose inner humanity is untainted by their relationships with several men. Although Andal has not been a chaste woman like Periyanni, she is valorized for her intelligence and resourcefulness (1968: 201). Shortly before his death, Gopal glorifies Andal for her 'gentle ... humanness ... for saying the truth' (1968: 340). In contrast, the chaste Periyanni is the root cause of the crisis that transforms Sattanathan's life when she slanders his relationship with Kunjammal. But towards the end of her life, Periyanni turns to religious worship to atone for her mistakes. Even her death by starvation is interpreted as a divine or even self-inflicted punishment for the dereliction of her conjugal duties. Before she dies she begs Gopal and Kunjammal for their forgiveness.

Periyanni functions as a foil to Andal and Buvana. The narrator's description of Buvana's idealized beauty echoes descriptions of Yamuna, Alankaram, and Indu. From the moment she is introduced, Buvana embodies the air of divine auspiciousness that pervades her house. She is named after her father's patron deity, the goddess Buvanesvari, which matches her divine appearance: 'Another form appeared from within. A woman. His eyes were suddenly struck by her large eyes and the golden hue that blossomed from her fair body. Sattanathan unconsciously averted his eyes. The impression of her turmeric smeared arms and legs could still be seen.... A slight smell of turmeric seemed to waft in the air ...' (1968: 41).

Sattanathan's first impression of Buvana is that of an inscrutable and extraordinary woman who stands apart from the rest of her family. He is struck by the quiet efficiency and almost divine air of equanimity with which she manages and negotiates differences in a large family. Although Sattanathan confides his past love for Kunjammal, Buvana is initially unaffected by his confession; he marvels at the apparent ease with which she handles her sisters-in-law's insecurities and takes care of the growing needs of several children, including her own. Her ability to make light of their growing financial burdens particularly in a time of scarcity amazes and comforts Sattanathan. Buvana's inner strength is repeatedly contrasted to Sattanathan's emotional fragility, particularly when he is troubled by his sisters-in-law's accusations. It is her perfect understanding and acceptance of Periyanni and Kunjammal that helps Sattanathan cope with his inner conflict and the growing crisis in his family and marriage. In short, Buvana represents the ideal wife who understands her husband's struggles and is able to negotiate with the other members of the family.

Buvana is associated with the eponymous motif of the novel, the *cemparutti* or hibiscus flowers that she always wears in her hair.

The flower that is believed to be the goddess Buvaneswari/Ambal's favourite flower is a metaphor that equates the goddess with Buvana's aesthetic purity and perfection. From her father's description of Buvana's tended hibiscus garden, the hibiscus attains the status of an aesthetic order that is beyond the utilitarian. Despite her mother's entreaties to grow vegetables, Buvana plants several hibiscus saplings that thrive under her attentive care. Thus, the flower is closely associated with Buvana's selfless domesticity and anticipates her ability to hold together an increasingly fragmented family. By the end of the novel, the pair of red hibiscus flowers in Buvana's hair comes to symbolize for Sattanathan, the uneasy intimacy between the self and an other that can never become one.

Buvana's character is effectively twinned with that of her father Senbagavanam Pillai whose piety extends the novel's initial emphasis on piety as a source of hope and redemption.

> A voice could be heard from inside. A voice worshipping god. A sweet voice. As though two people were singing together ... ten seconds later a unique sweetness flowed through it. A voice like bees flying in the sky.... A large body. Dusky complexioned. A large head that suited the large body. A bald head. A necklace of rosary beads around the neck. A silk white dhoti with a brick red border wrapped around his waist.... Bare-chested, with no mole or hair or wrinkles, his sandal and sacred ash smeared body sparkled.... (1968: 40–2)

Music in the form of the singing voice plays an important role in *Cemparutti*, as it does in Janakiraman's earlier novels. Sattanathan is visibly moved by the otherworldly experience of listening to Senbagavanam's devotional songs in praise of the goddess. He experiences a hitherto unknown sense of solitude that enables him to distance himself from his cares and reconfigure his relationship to himself and the world. When Sattanathan asks him for spiritual guidance, Senbagavanam cautions him not to practice religious meditation at the risk of neglecting his domestic responsibilities. Sattanathan's life is a constant negotiation between the self and the other, between the individual and the collective. Even as he is determined to prove his sisters-in-law's accusations about his amassing wealth for his own family, Sattanathan cynically admits the selfishness that characterizes worldly life. Religion, like family and marriage, can no longer command Sattanathan's faith, and in the hope for a more inclusive future, he decides to renounce his life as a householder. He is determined to shed all greed and ambition in an attempt to experience a selfless form of love that can reach out to the poor and underprivileged in a world ravaged by the Second World War.

In the third section of the novel, Sattanathan wonders if he was an honest and impartial provider. He is filled with guilt at the thought of having betrayed everyone and begins to question the value of his life. His overwhelming sense of worthlessness is fuelled by his envy and admiration of the revolutionaries and freedom fighters he knows. Sattanathan feels guilty for getting married when he sees that the police have beaten and fractured the arm of his store assistant for picketing foreign cloth and liquor stores. This was in 1930, when Gandhi's call for a non-violent mass movement against foreign cloth and liquor led many youth away from their jobs to participate in the widespread anti-colonial agitations. Some of Sattanathan's other acquaintances die in hospitals because of a shortage of medicines, or languish in prisons for their involvement in the 1942 Quit India protests. At a time of extreme poverty, mass shortage of food, and high prices of essential commodities, Sattanathan becomes the recipient of several bronze idols that were unearthed from his ancestral lands by his tenant. His first impulse is to distribute his newfound wealth in the family. Later, he regrets not giving his wealth to the beggars in the trains. He grows ashamed of his relatively privileged status as he reflects on the problem of poverty and inequality in the world.

Sattanathan's tender friendship with Sitapati also known as Bommai Iyer, a communist, partly redeems his sense of worthlessness. During a disagreement with Iyer, Sattanathan concedes that one does not have to sacrifice one's life for the nationalist cause to have a sense of accomplishment. Iyer, an itinerant communist who renounced his family and does not directly participate in the nationalist struggle, tries to convince Sattanathan that his self-deprecation shows a lack of self-love, which contradicts his faith in god. He questions Sattanathan's faith in a god who does nothing to help him overcome his low self-esteem. For Iyer, an ethical life that does not involve 'lying, theft, deception' is equal to a life sacrificed for the nation (1968: 422). Like the sensual intimacy of Babu's friendship with Rajam in *Mokamul*, Sattanathan's intimate friendship with Iyer is a source of self-affirmation and is the only significant relationship he has without the selfish ties of kinship and marriage. Their ideal friendship is couched in conjugal terms, '... Sattanathan had told him his family matters seeing his feminine heart. Bommai was the only friend he had found in this life, in this world. He would open his heart to him out of the elation and infatuation of having found a nonexistent love' (1968: 422).

Through Iyer, the novel offers a Marxist critique of the institutions of religion, family, and private property, which fuel human greed. Iyer has a decisive influence on Sattanathan, who, towards the end of the novel, renounces the institutionalized corruption and hypocrisy of religion and religious texts and turns to modern European literary classics, the Russian writer Leo Tolstoy, and the Bengali writers Rabindranath Tagore and Sarat Chandra Chattopadhyay for their noble ideals of selfless love. When Iyer is murdered for being a communist—this was a time when communists were perceived as enemies of the state—Sattanathan is confronted by the inescapable solitude that shadows every other person and the impossibility of a permanent union with other. He realizes that true freedom is found not in family or possessions but in a detached sense of solitude and selflessness that transforms into an ongoing attempt to negotiate the mass violence and poverty that characterize the historical setting of the novel, the Second World War and its aftermath. His marriage to Buvana also undergoes a spiritual transformation. Sattanathan's detachment thwarts Buvana's sexual love for him, which makes her suspect his love for Kunjammal. She turns delusional and imagines that he is having an affair. In due course, her health improves with psychiatric treatment, and she spends all her time writing god's name on a book. For her, this ritual religiosity is a way of effacing her sense of self by temporarily withdrawing from worldly existence. This is an ironic contrast to Sattanathan's religious scepticism. Now it is his turn to feel neglected by Buvana, who he feels he has lost to god. It is, however, Iyer's sudden murder that spells the end of Buvana's religious faith. In death, Iyer becomes the greatest symbol of humanity; for someone who cared so much for everyone, he had no faith in god or family. In the conflict between desire and filial duty, there emerges a more fundamental inquiry into the true nature of that freedom which lies in dismantling family and marriage, and the selfishness that underlies these structures. Freedom is not unlimited power, but precisely the process of negotiating the relations between the self and the other, the individual and the social, through the idiom of selfless care.

Marappacu (The Wooden Cow: 1975)

Marappacu, like Janakiraman's other novels, represents the sensual as a mode of embodied perception that transforms intersubjective relations. In this novel, the transformative potential of the sensual lies in the power of touch to blur and reconfigure the opposition between subject and object. Unlike most of Janakiraman's narratives, which feature male protagonists, *Marappacu* has a young Brahman woman, Ammani, at the centre of the story. Her tactile relationships cut across social distinctions and recreate meaning and subjectivity. The inter-corporeal act of touching holds the potential to negotiate and rework social relations of power to produce ever new and shifting forms of intersubjectivity. What is suggested through the novel's central character is that the tactile body, unlike the mind or soul, is the ultimate material reality, where norms are inscribed and potentially challenged. The novel's increasingly Marxist attitude towards religion, family, and marriage brings it thematically close to *Cemparutti*.

Ammani is the daughter of the secretary of the wealthy zamindar Kandu. Her parents entrust her education to him, and it is under Kandu's care that the young Ammani witnesses the cruelty and hypocrisy of marriage and family. The opening chapter of the novel describes Ammani's mockery of social conventions, which she openly expresses through defiant laughter. She laughs at the apparent joy and sorrow of relatives at weddings and funerals, and at her aunt's class arrogance; she is amused by her hypocritical friends, the 'unkempt Draupadis' (Janakiraman 1975: 4) who romanticize armed revolution as the only solution to poverty and inequality, but discard their ethical integrity at the prospect of disinheritance and turn into compliant, silk sari-clad women. She exposes the sexual hypocrisy of men who derive voyeuristic pleasure from the sight of a nude woman bathing even as they uphold the virtue of female modesty. As a young girl, she refuses to wear clothes just to embarrass her mother. The only time she doesn't laugh is when she sees herself in the mirror. If laughter insinuates her position as a detached spectator to social hypocrisy, the silent recognition of her reflection marks her inevitable implication in the very structures of convention that she dismisses. The novel explores the complex negotiations between individual agency and the social structures of power through the trope of touch.

Of all the senses, touch is an ambiguous form of bodily perception that manifests the body as both an idea and experience. As Merleau-Ponty argues in *Phenomenology of Perception* (2012), touch, particularly between bodies, is a bidirectional act that blurs the opposition between subject and object. The ambiguity of touch and its ability to transform its subject and the object is evident in the novel, where touch is not merely a physical experience but also an imagined one. The novel is focalized through Ammani and her urge to 'know' other bodies, and relies not only on physical touch but also on a tactile imagination of working-class bodies. The novel suggests the partial displacement of the devout Brahman body by the working-class body that possesses the potential to bring about change. I return to this point later in my discussion of the novel.

The early chapters of the novel invest touch with an ethical impulse to acknowledge disempowered bodies and subvert social norms. Ammani is driven by an urge to touch victims of stigma and authority. She feels the need to comfort Visvam, Kandu's disciple, when he is unceremoniously disowned for learning Sanskrit from other gurus. She is disturbed by the sight of Kandu's young daughter being subject to the austerities of widowhood. Unlike her parents, she refuses to be subservient to Kandu's authority and marry his son. Her tactile friendship with a judge's daughter enables the latter to confide her resentment for her authoritarian father. She 'pollutes' a priest when she touches him with the apparent intention of gaining indirect access to the untouchable idol of god in a temple. As an act of renouncing god she publicly burns her aunt's idols. She also longs to breach the sexual segregation in school through touch. She nurses a male classmate when he is beaten for drawing in class. That her relationship with the classmate is slandered only strengthens Ammani's determination to care for him. When a friend questions her impulse to touch people she replies:

> I'm not lecturing or being superstitious. I'm not talking about spiritual or body revolutions.... I doubt the soul and the mind exist. I only have this body.... It is not enough [for me to see someone]. I feel as if I can only understand someone if I touch them. If someone doesn't touch me I feel as if I have lost something, as though something is missing. (1975: 34)

Ammani goes to live with her aunt and uncle who initially seem to be the liberal parents she never had, but they disown her when she admits her relationship with a much older singer named Gopali. For a man who is uncomfortable with being touched, she ironically feels her uncle's love and concern most when she is beaten for her illicit relationship. Ammani emerges as an avowedly Marxist character whose experience of stigma and humiliation compel her to renounce god, marriage, and family. She embodies the sensuous possibilities of what she calls 'free love', which can never be limited to the exclusivity of marriage. Her sensuous relationship with several men including Gopali possesses the social potential of creating shifting forms of embodied intersubjectivity. These relationships are irreducible to the sexual act and subsist in the unspoken indeterminacy of tactile intimacy. Her attraction to Gopali is initially tied to the sensuality of his beauty and his singing voice, and not to his speech or his touch that to her only betray pretence. Gopali's singing voice is an embodiment of Ammani's ideal of a subaltern love with the power to draw and 'touch' marginalized sections of society. She embraces Gopali when he refuses to accept a fee to sing at her cousin's wedding and asks his poor driver be paid for the trip. On one hand, Gopali's apparent simplicity makes him appear as a spectacular symbol of the working class; this is suggested by the contrast between his near illiteracy and his versatile voice. While his classical songs attract the attention of the Brahman men in the audience, his ability to sing different genres of folk music caters to the popular tastes of the marginalized—women and children, lower-caste men, and other poor, working-class bystanders. Except for her uncle, the Brahman men in the audience disapprove of his folk songs. Gopali reminds Ammani of Krishna and Jesus Christ, both of whom appear to her as symbols of subaltern and promiscuous love that led women and children away from the bondage of marriage and family. On the other hand, the sight of Gopali singing is at once a self-divesting and solipsistic activity that runs counter to the possibility of a sensuous relationship with humanity. The memory of Gopali abruptly ending a public performance because of whispers in the audience and his subsequent private performance for Kandu convinces Ammani of his self-absorption. While she is drawn to his singing body, his seemingly filial touch and speech are a pretence that betrays his desire for her.

Ammani moves to Madras with Gopali, where he finds her an apartment. A solitary life in a quiet and green part of the city implies freedom from a rural world stultified by religious ritualism and exploitation. Ammani develops a keen awareness of the natural world around her and realizes the meaninglessness of habits designed to make life meaningful. Her desire for sensuous relationships with men across the world is an attempt, I suggest, to reject a sense of purposelessness in a mundane and provincial world. For Ammani, free love is the truth of human existence that has been artificially circumscribed by the exclusivity of marriage. Ammani's open love for the world is implicitly identified with a masculine disposition to be an autonomous and promiscuous subject that can never be owned or exchanged. In contrast, Gopali is represented as a provincial man whose beauty, self-indulgence, and musical sensibility are (even self-) identified with a feminine disposition to be self-effacing and yet be validated by everyone. He is feminized further by becoming a substitutable object of Ammani's love. But Gopali also exercises his prerogative as a man to make claims on Ammani's love and body. He pretends to be her adoptive father in the city unlike Ammani who declares their relationship openly to her aunt and uncle. Many of Gopali's friends compete for her attention, much to his jealousy.

Gopali's sexual double standards are undercut by Ammani's genuine endorsement of free love. This is evident in the encounter with the Bennets, a British family who assume that Ammani is Gopali's wife. Although Gopali is happy to go along with this assumption, Ammani declares her rejection of monogamy. (For Gopali, love is characterized by a sense of ownership and exclusivity even though this applies only to women. He is anxious to preserve his loveless marriage to an ugly wife to retain his reputation, but he knows that Ammani will leave him for another man if she loses interest.) What makes

Gopali's love conform to a conjugal understanding of the concept is its partiality and singularity. This is in contrast to Ammani's expansive ideal of sensual love that is indistinguishable from care that aims to humanize the world through touch while still being premised on conflict. In the ensuing conversation, Ammani suggests that freedom from conflict and violence is an impossible ideal. Even if economic and social equality were to bring about 'Marx's Ramrajyam' (1975: 200), it does not guarantee lasting peace and happiness. But Mr Bennet makes a distinction between the exclusivity of conjugal love and the all-inclusive nature of selfless love for the world. He is unsettled by Ammani's ideal of free love, which offers no guarantee or security, subsists purely on self-reliance, and is consistent with her claim to be god. While he identifies selfless love for the world as a manifestation of god, he challenges the inclusivity of her free love, which does not include diseased and disabled bodies. For Bennet, the fulfilment of man's basic needs is sufficient to eliminate all conflict that arises from greed. But for Ammani, even a perfect world can never remain perfect because it is necessarily premised on the condition of conflict that promises historical change. Her sensual notion of love is thus a historical factor that hinges on the very dialectic between the self and the other, and between identity and difference.

As a self-styled Marxist, Ammani initially idealizes the apparent self-sufficiency of labouring and working-class bodies. These bodies are barely invested with any interiority as they are manifest purely through the acts of labour that seemingly attest their authenticity This is evident in the motif of the Kaḷḷar man and woman, a community of bandits, warriors, and pastoral peasants known for their physical strength. The Brahman locality where Ammani grew up was adjacent to Kaḷḷar quarters. Ammani remembers a young and strong Kaḷḷar boy who threatens to assault Kandu for exploitation. She also recalls the stark contrast between the quiet efficiency of her mother's neighbour's maidservant, a shapely and dark Kaḷḷar woman, and her effete and sickly husband. The woman later has an affair with a landlord. Although the husband and the town finally acknowledge their affair, the landlord chops the woman's hand off in a furious altercation. She manages to go to the nearest hospital on her own and returns to work a month later. Ammani envies the woman's courage and resilience and wonders at the woman's future had she been educated, and later on she learns that Pattabi, Gopali's nephew, learnt a traditional martial sport from the Kaḷḷar men in his village and works as a cook to pay for his education. Gopali's devout aestheticism is displaced by the working-class body when Ammani has a sensual relationship with Pattabi. This shift is anticipated by Ammani's dreams of Lenin and Tolstoy toppling Tyagaraja, one of the greatest composers of south-Indian Carnatic music and a sacred object of Gopali's veneration. Her intense attraction for Pattabi is again premised on the idealized plenitude of a working-class body. Gopali arranges for Pattabi, a poor student, to stay with Ammani while he finishes his schooling. Over the months she comes to admire his strong presence and domestic efficiency. Although Pattabi resembles Gopali in appearance, they could not be more different. If Gopali represents the privileged, spiritual aesthetic of music, Pattabi represents a material engagement with the phenomenal world. His 'scientific' interest in music does not privilege songs, but extends to a whole range of sounds that betrays a keen awareness of the everyday. While Gopali grows jealous of Ammani's intimacies with other men, Pattabi remains indifferent. He even physically intervenes and overpowers one of Gopali's older friends when he makes advances towards her. In his long absences, Ammani remembers him as someone who occupied multiple roles as a caregiver, 'a nurse, a man, a mother, a husband, a make-up artist, a father, a brother' (1975: 159). Their relationship is not characterized by conversational intimacy, but by largely unspoken acts of selfless labour that seem to reflect Pattabi's reliability and love for her.

> I am not in his tongue. I am in his hands that work. In the legs that run. In the taste of the food he makes. I was in his mute aggressiveness towards a seductive person like Sundaram. When I was down with influenza, he would sit beside me and I was in the blank stare looking at nothingness with a bovine look bearing anguish. I was in the flowers he bought me. I was also in the kindness and quickness with which he folded my saris.... Why does every part of his body seem seemly to me? An unfailing hand, an unfailing foot, an unfailing eye, unfailing speech, unfailing desire, unfailing aggressiveness, unfailing courage, unfailing kindness for me.... (1975: 174–5)

Pattabi does not embody a distinct character inasmuch as he embodies the irresolvable question that unsettles Ammani's restless urge to love the world, 'What do I want?' (1975: 219). This is a far cry from the detached spectator in the opening chapter who laughs derisively at conventions; the older Ammani realizes her laughter is really a sign of her inability to be absolutely free of all conventions. She discards her international career as a reputed dancer: dancing now seems a mechanical habit that forecloses the possibility of novelty. When her servant Pachaiyappan announces his marriage to his cousin Maragatham, Ammani warns him of the risk of getting married: marriage is a meaningless ritual that blocks 'the circulation of life blood and emotions ... [when one] suddenly grows old' (1975: 235–7). For Ammani, marriage pre-empts the productive dynamism of promiscuity and binds the destinies of two individuals with a deadening sense of finality. She is disappointed by the hypocrisy of even some of her upper-caste Marxist friends who ensure they marry within the same caste.

Towards the end of the novel, Ammani realizes that true freedom does not lie in the impulse to touch or make love to everyone. Rather, a social understanding of freedom and power emerges through Ammani's encounters with Maragatham and Bruce, a Vietnam War soldier she meets on a trip to England. This understanding is premised on a collective negotiation of authority and not on individual transgressions of norms and practices. Ammani idealizes Maragatham's perfectly symmetrical and dark beauty as a symbol of the stability of domesticity. She has what she describes as a manly urge to possess and protect her beauty and chastity from the attention of other men, particularly Gopali, who makes advances at her in Ammani's absence. Maragatham's chastity reminds Ammani of the loss of her innocence as a result of her promiscuous lifestyle. When she returns from her last dance tour abroad, she discovers that Maragatham and Pachaiyappan have left the house after Gopali's misbehaviour. She begins to identify with the pain and suffering of womankind that can only be redeemed through cross-gender partnerships. The security and familiarity of the domestic space that Maragatham incarnates lay to rest Ammani's tactile ideal of free love. She realizes the meaning of existence lies not in pursuing the new but in the mundane and the repetitive, and ends up in an exclusive relationship with Pattabi without getting married to him.

Similarly, her mutually transformative encounter with Bruce defeats her intention of avenging the historical disempowerment of women through free love. Whenever he sees a woman, Bruce is haunted by the contempt of a Vietnamese woman who had lost everything in the war. The guilt of having killed people in the war compels Bruce to acknowledge and embrace his own emasculation, and his vulnerability exposes Ammani's illusory autonomy. From his experience of the war, Bruce comes to the conclusion that the world is fundamentally divided into two classes—those who have knowledge, and those who do not. Knowledge, he argues, is the ultimate form of power and exploitation. Bruce's criticism is also directed towards Ammani's impulse to know everyone through touch; an impulse that rejects the possibility of being grounded in the familiar in the constant search for meaning in the new. If the human quest for recognition and identity is never fulfilled, Bruce represents the necessity of grounding an otherwise rudderless life in belief and habit. Bruce is unmarried, but his attachment to his home and family restores Ammani's faith in a secure home. She realizes that her life of novelty has reduced her to a wooden cow in an exhibition that does not recognize the temporal rhythms of life and death. She is truly humanized through Bruce when she embraces old age and death, and realizes she will still be loved.

Janakiraman's novels begin with male desire for an idealized woman; when this woman asserts her desiring self, the perception of her as an ideal is challenged. This was a strategy that the men employed to disown their desire and vulnerability in the face of the cultural expectation of a life of celibate religiosity. *Marappacu* brings a slight reversal to this theme, where Ammani's encounter with Bruce, an obviously vulnerable man undermines her illusory autonomy and urges her to settle down to a domestic life of monogamy, albeit without marriage. Again, the woman is not free of men's perception of her, yet she appears pure despite her inexplicable impulse to experience the world through touch. In the end it is Gopali's guilt, his attachment to his own family, and Ammani's identification with a domestic working-class woman that domesticates her ideal of free love. She embraces the possibility of a man's companionship even if it requires embracing her own dependency and finitude. In the next two chapters, on Karichan Kunju, M.V. Venkatram, and Mauni,

I track similar engagements with male desire for idealized women, and the shedding of this idealization with the acknowledgement of (female and male) sexuality. In the case of Karichan Kunju and M.V. Venkatram though, the imagined conflicts between sexuality, spirituality and religiosity are embodied in the diseased male body.

Note

1. Devadasis were women who were dedicated to temples where they performed dance and music. Largely independent, they had their own families and had relationships with their male patrons.

3

Karichan Kunju and M.V. Venkatram

Between Desire and Disease

Like their contemporary T. Janakiraman, R. Narayanasami (1919–1992), better known as Karichan Kunju, and M.V. Venkatram (1920–2000) were influenced by K.P. Rajagopalan's writings and shared his preoccupation with the inner workings of the sexual subject.[1] Janakiraman, Kunju, and Venkatram explored the fraught intersections of sexuality and religiosity as embodied in the Brahman man. In Janakiraman's novels, for the most part, male desire cannot be distinguished from devotion or duty, and is partly sublimated in art or music, or care and responsibility. In Kunju and Venkatram's work, the male protagonists are torn between their illicit sexual desires and their religious and spiritual impulse to transcend desire and the body. However, in both Kunju and Venkatram's works, forbidden male desire is embodied as disease. In such cases, the male protagonists view disease as both a religious experience of sexual redemption and as a particular mode of sensuality. The turn to piety and asceticism in these texts fails to resolve the untenable contradiction between the religious and the erotic.

Let me here briefly clarify my use of the word 'disease'. I use the word in its accepted sense as a state of physical disorder and in a more general sense to refer to a dis-ease or uneasiness that the protagonists experience in relation to their sense of self and the world at large. While I am aware that these two scenarios of disease in the narratives may not share the same etiology, manifestations, or long-term effects in the narratives, they produce similar kinds of physical impairment, social oppression, and psychological imbalance. Here, I am only concerned with the ontological significance of disease that operates in creating holistic and self-affirmative ways of being in the world.

Historically, the colonial model of masculinity, and its construction of Hindu ascetic masculinity, has predominated scholarship on south Asia. While the idea of the ascetic has been associated with the premodern and the religious Hindu, the colonial model has been understood as a model of South Asian masculinity affected by its exchanges with the colonial state. As Mrinalini Sinha argues in *Colonial Masculinity*, modern, Western masculinity and traditional Hindu conceptions of it were correlated in imperial politics. Certain professed ideals of colonial masculinity, such as martial valour, were introduced to justify racial exclusions in various spheres of the colonial machinery as seen in the army and the public service commission. Chandrima Chakraborty's book *Masculinity, Asceticism, Hinduism: Past and Present Imaginings of India* (2011) addresses the same question from the perspective of the nationalist discourse, from Gandhi to leaders of the Hindu right, and the ways in which traditional, Hindu conceptions of masculinity and asceticism were reworked for anti-colonial purposes. Even in the colonial period, political leaders and the literati made efforts to contest the colonialist views of Hindu effeminacy.

This modern construct of male asceticism is, by virtue of its apparent integrity, a fragile one shot through with sexual anxieties. The Brahman man came to be historically imagined as a man of religious and cultural capital, and, therefore, also a man of intellect. Because his life was far removed from a life of labour, and, in fact depended on the labour of lower-caste men (and women), he did not conform to conventional notions of masculine strength. His masculinity was a function of sensual abstinence and an austere lifestyle that regulated his desire, if any, to cater to the needs of the procreative family. Paradoxically, since masculinity has conventionally been linked to physical labour as well as sexual autonomy and control, the assumption that he was abstinent or celibate undermined his masculinity. This is evident in the now-stereotypical representation of the Brahman/upper-caste ascetic in innumerable stories in the Puranic and Buddhist imagination who loses his spiritual merit and sexual integrity to a divine dancer or courtesan and often ends up fathering her child. Even in the Orientalist imagination, the Brahman man is either depicted as a wily person who exploits others with his cunning or again as an intellectual with a soft, effeminate body. If masculinity has been typically associated with strength and moral self-restraint, the male protagonists of the following texts represent a crisis in masculinity with their lack of sexual restraint and capacity; a crisis that is (retrospectively) figured as disease. But this moral interpretation of disease is also limited or contradicted by the fact that the diseased male body is also seen as a field of sexually productive possibilities.

The modern figure who loomed large in the religious imagination of this generation of Tamil writers was Mohandas Karamchand Gandhi. His growing popularity from the 1920s and the 1930s inspired the writings of many self-styled Gandhian writers in Tamil and other Indian languages. Gandhi's ideals of non-violent resistance, spiritual abstinence, and social reform were widely and even loosely fictionalized by some early Tamil women writers (particularly in V.M. Kodainayagiammal and in the early works of Rajam Krishnan), who could for the first time imagine women sharing public spaces with men while protesting against foreign cloth and liquor. So even if a direct allusion to Gandhi or his mass movement was absent, the Gandhian reformist spirit, as it were, pervaded a plethora of characters. While some of these female writers imagined characters who were against alcoholism and domestic violence, their male counterparts created pious and restrained male characters whose conflicts with sexuality resemble, even if somewhat crudely, a Gandhian model of abstinent masculinity. For instance, the protagonist of Kunju's novel *Pacittamāṉiṭam* (1978) attempts to redeem his sexuality by re-channelizing his desire in altruism, representing a political model of masculinity driven by a salvific vision of social justice.

Karichan Kunju's *Pacittamāṉiṭam* (Hungry Humanity: 1978)

Much of what is known about Kunju's life can be gathered from his moving account of K.P. Rajagopalan's life and writings. In the last two chapters of his book *Ku.Pa.Ra. Cila Niṉaivukaḷ* (Ku.Pa.Ra.: Some Memories, Parts I and II), Kunju says he learnt Sanskrit from the age of eight to fifteen in Bangalore (now Bengaluru) before returning to Kumbakonam (see Seshadri). He then studied in the Madurai Rameshwaram Devasthanam School from 1936 to 1940, where he earned a bachelor's degree in Sanskrit and Tamil. He started studying Tamil in 1934, and from 1940 to his retirement in 1977, worked as a Tamil lecturer at the Kumbakonam Government College. It was Janakiraman, then a student at the college, who introduced Kunju to modern literature, particularly the poems of Subramania Barati. Janakiraman also introduced him to Rajagopalan and encouraged him to publish his own stories in *Maṇikkoṭi*, *Kalaimakaḷ*, *Āṉanta Vikaṭaṉ*, and *Kirāma Uḻiyaṉ*. Since Janakiraman and Kunju had formally studied Sanskrit, they read and interpreted lines from Kalidasa and Bhavabhuti's plays and verses from the Upanishads to Rajagopalan. In turn, Rajagopalan critiqued their stories and honed their literary skills.

Karichan Kunju was part of a small literary organization called 'Jeyamāruti Vācakacālai' that conducted literary discussions in one of the halls of the Sarangapani temple in Kumbakonam in the 1940s. This group included the artist Gopulu, famous in the world of Tamil journalism for his illustrations; Savithi, who wrote for *Āṉanta Vikaṭaṉ*; R.K. Rangarajan, who wrote detective stories for *Kumutam*; and K.R. Gopalan, who, along with the others, produced handwritten literary journals. Rajagopalan was also a part of these discussions. Another space where writers met to discuss literature was a shop in front of the Kumbakonam High School called 'Toṇṭar Kaṭai', owned by one of Rajagopalan's ardent followers. Here, Rajagopalan ran a small bookstore that was mostly unsuccessful. Students, teachers, and writers of the Jeyamāruti group also met here to discuss the form and function of literature and nationalist politics, particularly those of Gandhi and Nehru. Kunju also interacted with senior writers like P.G. Sundararajan or 'Chitti', and Chidambara Subramaniam at Rajagopalan's house.

Like his contemporaries, Karichan Kunju represented the life of the Brahman man as one of conflict between sexuality and religiosity. Here the term religiosity may not refer to any specific form of Brahmanism and is often conflated with spirituality or the Advaita doctrine as something that characterizes the metaphysical identity between atman and Brahman. Kunju's protagonists are divided by their illicit sexuality and their religious and spiritual impulse to transcend desire and the body. But the conventional opposition between sexuality and Hindu male asceticism is complicated by three factors: firstly, the interpenetration of the religious, the spiritual, and the sexual; secondly, the coincidence of the sexual and the religious in disease; and thirdly, through protagonists who try to practice abstinence without being able to altogether renounce worldly life. These protagonists experience disease both as a religious experience of sexual redemption and as a self-affirmative and empathetic mode of sensuality. To be precise, the experience of shame and suffering is a transformative and empowering one that compels the protagonist to empathize and literally reach out to other outcastes, often through touch. Thus, what is posited as an untenable contradiction between the religious and the erotic reveals a more fundamental disjunction between the mind and the body. If dominant masculinity has been typically associated with strength and moral self-restraint, the male protagonist in *Pacittamāṉiṭam*, with his lack of sexual restraint and capacity, represents a crisis in masculinity a crisis that is, in retrospect, constituted by disease. His moral interpretation of disease is also limited, or contradicted, by the fact that the diseased male body is a field of sensual and ethical possibilities that potentially overcomes the ontological disparity between body and mind, the self and the other.

A reading of Karichan Kunju's writings suggests an analogy between sexuality and spirituality. This is seen in the short stories that suggest the mutual implication of desire and love, with a mostly spiritual imagination of disease, violence, and, in some cases, even death. The experience of disease enables certain modes of sensuality that are directed to the body but also attempt to transcend the body to attain a sense of plenitude. I argue that desire for the body is inextricably linked to the desire for transcendence and it is precisely the repeated failure of desire to transcend the limits of the embodied self that enables the possibility of reconfiguring meaning and subjectivity.

I begin with a discussion of Kunju's only novel *Pacittamāṉiṭam*. The embodied self-image of the male protagonist is visibly impaired by his experience of disease. But certain sensual possibilities are opened up and persist despite his diseased body at the cost of foreclosing others that were contingent on the healthy body. This is not to preclude the stigma and humiliation of disease but consider the sexually empowering implications of the diseased body whose social absence affords certain sexual liberties. That the disease in question results from leprosy, an acquired and not congenital disease that could not be cured, complicates, however, a unilateral and permanent shift from health to disease. The novel dramatizes the inner struggles of a male subject divided between two temporalities, of erotic dreams and memories of an able past that persist uneasily with the realities of a diseased present. What characterizes the partial shift from health to disease is a shift in emphasis from one mode of sensuality to another, that is, from touch to sight. While the idealized healthy body of the past can enjoy tactile pleasure and intimacy, the diseased body resorts to voyeurism, although a longing for touch persists. The social anonymity of the diseased male body enables the erotic gaze to function as an exclusive form of sexual gratification even in the most public spaces. Towards the end, however, the novel sets up a rather indefensible moral equation between sexual excess and disease. Although the protagonist's sexual desire is initially unaffected by his disabled state, the moral interpretation of his disease and the sublimation of desire in expiatory acts of compassion and asceticism promises a miraculous cure and potential transcendence.

To summarize the rather circuitous plot of the novel, Ganeshan returns after 40 years to the holy town of Kumbakonam, where he grew up. He has returned after a life of sexual debauchery and exploitation and is in need of medical treatment for leprosy. He is convinced his disease is an expiatory sign of his homosexual past that he feels he has to suffer to attain redemption and transcendence.

But his moral perception of his diseased condition is contradicted by irrepressible sexual desires that are expressed through erotic memories and dreams. He is on the verge of recovering at a charitable hospital run by Christian missionaries when, to his dismay, his suppressed sexual desire for the white nurses surfaces with a vengeance. So he leaves the hospital to tour the province as an itinerant beggar. He accidentally encounters his friend Kitta and his wife Ammu, whose older sister Machi had a childhood affair with Ganeshan. This triggers memories of Ammu and Machi's youthful beauty and his once able body. The novel traces Ganeshan's gradual decline from an idealized childhood to same-sex indulgence and exploitation at the hands of Singaram (a mirasdar), which in the end is only redeemed by his expiatory acts of compassion and asceticism. The novel also presents Kitta, another male outcast as a foil to Ganeshan. The young, unemployed Kitta escapes the town that humiliated him for his licentiousness, determined to earn his own living with the help of a network of friends and relatives. But even after he becomes a successful businessman, his sexual affairs create a domestic crisis that upsets his authority and power over his family and employees. He loses his family's esteem and his son tries to undermine his authority by taking his place in the business. He is reformed by his final encounter with Ganeshan, who encourages him to renounce the world to attain spiritual liberation.

Although he is raised by a childless Brahman couple, Ganeshan is 'adopted' by his entire village that loves and celebrates his beauty and intelligence. He is the beloved, orphaned child who belongs to everyone precisely because he exclusively belongs to no one. This is literally suggested by Ganeshan's liberty to inhabit all the households in the Brahman locality and become a welcome part of several surrogate families. The entire Brahman community in the village organizes and celebrates Ganeshan's sacred thread ceremony, which his religious boarding school at Mannarkudi requires him to do. It is at this neighbouring town that he is spotted by the wealthy and influential mirasdar, Singaram Rauthu. The brief happiness and security of his childhood is interrupted when Singaram seduces him with the comforts of a luxurious life in exchange for his sexual companionship. 'When I see beautiful boys I'm enchanted and feel like taking them home to live with me. Then one day I told my mother you look just like my [dead orphaned] nephew. Ever since then she has been insisting that I bring you home ...' (1978: 208).

There is a persistent contradiction between the narrator's idealization of Ganeshan's childhood freedom and his later seduction and incarceration by Singaram. His relationship with Singaram begins on an exploitative note that does not preclude the possibility of intimacy. At the time of his imprisonment by Singaram, the spatial and sexual regulation of Ganeshan's body sustains and interrupts the possibility of effeminacy and same-sex intimacy. What is important to note is that the narrative invokes Ganeshan's body as a concealed and feminized presence. On his intimate train journeys with Ganeshan, Singaram is particular to travel by night in separate cabins that have been reserved for them. Singaram derives pleasure in concealing Ganeshan from the outside world, 'On all their travels, Ganeshan was hidden from the eyes of others like veiled women', that explains his ignorance of the world he inhabits (1978: 215). He is initially a feminized object of desire coveted by Singaram's close friends until Singaram fashions him in his own virile body-image. He encourages Ganeshan to consume meat and exercise his body, introduces him to alcohol, and adorns his body with chunky golden jewellery to suggest virile power and formidable authority. Thus, through his association with Singaram, Ganeshan seems to undergo a rite of passage to a form of manhood that is shorn not just of pious Brahmanhood but also effeminacy, the two being equated in the novel. The growing masculinization of his body compels, as it were, the acknowledgement of his latent desire for women. Thus the possibility of establishing a homosexual identity is averted through a narrative equation of gender with sexuality or masculinity with heterosexuality.

Over the course of the story, Ganeshan's body undergoes a reversible process of recovering and again losing the visible markers of Brahman masculinity like the sacred thread, which through his association with Singaram, he is forced to cast off. Singaram grants his plea for freedom, gets him a job, and marries him to Sundari, a poor, orphaned ex-classmate that Ganeshan accidentally encounters while trying to escape anti-colonial riots. Although Sundari is only partly Brahman herself, she eroticizes Ganeshan's Brahman-ness, pressing him to wear his sacred thread. She insists on observing Brahmanical rituals that regulate the preparation and consumption of food, and appoints a Brahman cook despite Ganeshan's disapproval. Ganeshan is freed of Sundari's ritual impositions when she dies following several miscarriages.

The final transformation that Ganeshan's body undergoes is from health to disease. Disease is first invoked as a corporeal metaphor for filial and romantic ties. During his life with Singaram, Ganeshan stumbles upon other boys, as well as Singaram's wife and children, trapped in another part of the house—and sees that their faces have been distorted beyond recognition by disease. Shortly after Sundari's death, Ganeshan has an affair with the woman doctor who operated on her. The doctor incarcerates him in her house lest her jealous politician lovers murder him. But the doctor soon abandons him when she discovers he has leprosy. From his disfigured appearance, the doctor anxiously assumes his condition is infectious. She lends him some money out of gratitude for their love and sends him to Tanjavur.

Ganeshan's body, which enjoyed the social recognition and purity of youth, is deracinated and imprisoned only to become a profane and exploited object of male desires. But his 'homosexuality', equated with his feminization, is countered by his 'masculinization', which, however, does not forestall his further confinement. He still has to negotiate with male and female desires in exchange for safety and survival. Even the possibility of (sexual) freedom is undermined by the onset of disease that renders Ganeshan's body uninhabitable and for which he is humiliated. Disease, I argue, constitutes the contradiction both within as well as between the body and the psyche. There is a clear discontinuity between material and psychic (self-)representations of the body, and between the incoherent image of the diseased body and its healthy past that is invoked in sensual dreams and memories. The opening chapters of the novel suggest the discordance between two contrasting body-images—of a body confined by disease, spatially unrestricted, and of a healthy body that loses its mobility and freedom. Ganeshan's incoherent body-image is correlated to his diseased body, which continues to bear nostalgic memories of its healthy, mobile past. He recognizes the diseased transformation of his body in the mirror only because he still has 'the same mind' that recalls and idealizes his once coherent body-image (1978: 23). There is thus a fundamental disjuncture between the body as an idea and the body as an experience (see Merleau-Ponty). Thus, to be embodied is also to have a perception and experience of the body in its relation to the world. In such a context, desire arises from the mind or memory, and is tied to an able body that once enjoyed tactile forms of intimacy and recognition.[2] But even the moral interpretation of the diseased body as punishment for sexual excess is unable to contain the stubborn persistence of desire, whose ultimate aim is self-recognition.

The longing for touch persists even as Ganeshan derives pleasure from gazing at women. His tactile exchanges with the beautiful Swedish nurses at the missionary run hospital are initially indistinguishable from his appreciation of the Christian virtues of care and compassion. Through the nurses, the narrator admires Ganeshan's body to salvage him from complete degradation.

> Ganeshan now became the owner of that voice that reminded one of the earlier beauty of that unrecognizably transformed face. Some of the parts of his body attested his pure beauty. He and his disease were enigmas to them [the nurses] ... Ganeshan's disease was of a new kind. It was not just the beauty of his face but his very body that had been completely transformed by the disease. His round, beautiful face was disfigured—it spread out like a flat plate and had swollen. The long fingers of his long arms that stretched down to his knees were disfigured; they had swollen up and cracked ... otherwise his body was alright to a certain extent. Its seductive fair complexion had not disappeared. The force and depth of his ringing voice that arrested and attracted the attention of its listeners had not been affected. One could see him struggling to walk because his toes were short and swollen up and were twisted and crooked like balls and his toenails had withered and shriveled up. But he had not lost his dignity and majestic bearing. (1978: 55–9)

Ganeshan's embodied self is fundamentally tied to his sexuality; his longing for self-recognition cannot be distinguished from his desire for tactile intimacy. The sight of his recovering body is accompanied by the resurfacing of his sexual fantasies of the nurses' beauty. Betrayed by what he believes to be his failure to pass a spiritual test, Ganeshan escapes the hospital in his quest for spiritual freedom. 'He was deceived by the thought of having lost the opportunity to transcend himself; of retrieving his lost soul; of polishing the filth of his old mind ... that was within this new body that melted and dripped ...' (1978: 59).

There is an untenable discordance between the sexual liberties enjoyed by the diseased body and the moral closure of the novel. On the one hand, there is the moral interpretation of the involuntary and ultimately inscrutable experience of disease as punishment for illicit desire and on the other, there is the inability to suppress the sexual possibilities that are opened up by the diseased body. While Ganeshan's disfigured appearance deprives him of personhood, it gives him social immunity to derive voyeuristic pleasure from exposed female bodies. For instance, on a trip to a holy town he encounters Ammu, Kitta's wife, whom he mistakes for her older sister Machi. He remembers his sensuous affair with the young Machi and his promises of marriage. However, years later he is unable to distinguish her from her sister, Ammu. To his erotic gaze, the Swedish nurses, Machi, and Ammu are mutually substitutable metonyms as his desire shifts from one to the other.

If self-affirmation is possible only through the relational act of recognition between the self and other, the disabling of social relations is continuous with Ganeshan's diseased state of self-estrangement. I argue that his ailing body is a corporeal metaphor for a structural and existential state of shame and abjection. Ganeshan simultaneously identifies and de-identifies with his diseased condition. He silently admits that leprosy has left him feeling 'doubly orphaned' and self-alienated (1978: 20). He associates the onset of leprosy with the death of his parents, his neglected childhood as an errand boy, and the loss of the comforts of domesticity and almost all his inherited wealth. He realizes his life is nothing but a shift from one form of incarceration and depersonalization to another—from his healthy and luxurious but imprisoned past to the misery and privation of disease that makes his body uninhabitable. He resigns himself to his apparently incurable disease by rationalizing his shame and suffering as a 'penance' in itself, which may or may not promise self-transcendence (1978: 23).

The embodied signs of Ganeshan's wealth threatens his survival even as it negotiates potential stigma and humiliation owing to his diseased body. On the one hand, his wealthy appearance makes him vulnerable to violence and theft—he considers his money and bejewelled body constant liabilities that could cost him his life. On the other hand, wealth empowers him with a certain degree of social impunity that mitigates the discrimination and humiliation of disease. Thus, his bodily integrity and being are at once compromised by shame and impairment, and secured by the visible signs of social class. Although his disfigured appearance pre-empts his entrance in most of the stores that have notices forbidding entry to people with 'diseases', his elite body is read as a marker of social privilege and dignity. Ganeshan's presence thus evokes an ambiguous response of respect and disgust (1978: 18). The narrator betrays an admiration for Ganeshan's dignified bearing by imagining Vaithi, the coffee-shop owner's amazement at the sight of the leper 'dressed in a respectable shirt and vēṣṭi ... [with a] leather suitcase and a stylish bag'. The narrator says, 'the owner was probably only accustomed to seeing beggars who were afflicted by leprosy but not well dressed lepers' (1978: 18). Although Vaithi fails to recognize his former classmate, his attentive hospitality consoles Ganeshan. However, the possibility of being recognized by him only reinforces Ganeshan's fear and shame. As Ganeshan is about to reveal his identity, the sight of his disfigured hand fills him with disgust, and he lies to Vaithi about being a friend of Ganeshan, who is dead (1978: 19).

If the act of identification is a relational one that operates through the other, it takes the other to either recognize or fail to recognize the self. The crisis of identity and the failure of recognition operate at different levels here: Vaithi's—and the world's—failure to recognize Ganeshan adds to his self-estrangement, and the possibility of being recognized as a familiar person is an even greater cause for shame and anguish. Ganeshan's disfigured but elite appearance invokes contradictory impulses. While he is forbidden entry from stores, his presence also suggests privilege and dignity. He is reminded of the greedy doctors who refused to touch his diseased body and made him feel 'like an untouchable' who no longer recognizes his own body (1978: 21). In one of the later chapters of the novel, Ganeshan is ashamed of being recognized by a doctor. The doctor, who represents the rational voice of science, tries to convince Ganeshan that leprosy is, contrary to popular belief, neither incurable nor infectious. Although Ganeshan is particularly mortified at the prospect of being recognized by someone from his youth, the doctor consoles him and encourages him to overcome his shame. He tells him that people confuse the disfiguring effects of leprosy with contagiousness and puts him in touch with a Christian missionary-run hospital reputed for curing leprosy. Ganeshan later realizes the doctor is the husband of his childhood love Padma. Like his other childhood memories of women, his sensuous memory of Padma is a purely tactile one, associated with a desirable and coherent image of a once healthy body. He is reminded of 'Padma's touch and the keen awareness of their bodies when they had to stay awake and performed night long plays for their families during the auspicious nights of *Civarāttiri* when there was no electricity' (1978: 45). Ganeshan discovers from the doctor that Padma died of an incapacitating sickness that the doctor suggests was a symptom of her longing to have more children. Here, disease has a symptomatic status in the way it signifies a woman's sexual dissatisfaction with an abstinent Gandhian husband and her longing for her childhood lover. The doctor tells Ganeshan that 'she died muttering [your] name deliriously remembering your last childhood encounter' (1978: 48). The novel implicitly valorizes a spiritual ideal of sexual abstinence and the doctor's nationalist aspirations, while Padma is 'punished' for her sexuality, even though it is couched as a desire for motherhood.

Ganeshan is unable to suppress his erotic fantasies that constantly foreground his incoherent body-image, even as they gesture at alternative possibilities of sexual pleasure. There is a clear disjunction between his mental representations of his once healthy and desirable body and the image of his diseased body that is deprived of personal value. He has masturbatory dreams of his sexual past that conjure tactile images of male and female lovers, and the suitcase of money that Ganeshan carried around on his journey unexpectedly turns into a man or a woman. The narrative suggests an equation between money and male sexuality. If money is understood as a general equivalent and measurer of everything and possesses infinite exchange value, it has the same indiscriminate circulatory power as male desire. But if masculinity and male sexuality are the general equivalents in an androcentric sexual economy that enjoys stability and resists evaluation, they are actually fragile and insecure. Thus, both money and masculinity are, in reality, not idealized and privileged signifiers against which other signifiers are relatively measured, but are themselves as unstable and secondary as the objects they measure.[3] Ganeshan is visibly debilitated by his erotic dreams that are barely distinguishable from his waking life, 'from the reality of his consciousness of the wet stain on his vēṣṭi' (1978: 35). His involuntary ejaculation suggests the loss of male integrity. His dreams betray a longing for a self-assuring sense of intimacy that is now compromised by his disfigured condition.

> [D]reams are not lies, complete lies ... a few rumors mixed with some old experiences ... dreams of speaking to his old male friend and his female friends without moving his tongue, he saw their bodies, the pleasurable parts of their body; without opening his eyes he conversed with them and experienced the happiness of touch lying on the floor without moving his arms and legs.... (1978: 35)

In another instance, his disfigured appearance forestalls the sexual consummation of his desire but enables the possibility of deriving voyeuristic pleasure by invoking his body as an absence that deflects social attention. Ganeshan secretly watches some women bathing at the riverfront. The sight of the partially exposed female bodies moving to the rhythms of bathing conjures a sexualized image of female movement and vitality that is lacking in Ganeshan's own body. For someone who has hitherto led a sheltered and confined life, the sight of women bathing is a sexual novelty.

> He was relieved that he was surrounded by women. Women of all ages dived and bathed peacefully in a large crowd in the open space at the riverfront. Even if some didn't swim they immersed themselves and emerged and jumped and frolicked in the water. Their arms and legs were uncontrollable. Bodies swayed in every direction. They lay on their backs and rinsed their long hair. The bathers did not have to bother about their colorful clothes that wrapped their bodies and slipped when they dipped themselves in the water. For, there were only women. Even on that auspicious day when they immersed themselves in the holy water, some had not forgotten their soaps. Some scrubbed their legs, arms, shoulders and breasts until they were covered with froth before emerging from the river.... They were dripping as they emerged from the river. The sight of city women not used to bathing in the river, struggling to wring their saris before wearing them was food to Ganeshan's ravenous eyes. He similarly consumed the rare sight of those who were familiar with the river, quickly removing their blouse and slipping on a new one like lightening. These were truly new experiences for him. (1978: 85)

If self-identity is a fiction that is produced through an act of (mis) recognition between the self and the other, such a fiction is made possible through Ganeshan's encounter with a young, blind beggar woman. There is a return to touch from sight as an ostensibly more immediate and mutual mode of recognition. The valorization of touch over other modes of sensuality persists throughout the novel, particularly in Ganeshan's fond memories of his childhood loves or of the filial caresses of his father's friend. While the beggar woman's reliance on touch for recognition redeems Ganeshan's compromised selfhood, her inability to see further diminishes his physical presence. The unreturned gaze of the blind woman paradoxically undermines and assures self-recognition: it enables him to be the voyeur who can see without being seen. His fragmentary perception of her is reminiscent of his disconnected perceptions of women who reflect his own sense of fragmentation. Thus, any embodied act of recognition through bodily senses of sight, hearing, touch, smell, and so on never promises absolute identity. But there is a qualitative difference in the way Ganeshan's perception of the beggar woman goes beyond her filthy and unkempt appearance to her unblemished beauty, which, for him, is an index of her nobility. He notices, 'her oiled and neatly kept hair, her long slender face and her elegant nose and her pierced nose and ears' that belie her beggarly state (1978: 85). Her upright posture and the beauty and elegance of the exposed parts of her sari-clad body suggest her ideal femininity. He notices that one of her heels is shiny and smooth 'like folded blossoms' and without any cracks that betrays her upper-class status (1978: 85). The idealized encounter represents the possibilities of an altruistic and mutually redemptive union that enables Ganeshan to transcend his desire for her.

The lives of Ganeshan and the beggar are similar, in that she is also an orphan who escaped a cruel marriage to a man who seduced and abandoned her, leaving her with a child. Ganeshan's relationship with the beggar woman and her son gives him a self-assuring sense of power and responsibility. His act of naming the unnamed woman Kodai and her son Vanmali identifies them as dependents in need of his protection and support. Kodai is initially anxious for Vanmali's life when she learns of Ganeshan's leprosy from neighbours who suspect them of having an affair. Ganeshan later convinces Kodai that leprosy is not infectious. When Kodai remorsefully insists on having an intimate relationship with him, Ganeshan refuses to surrender to his desire. His compassionate acts of teaching Vanmali English and taking care of Kodai's needs redeem his hitherto debauched life as he discovers the disfiguring manifestations of leprosy miraculously receding from his body. His morally ambiguous perception of money is conveyed by his fear of the corrupting effects of money and the altruistic benefits of money that he believes may promise redemption.

The opposition between sexuality and spirituality is seen in Ganeshan's encounter with Pasupati, a policeman. The narrator's erotic and spiritual investment in Ganeshan is implied through Pasupati's attempt to salvage him from utter degradation. Like Kodai earlier, Pasupati's life reflects that of Ganeshan's—Pasupati loses his parents at an early age and honours his promise to his father to feed the poor. His altruism and ascetic aspirations make Pasupati a mirror image of Ganeshan's own transformation. It is Pasupati's faith in Ganeshan's apparently enlightened status that redeems his guilt and ultimately affirms his faith in his own spirituality. Initially, Ganeshan's disciplined appearance and self-absorbed indifference to the world wins Pasupati's veneration. His self-deprecatory attempt to convince Pasupati of his ordinariness only strengthens the latter's faith in his spiritual greatness. Pasupati believes his human fallibility pre-empts the possibility of truly understanding Ganeshan. When Ganeshan mentions the loss 'of his old body', Pasupati interprets his statement as an allusion to the meaninglessness of life, 'How long should I wander in this dead body? I'm dead without dying ...' Pasupati is convinced that Ganeshan's 'eroticism; his conjugal relationship with the blind woman and his leprosy are apparent, deceptive' signs of his incorruptible spirituality (1978: 290). Even as Pasupati considers Ganeshan his spiritual guru, Ganeshan acknowledges Pasupati as his spiritual guide who will help him realize his goal.

A final test of Ganeshan's spiritual transformation is shown in his encounter with Kitta. Kitta functions as a foil to Ganeshan, his greed and sexual promiscuity serve to emphasize Ganeshan's noble suffering and victimhood. While the narrator's (and presumably the reader's) sympathies lie with Ganeshan, there is no sympathy for Kitta who is degraded beyond repair by his sexual corruption and greed. If Ganeshan is portrayed as a victim who enjoys illicit pleasures by exploiting the social insignificance of his diseased body, Kitta, who does not have the advantage of being a diseased orphan as compared to Ganeshan who is constantly sympathized with for being one, is 'punished' for manipulating women to fulfil his reckless greed for financial power. Unlike Ganeshan, Kitta is represented as an agential man who escapes his hometown when he is shamed for secretly looking at the temple priest's daughter bathing. Determined to prove his own worth, his persistent efforts and (sexual) negotiations with a network of friends and relatives pay off. He uses his financial authority to legitimize his affairs with other women, including his widowed sister-in-law, who relies on his financial support, and his business partner's wife Buma, who is instrumental in his financial success. Buma and Kitta's affair turns out to be mutually beneficial: Buma offers to sell her jewellery to finance Kitta's medical store, which establishes her husband's career and improves their marriage. But the legitimacy of his financial authority is soon undermined by a growing crisis in his relationship with his wife, who refuses to tolerate his sexual hypocrisy. Kitta's sexual hypocrisy suggests at once his attempts to legitimize the sexual license he was denied as an unemployed youth with financial power and the fear of potentially losing his wife, thus threatening his authority. Kitta suspects his wife Ammu of having an affair with Ganeshan when he sees him staring at her as they are driving back from a pilgrimage. Although Kitta does not recognize Ganeshan, his memories of him indicate his jealousy of the town's beloved orphan.

Kitta's financial independence does not give him a lasting sense of self-ownership. His sexual suspicion costs him his marriage—he feels disempowered when his wife Ammu begins to trivialize his authority. His niece Machi and her husband who are his dependents decide to leave him to return to their village. Kitta's authority is temporarily undermined when his younger son, who assumes some of his responsibilities at the medical store, violently rebels against his authority and imprisons him. One of the signs of Kitta's disenfranchisement is his emasculation, depicted through his seemingly deficient paternity. He has a mentally and physically disabled son who is entirely dependent on his family for his survival. And we later discover that Kitta owes his financial independence to his mentally disabled older brother's accumulated savings as a beggar. Kitta's encounter with Ganeshan at the end of the novel proves to be his only escape from insecurity. His hedonistic lifestyle becomes a moral burden that finally has to be abandoned to attain spiritual transcendence and peace. Ganeshan urges him to renounce his worldly privileges, which Kitta realizes have become futile liabilities that impede his quest for peace. If Ganeshan's sexual reformation reinstates the novel's moral didacticism, nothing instantiates this better than this reformative encounter with Kitta.

The novel's final vision of life rests on the idea that pain and suffering have to be embraced in order to detach oneself from the phenomenal world. For Ganeshan, the possibility of transcendence ideally entails a purely spontaneous existence that is not deliberate. He derives comfort from the fact that his life has been a set of involuntary experiences, from the disfigurement of leprosy to being sacralized and humiliated for looking like a spiritually enlightened beggar, that is, his appearance as a beggar often evokes contradictory responses of pity and devotion. Devotees at the temple throw coins at the sight of his destitute and disfigured appearance 'to acquire divine merit or redeem their sins' (1978: 77). Others assume he is a holy man when they smear sacred ash on his body. His inability to disavow his leprosy is suggested by his identification and de-identification with other poor and hungry lepers. But ultimately, his bodily needs for food and sex tie him to the physical world. Kodai's sudden death from an illness paves the way for Ganeshan's freedom from worldly responsibilities. In a move that echoes his own childhood, Ganeshan 'adopts' Vanmali and sends him to a boarding school, while he gradually turns into a solitary, self-absorbed man who spends his time lost in meditation. His growing indifference to 'worldly attachments and hunger ... to overcome the self and become one with the world' suggests that a metaphysical identity with the world can be potentially acquired, initially through touch, but ultimately, by detaching oneself from an embodied existence (1978: 307). If spiritual identity with the world is attained, would that entail a definitive end to desire and the sexually marked body?

M.V. Venkatram's *Kātukaḷ* (Ears: 1992)

M.V. Venkatram was born to a Saurashtrian Brahman family in Kumbakonam. He obtained a degree in economics and was involved in the silk and zari business. He first published his works in the 1930s in *Maṇikkoṭi* and was part of the literary circle influenced by K.P. Rajagopalan, which included Karichan Kunju, T. Janakiraman, Thiruloka Seetaram, Dhenuka, Tanjai Prakash, N. Vichuvanathan, C.M. Muthu, and Podhikaiverpan. His works have been published in journals like *Kalāmōkiṉi, Kirāma Uḻiyaṉ,* and *Civāji.* He also ran a literary journal named *Tēṉī* briefly, where he published Karichan Kunju and Mauni's stories. He has written over 200 stories and novels. *Nityakaṉṉi, Kātukaḷ,* and *Vēḷvittī* are his most noted works. He also wrote more than 60 short biographies of various national figures and translated over 10 books for the National Book Trust of India. In 1993, he was given the Sahitya Akademi Award for Tamil writing for his novel *Kātukaḷ.*

Unlike Karichan Kunju's *Pacittamāṉiṭam,* M.V. Venkatram's novel *Kātukaḷ* engages with the figure of the diseased male outcaste whose body is a projection of an embattled (sexual) identity. Disease in this novel does not assume a visible form as it does in *Pacittamāṉiṭam,* although it similarly foregrounds the self-estranging disjuncture both within and between the body and psyche. In this novel, it takes the form of visual and aural hallucinations that appear as ironic and reversible signs of self-affirmation and self-estrangement. I suggest that the protagonist's projected hallucinations function as a formal narrative device that simulate an imagined reality that repeatedly evokes and exorcises the desire for (sexual and religious) meaning and truth. I am interested in exploring the phantasmatic nature of this apparent reality that sustains the uncertainty of sexual meaning. What characterizes such an imaginary reality is the reversibility of its signs that break the referentiality of sex, where sex is transformed into signs, into what Baudrillard in *Seduction* calls a gestural, ritual, and sensual game that alternatively evokes and disappoints religious faith and sexual desire. The male protagonist Mahalingam's fantasies thus repeatedly dramatize the desire to remain a lacking or desiring subject whose desire for meaning is only momentarily achieved before being frustrated again. His attempts to establish meaning is couched in an unstable rhetoric of sexual desire and religious/spiritual faith that, unlike *Pacittamāṉiṭam,* does not gesture at the possibility of spiritual liberation, but ultimately ends in an identity crisis that resists narrative closure.

The advantage of the free, indirect narrative that shifts between the perspectives of the protagonist and the narrator lies in retaining the distinction between the imaginary, projected world of the male protagonist and social reality; a distinction that by the end of the novel is briefly collapsed at the level of narrative and story. The novel suggests that the only way the orphaned Mahalingam can counter the isolating and estranging effects of his projected fantasies is precisely through the projection of an alternative fantasy of self-empowerment; in this manner, signs of self-alienation are juxtaposed against signs of self-affirmation. My interpretation of the fantasy sequences in the novel is neither a symptomatic one that tries to reveal the latent from the manifest meaning, nor one that pathologizes the protagonist. I am concerned with the articulation of certain unconscious desires and affects that determine the distorted form of the protagonist's fantasies (see Žižek). Both *Pacittamāṉiṭam* and *Kātukaḷ* are related in their representation of the simultaneously disempowering and empowering possibilities of the diseased and disabled body, although the kind of male subjects produced relies on the difference between a visible and an invisible disease.

The early part of this autobiographical narrative describes Mahalingam's childhood in a religious household. His devout parents, the narrator says, 'privileged and were empowered by their simple religious faith ... by their piety that was like an infectious familial disease they had inherited that redeemed their illiteracy' (Venkatram 1992: 10). His father is a shopkeeper whose elaborate religious and ritual observances are perceived as frustrating impediments to the immediate satiation of Mahalingam's constant hunger. His illiterate father tries to redeem his own lack of scriptural knowledge by fashioning him in the idealized image of a literate, devotional singer. He employs traditional teachers of devotional music to teach Mahalingam who is, however, too embarrassed to sing despite his father's entreaties. Mahalingam's diffidence proves to be crippling; he is too uncomfortable of being with strangers and his father scolds him for his 'effeminate shyness' (1992: 14). His father is later reassured by his son's rather intense engagement with Tamil literature and his incipient career as a fictional writer, which adversely affects his academic progress. Reading and writing romantic fiction provides Mahalingam with the only available means of expressing romantic ideals of women he secretly desires but is too ashamed to acknowledge. The writings of spiritual thinkers like Vivekananda, Aurobindo, and Ramakrishna Paramahansa create an impression on his young mind, inspiring him to emulate their celibacy. His determination to remain celibate 'does not formalize but transforms his religious piety into emotional gestures' (1992: 16).

Spiritual literature and romantic fiction play a crucial role in constituting Mahalingam's self-perception. His initial desire to remain celibate to pursue his spiritual ideals and literary ambitions is rendered uncertain by his desire to realize his sexual and romantic ideals. But both desires finally turn out to be ironic and he finally agrees to fulfil his father's desperate desire for an heir by marrying a woman of his father's choice. He has a sexually active relationship with her, although he is clearly not attracted to her. His relationship with his wife is premised not on a sense of lack or desire but is a purely narcissistic exercise that only reveals his self-alienation. He resorts to the empowering promises of religion despite his irreligious youth as a desperate measure against the onslaught of his hallucinations. Similarly, the potential consummation of a younger married woman's desire for him later in the novel is interrupted by his repulsion for her apparently malodorous body. He is even repelled by the apparent stench of his dream about her seduction, which reassures him of his integrity. Thus, both sexual desire and spirituality fail to provide self-identity.

Mahalingam's marriage turns out to be a hindrance to his literary and spiritual interests, which are doomed when his father's business competitors exploit his naivety and swindle him of his wealth. With nothing but bankruptcy and debts to bequeath his son, his father ends up losing his memory and eventually dies after a prolonged illness. Mahalingam's wife abandons him when her mother rescues her from imminent destitution. Faced with the responsibility of redeeming his father's debts and supporting a widowed mother, Mahalingam has to forego his dreams of becoming a successful writer and having a spiritual life. His experience of hardship and sexual frustration challenges his faith in God.

The narrative's identification of Mahalingam's identification with his father is suggested by their similar financial misfortunes—their naive and unquestioning faith in their deceptive friends brings them to bankruptcy and destitution. Mahalingam's relationship with his father is clearly fraught by a childhood resentment of his authority and religiosity that hindered the immediate gratification of hunger. The internalization of his father's humiliation, and his inability to conform to his father's ideals, only confirms his low self-worth. His father's insolvency and his consequent death undermine Mahalingam's identification with his father's authority. The loss of the father's status and authority later mediates Mahalingam's own disempowered status. Financial constraints and domestic responsibilities make it impossible for Mahalingam to pursue his literary interests without his father's financial support; survival itself is threatened. Faced by bankruptcy and imminent destitution, Mahalingam realizes he can only redeem his emasculation or even rationalize his misfortune through his monotheistic religiosity. The strength of his religious faith is immaterial and ultimately indeterminable; what matters are the seemingly self-affirming possibilities of religiosity, that have to be constantly reinforced against the onslaught of irrepressible sexual desires, poverty, and hunger. I argue that Mahalingam's fantasies are an articulation of his alternating faith and scepticism that evoke and exorcise his desire for meaning and self-affirmation. The idea of his own divine status—of being under Lord Murugan's protection—gained from his aural hallucinations is momentarily empowering, but is repeatedly dispelled by his own doubts. The sound of Murugan's words contradicts his notions about God that are determined by his readings of religious literature. Mahalingam's fantasies parody the seductive signs of God's favour:

> Mahalingam had read about God speaking to great men but no book had the statistics of how many words He spoke. He knew some books said God had silently guided people but this was a contradiction. They say the devotee hesitates when God appears before him pleased with his penance and grants him a boon. But here it felt God had meditated on Mali and was blabbering in joy at his sight. (1992: 31–2)

Mahalingam's religious scepticism is affirmed by multiple, unidentifiable voices, which are followed by the voice of a seductive and vengeful female who claims to be the bloodthirsty goddess Kali. He momentarily imagines it is the divine voice of Murugan, who pleased by his devotion, has come to his rescue. But his pious hope is disillusioned when Kali swears to destroy him and his family for insulting her. She accuses him of betraying her by shifting his loyalties to Murugan and Rama. Mahalingam defensively asserts his belief in monotheism and expresses his indifference to nominal differences between gods. Kali avows her exclusive divinity and chastises Mahalingam for not worshipping her in his previous lives. Mahalingam's doubt about Kali's divine status is confirmed by her threat to destroy his family for his betrayal.

Mahalingam's hallucinations dramatize his self-estrangement through the imagined encounter of seemingly opposing voices and images that are composite projections of his self. Whether these voices allude to a real or discrete person from Mahalingam's life is neither certain nor relevant. What concerns me is the fact that while the male voices can be identified with the emasculation of Mahalingam and his father, the female voices conjure a contradictory image of woman as alternatingly submissive, seductive, and threatening. To use Lacan's words, she is phallic and lacking, castrated and castrating. Mahalingam's hallucinations suggest he both identifies with and disavows the feminine, which is at once a reassuring symbol of plenitude and a lack that threatens his unity and autonomy. The only defence against this threat is fetishizing the feminine as a derivative of the masculine or as the maternal body that internalizes and transmits patrimony. The emasculating effects of Mahalingam's financial loss, for instance, take the form of an imaginary argument between a composite male and female voice that represent multiple characters. The female voice is an allusion to the goddess Kali whose unexpectedly malodorous body recalls Mahalingam's earlier dream about an abused younger woman who sought his protection from her mother-in-law's cruelty and her allegedly impotent and effeminate husband. She tries to seduce Mahalingam by evoking his sympathy and dresses up once she senses his relenting compassion; she even expresses a wish to have a son like his. He nearly succumbs to her advances, when, after a moment of guilt, he is suddenly repelled by her malodorous body. In the dream she visits him and implores his protection from her in-laws when her brother comes in search of her and threatens to return her to her husband. She refuses and defiantly insists on living with Mahalingam. In another scene, the male voice claims to be the goddess/young wife's jealous husband and alludes to one of Mahalingam's creditors. The male voice ridicules his hope of retrieving his lost status and, demanding his dues, warns him of imminent destitution. The female voice, a distorted allusion to the goddess/young wife, defends Mahalingam with a profession of wifely love. Their imaginary conversation soon turns into a violent fight between a jealous husband who demands the goddess' acceptance of his conjugal rights over her and an amorous goddess who fiercely defends her wifely loyalty to Mahalingam. When the creditor ridicules her wifely devotion, she severs his penis in a fit of rage that leaves him lamenting his castration, thereby referring to Mahalingam's own state of emasculation.

Mahalingam tries to believe his hallucinations are divine retribution for past sins that can only be redeemed through worship, but the impossibility of discovering signs of divine favour both undermine and reinforce his religious faith. When he reluctantly agrees to visit an ascetic known for his curative powers, he is assaulted by a hallucinatory dialogue between a male and a female actor preparing for a play. The actors do not necessarily refer to distinct or real individuals from Mahalingam's life but are signs of his religious belief and faith in his own spiritual integrity. His embattled identity is dramatized in the following 'secret' conversation that ridicules his apparent sophistication and intellectualism; expresses his forbidden desires by sexualizing his piety for an amorous 'goddess', and finally suggests his identity with an effete and infantilized God Murugan.

[Male Voice] Mother, who am I? [Female Voice] ... If you keep asking yourself this question you will gain spiritual knowledge. [Male Voice] If I'm enlightened I won't be able to have affairs or eat whatever I like. I don't want knowledge ... Mali [Mahalingam] sir is confused not knowing who I am ... I'm Ku.Pa.Ra's [K.P. Rajagopalan's] fan, I can briefly describe you in four words.... [Female Voice] You don't need to describe me. I know who I am.... I'm the complete form of knowledge. [Male Voice] Oh! That's why you stink so much.... Just because you are enlightened shouldn't you bathe even when you are menstruating? [Female Voice (whispers as if telling a secret)] Mali is very sophisticated.... He doesn't like it if you're vulgar.... [Male Voice] Why should he listen to our secrets? ... [Female Voice] Idiot! Did you forget we are speaking like this so that Mali can hear? ... [Male Voice] ... He's deaf in any case ... why are you speaking like a college student with English mixed in her Tamil? ... [Female Voice] ... Shouldn't Mali know I'm educated ... Mali is an intellectual; an intellectual will only love an intellectual ... [Male Voice] ... Isn't that why you're sleeping with him? [Female Voice] You're again being vulgar ... [Male Voice] ... Mother who are you? [Female Voice] I am the empress of millions of worlds. Ghosts, demons, spirits, gods ... I'm them all. I'm sound, I'm the seed [the Sanskrit word *vindu* also means seed or semen] ... [Male Voice] ... Where's the seed? You tempted me to come by saying Mali has a lot of it. I didn't even find a drop ... [Female Voice] ... if you keep saying 'seed' Mali will be disgusted. [Male Voice] But he sings '*Naadavindu Kalaadi*' [a sixteenth-century devotional poet Arunagirinaathar whose song '*God is everywhere*' was dedicated to Murugan] ... is he disgusted when he sings? ... Where did you find Mali? [Female Voice] Mali has been crying 'Muruga, Muruga!' for some lives ... [Male Voice] Oh that Muruga who was born to you after you had an affair with that Shiva fellow? [Female Voice] Yes that very Murugan. Mali has been praying to Murugan for several lives. But Murugan refuses to remove his mouth from my noble breast ... Mali's voice hasn't reached his ears. Murugan is a child; he's at an irresponsible age. Can I be like that? ... I'm going to make him [Mali] the transcendental ... I'm going to make him a pauper first ... [Male Voice] So you're going to turn him into a madman? ... [Female Voice] In this country a madman is praised for being an enlightened person, an intellectual.... He calls himself a monist ... what's cooking? [Male Voice] Mali's blood, Kamakshi's blood, their children's blood to quench your thirst.... (1992: 84–5)

Mahalingam's hopeless and self-deprecating hallucinations have destructive effects on his family. He is suddenly aroused by another imaginary and rather sexually provocative conversation that makes him rape his pregnant wife, who later gives birth to a stillborn child. His young son's obstinate refusal to eat provokes Mahalingam's violent rage; he beats the boy and expels him from the house.

Mahalingam's religious identification with Murugan is only a fragile defence against his identification and desire for the feminine, which undermines his faith and self-possession. He is prepared to bear any amount of suffering if he is assured of Murugan's blessings. His attempt to affirm his sense of self is suggested in another dream about two disembodied voices that represent Mahalingam's fragmented self. The voices sexually parody his spiritual and literary/intellectual ideals. An imaginary female friend who calls herself Chaya recalls the earlier voice of the goddess and the young wife. She tries to seduce him by praising his literary talent and tries to poison him against Murugan, whose indifference she declares is responsible for his poverty. She offers him money and sexual pleasure that 'is the ultimate joy' in exchange for devotion (1992: 97). She derisively remarks, 'Even to achieve spiritual transcendence you need to experience the pleasures of the body ...' (1992: 95). This is followed by a male voice that chastises him for rejecting her advances and ridicules his impotence, which he equates to that of Murugan, the youthful, abstinent boy-God who spurns women.

Mahalingam awakens from the dream and feels his body has become a stage where his conflicted subjectivity is being projected and dramatized. There are moments where he feels he enjoys what seems to be a radio and then a television play. He suddenly hears the deafening auspicious sound of 'Om' as he sets out with a friend to meet Sage Ramdas reputed for his spiritual powers. He hears rebellious voices preparing to battle Ramdas's spiritual powers that chastise Mahalingam for his powerlessness and ridicule his cowardly non-violent Gandhianism. When Mahalingam implores Ramdas to cure him, the sage tells him that his ability to dissociate himself from his madness, which is a divine test of his spiritual resilience, is itself a sign of divine favour. Mahalingam, not convinced by Ramdas's reassurance, demands evidence. Ramdas says that divine protection is suggested by Mahalingam's ability to objectify and narrativize (tell as a story) his delusion in conversation without being overwhelmed by it (1992: 97). In some sense this gestures at the very redemptive function of this autobiographical narrative, which is shown through the act of objectifying and thereby distancing oneself from the unconscious by putting it into language.

By the end of the novel, the distinction between past and present, between reality and Mahalingam's projected, hallucinatory world becomes ambiguous. Mahalingam is overwhelmed by his financial hardships when his daughter almost succumbs to a high fever. With just enough money to take care of her medical expenses the desperate and destitute Mahalingam rushes to the temple to pray but then briefly realizes he has to be 'practical' (1992: 105). On his way to the doctor, he is haunted by hallucinatory images of suicide. He equates the 'amusing' sight of an emaciated beggar hanging from a low tree with the image of another beggar from his childhood who similarly committed suicide by hanging himself. This image is then conflated with another childhood memory of a body suspended from a tree that bears sartorial signs of the dead man's elite status. He realizes that the beggar and the rich man made careful arrangements to ensure the impossibility of saving themselves or being rescued when they committed suicide. Mahalingam is reminded of his friend from college who committed suicide by strangling himself with a rope, unable to support his destitute family. Even as he contemplates suicide, Mahalingam is scared of the possibility of a painful death. He realizes the beggar and the rich man, unlike his college friend, 'smartly used cloth rather than rope to die relatively comfortable deaths' (1992: 105). He is tempted to put an end to his hunger, poverty, and psychological disorder, and imagines seeing his wife and children mourning his death. He is overjoyed to see images of his dead bodies from his previous lives, which suggests the renewed possibility of escaping everlasting suffering and unhappiness. He imagines witnessing his daughter's funeral procession and assumes the hungry Kali devoured her and his two stillborn children. He briefly thinks his wife is dead but his resilience prevents him from completely succumbing to his hallucinations. His hopes are later realized when, after worshipping Murugan at the temple, he sees his wife is alive and his daughter has recovered. The novel ends with the narrator/author's autobiographical note that expresses admiration for Mahalingam's resilience and suggests that the only way of countering the representative reality of his hallucinatory world is precisely through the representation of an alternative but equally imaginary reality that is self-empowering.

In conclusion, both Karichan Kunju and M.V. Venkatram share a moral or religious engagement with disease that compromises bodily and psychic integrity. These texts show how disease both constrains and enables alternative forms of sexual expression. The authors' moral interpretations of disease as expiatory signs of sexual excess are ultimately unsuccessful in renouncing desire. While the longing for spiritual transcendence in *Pacittamāṉiṭam* is a pretext for the protagonist to strive—and ultimately fail—to attain sexual identity and recognition, the narrative of sexual irony in *Kātukaḷ* dramatizes the tension between desire and religion in an embattled sexual subject without achieving narrative closure.

In my next chapter on Mauni, I trace the influence of Karichan Kunju and M.V. Venkatram's spiritualization of desire. There is again the idealization and de-idealization of the woman and her sexuality;

an idea that also brings Mauni closer to Janakiraman. Unlike the latter though, Mauni engages with the temporality of romantic loss and agony in an impermanent world. Desire and love, and the identity they promise, become ever deferred ideals that can never be attained or sublimated within the constraints of an embodied existence.

Notes

1. D. Narayanasami was affectionately called Karichan Kunju, meaning 'baby drongo', by K.P. Rajagopalan, who wrote under several pseudonyms, one of which was Karichan.
2. In *The Ego and the Id* (1962), Sigmund Freud proposes a more robust understanding of an ego that resists an identification of itself and the id with the conscious and the unconscious, respectively. He suggests that the supposedly conscious ego is itself partly unconscious when it resists parts of itself. Thus, the act of repression forms an integral part of the ego. The ego merges with the id and is essentially a system of perception that is partly a set of preconscious ideas or 'verbal images'. The ego controls the id but is also obliged to conform to the desires of the id. As Freud argues, the ego is a 'modified portion' of the id that perceives the empirical world making it a 'body-ego', a mental projection of the surface of one's physical body. See Freud (1962).
3. For a discussion of the equivalence of money, the phallus, and language, see Goux (1990).

4

Mauni

Desire as Dream and Fantasy

Mauni (1907–1985) was another writer whose writing career was launched by *Maṇikkoṭi* in 1936. Like most of the other writers discussed in this book, Mauni, whose real name was S. Mani, was from the Tanjavur district. There are few details about his personal life: like K.P. Rajagopalan and N. Pichamurthy, he studied in Kumbakonam and graduated in mathematics. Following his marriage, he lived in Kumbakonam for 14 years, during which he had no formal employment, before moving to Chidambaram (which is now in Cuddalore district) to take care of family property and affairs. He had five children, two of whom died young in accidents. Another son became mentally disturbed after he graduated in Philosophy (see Kumar 1992 and Mauni 1997). These tragedies probably had an impact on Mauni's writing career, which mostly dealt with topics such as loss and death.

Mauni wrote 24 short stories that were published between 1936 and 1971. He was discovered in 1933 in Kumbakonam by B.S. Ramiah, editor of *Maṇikkoṭi* and Congress activist. Mauni sent six anonymous stories through his friends to Ramiah, who named and published them in *Maṇikkoṭi* in 1936.[1] Ramiah, who later discovered that the author of the stories was S. Mani, named him 'Mauni', the Silent One. The next set of nine stories that was published in 1937–8 contained themes that would persist in the rest of his work—the illusory nature of existence; the impermanence of all things; memory; time; and death. After *Maṇikkoṭi* shut down properly in 1939, Mauni's next two stories appeared after a long gap, in 1948 in *Tēṉī*, a journal edited by M.V. Venkatram. The last group of seven stories were written over 17 years and published as part of an anthology after Mauni's death in 1985.

Mauni was by no means a widely read writer, which partly had to do with the fact that he was not a prolific writer. The more significant reason for his limited reception had to do with the abstract and convoluted manner he used to describe the temporality of loss and death. He is a unique figure in the history of the Tamil short story unlike his contemporaries who produced more concrete and plot-driven stories that captured social reality. The kind of Western writers he read are a reflection of his own oeuvre—Jorge Luis Borges, Franz Kafka, and Robert Musil. Pudumaippittan, his contemporary, described him as the Tirumular[2] of the short story, 'He [Mauni] is the only one who can stand at the extreme frontiers of the imagination and capture those concepts, which have so far refused to be contained in words.' Mauni's stories are rather amorphous and lack distinct characters, many of whom are anonymous. In fact, most of his characters are unsubstantial and disembodied shades of one another, each contributing to a general disaffection with the impermanence of the world. This gives rise to a desire to escape this world to another metaphysical reality. His stories describe the slippages between sleeping and waking; the worldly and the otherworldly, and slide easily into dreams and hallucinations. As Lakshmi Holmström and Venkat Swaminathan say in their introductory essays to a translation of Mauni's stories, the general scepticism towards the illusory nature of the world places Mauni within the Vedantic tradition (see Swaminathan in Holmström 1997). There is a constant interplay between the psychological and the metaphysical that makes it impossible to think of a concrete reality in Mauni's fictional world. His anonymous characters are continuous with the anonymous spaces they occupy—a wasteland, the description of streets and trees, frontier spaces like railway stations, and windows and thresholds of the traditional Tamil house—that connote the transitory nature of time, existence, and so on.

Mauni's interview with the critic K.A. Satchidanandan was published in the literary journal *Tīpam* in 1967. In the interview, Mauni describes his recursive practice of writing and rewriting his stories and constantly changing their form. He even claims to have attached two half-finished stories written years apart to form another story. This is significant and perhaps not surprising, considering the fluid form of his stories and the way they merge into one another. This very quality made it difficult for other writer-editors like B.S. Ramiah, C.S. Chellappa, and K.N. Subramaniam to collect and publish his stories. He also mentions his literary discussions with K.P. Rajagopalan, who lived close to his house in Kumbakonam. It was Rajagopalan who first asked him to write a story for *Maṇikkoṭi* and an issue of *Tiṉamaṇi Malar* that was being edited by Pudumaippittan. Mauni's response to a question on his literary perspective sums up, I believe, the major thematic of his writings:

> The 'self' experiences itself very dimly. Yet it is aware too that it is full of truth and beauty. It recreates that fullness unconsciously, not as a 'self' standing opposite itself, but as another and as an objective thing. In this way, this self goes on assuming that this dimly expressed other is the truth. Art, philosophy and religion are all now in a similar state. In literary creativity, the artist and the *rasika* [fan/reader/aesthete] are alike in some ways. The artist does not write for any particular audience. Neither does the *rasika* read and appreciate a work because it was created by some particular person. True literature is not that which chooses a topic for its aesthetics or literary worth and then launches into some vague circuitous descriptions of it. Rather, it ought to be the intention of literature to take a palpable experience from a particular perspective or standpoint, become one with it, appreciate it with the mind and all the senses, and then represent it objectively, without being overwhelmed by emotion. (Satchidanandan quoted in Holmström 1997: 163; italics in the original)

What interests me is the idea of the imaginary identification of the self and the other that is always under the threat of dissolution. All of

Mauni's stories at some fundamental level foreground the disjunction between perception and reality. In Mauni's imaginary world, the presence of the unconscious is crucial as it appears precisely in the gap between perception and reality, and thus in the failure of language to capture reality. Mauni's stories corroborate his thoughts on the function of literature: they posit an 'objective' world where the opposition between subject and object is constantly dissolved and reoriented. His characters' perception is as unstable as the phenomenal world that fails to yield a stable or essential truth. But it is precisely in their quest for truth that the characters are able to constantly reorient their relationship to the world and to one another.

Mauni's early set of stories focus on the temporality of romantic agony and loss. His male protagonists imagine dreamlike scenarios of longing where desire and love remain ideals that fail to affect a union between the self and the other. There can be no truth or identity in these scenarios where there is a constant blurring and fragmentation of selves and bodies. In fact, one of the chief features of his stories is a fluid and fragmented notion of the self that traverses multiple characters. But this fluidity does not apply to sexually differentiated bodies, thus retaining sexual difference. Women in Mauni's stories can be categorized into two types: the first type includes women who are either young lovers or separated from their lovers, or are dead; the second type includes wives and the good devadasi. Most of these women, as they conform and subvert, are ideal projections of their male counterparts, although there are instances where they acquire a degree of autonomy. These women are often perceived as alluring but fearful incarnations of feminine power and desire that undo male integrity. This brings Mauni closer to the deified women in Janakiraman's works, or those in the stories of a later writer like L.S. Ramamirtham (1919–2007), but somewhat unlike the more discerning women in Rajagopalan. In some cases, Mauni's women possess self-reflexivity and cease to be mere reflections of the male self; in fact, they reflect the lack of male self-possession and imagine their own relationships with other men or women.

Mauni's 1937 short story '*Aḻiyā Cuṭar*' (The Undying Flame), for example, explores the psychological ruminations of a narrator who re-encounters a woman he once met in a temple. From his self-description, the narrator—like most of Mauni's characters—resembles

Mauni himself. He describes this re-encounter to a friend who is initially a passive listener, but later merges with the narrator's psychological landscape. The woman seems to be a projection of the narrator's imagination. All the characters are nameless. This story has a typical 'Maunian' setting: the narrator occupies an interstitial space at the threshold of a room by a window overlooking the street. Unlike Janakiraman or Karichan Kunju, who are rooted in their local environment and feature the Kaveri, the temples, and the Brahman *akrahāram* (a Brahman locality) of Kumbakonam or Tanjavur, there is nothing about this setting, or any of Mauni's settings, that is rooted in a local reality. Like Rajagopalan with the exception of his historical stories, Mauni's stories could be located anywhere. The narrator is looking at a withered tree that apparently reflects his own state of mind:

> The tree seemed to be to be standing alone, unkempt, disheveled, mourning silently. Birds which came swopping through the air to perch upon its branches, suddenly grew still, as if they had lost their lives and become one with that tree. Their cries sounded intermittently, like death calls. After a while, they flew away, as if with renewed life. [To the friend] '... Can you see it [the tree] groping for something that the skies do not possess, hands outspread, eyes shut, always searching? ... It cannot rest; its play is not yet over.... Clouds come and rest upon it, heavy with love. It shudders unable to bear their weight. Is it a royal whisk, outspread to cleanse away the clouds from the pathways of the skies? Or does it stand there, yearning for the raindrops, which will bring new shoots? Why does it stand? Why? (Mauni quoted in Holmström 1997: 45)[3]

Like Mauni's other stories, this one dramatizes the human failure to interpret existence. In Mauni's fictional world, the impulse to attribute meaning to the phenomenal world, including the world of the mind, is an attempt to rationalize loss and impermanence, which cannot be understood. It is not certain that the physical tree is the real object of the narrator's attention; rather, there is a blurring of the boundary between subject and object, where the object seems continuous with the subject's sense of loss. And yet the search for a causal logic—or the impulse to accord the idea of existence as loss a metaphorical status—fails to capture the truth of existence. Any attempt to capture an ideal or metaphysical realm only reinforces the inadequacy of language. The narrator nostalgically remembers his once youthful beauty, which he associates with his first encounter with the woman, then a young girl. They meet at the entrance of a temple as she is about to leave when she looks back at him. The narrator is unable to interpret the act of looking back as anything except a spontaneous act, which acquires its own causality. Even the sight of the girl praying before the deity appears to be a transcendental image of completeness that traverses the limits of space and time, 'her eyes seemed to have gone beyond the image of god, past the boundaries of life's beginning and end, to rejoice in some extraordinary happiness.... Time stood still, lost in her form, in that Presence' (1997: 47). Here, the location, the temple, and the act of praying can be seen as the exteriorization of a most private experience. The praying form of the girl is raised to the status of a transhistorical truth, the truth of self-dissolution to become one with the world. The narrator has the same transcendental experience when he meets her nine years later at the same temple. The veneer of her Western appearance is lost before her silent devotion. But again the narrator admits the futility of thought or language to understand or express this ecstatic experience. During both the encounters, the narrator imagines his silent love for the woman elicits the rage of the *yāḻis* and the idol in the temple.[4] The woman seems to tell him, 'I'm destiny's shadow. You see in me the seductive harshness of love' (1997: 50). Clearly, even the ideal of love embodied in the woman does not possess an essential truth. It does not promise a definitive way out of an embodied consciousness structured and divided by language.

The shadow is a recurrent motif in Mauni, used to describe the imaginary nature of the self. The word 'imaginary' should not be equated with falsity, but understood as a necessary yet fictional construction of the autonomous and unified subject that is constituted and undermined by the unconscious. In his seminar 'The Subject of the Unconscious' Lacan's central thesis is that the unconscious is structured like a language; indeed it is language. The unconscious is constituted through the subject's articulation in a transindividual symbolic order. By language, Lacan does not merely mean verbal or written language, but any signifying system that is based on differential relations. The unconscious is a signifying process that involves coding and decoding, ciphering and deciphering. And it comes into being in the gap between the signifier and the signified, and in the inability of meaning to be fixed. Like Freud earlier, Lacan describes the unconscious as a rupture between perception and consciousness; as a failure or impediment in the symbolic chain. This rupture explains the failure of language to express. As the friend listens to the narrator recount his experience, he imagines the temple not as a physical place but as a blurred frontier zone that borders the conscious and the unconscious:

> Yes bats, which are abroad even during the day, wandering about unaware that it is indeed day. Within that inner space, where daylight hesitates to enter more than halfway, in that dim twilight, the images stand, taking on radiant life. Were temples sculpted in order to nourish that great happiness at the silent centre of our deepest and most private experience? What truths does that *canniti* [sanctum sanctorum] wish to communicate, surrounded as it is by the corridor with hanging lights, where, to one's shocked surprise, there is no difference between the devotees and their shadows? Are all of us merely shadows? Of what then are we the moving shadows? (1997: 48)

The desire for a spiritual union with the world remains an imaginary ideal that is inherently estranged by the limitations of language and human existence. When there is no certainty to existence, the narrator says, one can only have faith in the possibility of discovering the truth. The only way of resolving the deadlock between the uncertainty of existence and free will is to resort to faith in destiny.

> What did she say? What had she asked me to do? Was it, after all, a dream? No, she never spoke. But what is there in sound or in words? Or indeed in form? They are all meaningless. They cannot make us aware of the truth.... There are these pointing fingers, though, which tell us not everything is *maya*. They point to something else—Look, up there!—yet they themselves disappear even before we learn to move in that direction. In the uncertainty of darkness, we are left with just the belief that unless we make that leap of chance, we may never reach the right path ... I heaved a great sigh, exhausted, aware that we will never really understand what lies above us ... [The friend] This morning he is not to be seen. Where he went and why, I do not know. I do not know if he knows that either. My only thought is that He alone knows everything. If indeed there is a He. (1998: 50–1; italics in the original)

The apparent correspondence between the human psyche and reality is the theme of '*Manakkōlam*' (Images: 1948), another short story from Mauni's middle period. Like the earlier story, this story focuses on woman as a transcendental ideal that ostensibly lends meaning to an otherwise aimless life. If there is no inherent purpose to life; if life cannot be predetermined, only the act of desiring orients the human subject towards an imagined future. The story suggests that reflection and experience are mutually oppositional categories: one cannot constantly reflect on existence by attributing meaning or causal logic to every incident without impeding the possibility of experiencing it. The fact that life is not predetermined or that everything that occurs is causeless and coincidental opens up the possibility of absolute freedom. The male protagonist of the story, Kesavan, is caught in the unavoidable divide between absolute freedom and his own subjectivity, which is the necessity of making a choice that limits this freedom. Like Mauni's other male protagonists, his inability to interpret the meaning of existence paralyzes his ability to act or make a choice. In the face of absolute uncertainty, even his memory, which operates on remembering and forgetting the past, is an unreliable resource to inform future action. He is paralyzed by a longing for his neighbour's wife, Gauri. The torment of his longing is mitigated by the calm and peace of the night and exacerbated by day. By night, she is invoked as a disembodied and, therefore, pervasive presence that subsists in the imagined sound of the veena or the fragrance of the flowers she wears in her hair. But the joy of fantasizing about Gauri renders the night brief, leaving Kesavan longing for the nights to come. Kesavan comes to the conclusion that one cannot always contemplate the purpose of life, and should also be open to experience. Of course, this cannot be a passive stance, for existence demands some form of action. His experience of Gauri is initially a disconnected event in his life, but later, the look of her eyes that shone like 'torch lights' gives his empty life a sense of purpose. He rejects her status as another man's life and identifies her with a self-assuring ideal of womanhood that exceeds the boundaries of marriage and only seeks to 'acknowledge male weakness and obscure female strength' to inspire 'repugnance' and 'fear' (1997: 68). Kesavan seems to internalize Gauri even as she appears in his dreams. His nightmare of being embraced by lusting serpents only reassures his own self through an imagined female other. Thus, even as Gauri is elevated to an ideal of feminine strength, she lacks subjectivity. She is a fragile projection of perfect identity that confronts the man with his own lack.

'*Maṉakkōlam*' anticipated a later story called *Cāvil Piṟanta Ciruṣṭi* (From Death, Creation: 1954). The three characters of the story, the husband, his wife, and a young man resonate with the characters in the earlier story. In fact, the names of the husband and wife are the same in both stories. In '*Maṉakkōlam*', Kesavan incarnates an ambiguity that blurs the past, the present, and the future, and is figured as the tension between tradition and modernity. In *Cāvil Piṟanta Ciruṣṭi*, the opposition between tradition and modernity is embodied in two characters, the husband and the young man, both named Subbayya. Without critiquing, the story reiterates the earlier formulation of marriage as an institution that reassures male insecurity and obscures female strength. The husband in this story is insecure and possessive of Gauri, his young and beautiful wife. Unable to acknowledge his insecurity, he assumes an outward appearance of self-sufficiency. He invents excuses to forbid her from meeting her parents, which she obeys. He convinces himself his decision is out of consideration for her convenience and not out of self-interest (1997: 72). Soon after she leaves for her sister's wedding, her husband experiences intense loneliness.

The Gauri of this story is a self-reflexive woman unlike the Gauri of '*Maṉakkōlam*'. Coming from a poor family, her parents have no choice but to get her married to an older but wealthy widower. Although Gauri appears inscrutable to the two men in the story, the narrator describes her as a young woman who matured rapidly after her marriage. She does not believe she has been sacrificed by marrying an older man and is steadfast in her love. Subbayya, who has only known Gauri to be a silent and submissive wife, is surprised and jealous to see her rejoice in the company of her family. In a fit of resentment, he forces her to leave with him the day after the marriage. On their way back they meet a young man, also named Subbayya, who represents another model of insecure masculinity. He embodies a synthetic notion of modern urbanity that is characterized by his fashionable clothes and the songs he sings to attract the attention of his co-passengers. His nervous response to Subbayya, who asks him if they have met, elicits Gauri's amusement. The narrator is careful to protect Gauri from potential criticism; she is described as an enigmatic but chaste woman, 'If her eyes fell upon a man, the next instant they would half close, as if they had been faintly tainted' (1997: 75).

The story dramatizes the psychological conflict within and among the three characters: Gauri is anxious that the men may impute their own desires to her behaviour. When the young man assumes Gauri to be Subbayya's daughter, Subbayya suppresses his insecurity by taunting Gauri. When he gets off at one of the stations, he claims to have mistaken a man for Subbini, a man who had once been considered as a groom for Gauri. He also compares Subbini to the young man on the train. Gauri is so accustomed to Subbayya's taunts that she is apparently incapable of feeling anymore pain. On realizing that Gauri is married to Subbayya, the young man believes he has lost all hope of happiness and envies her husband. But he is not sure if he would be happy to possess Gauri, were the older Subbayya to disappear. He feels trapped, unable to move away or be in their presence. To Gauri, the two men seem to merge as indistinct shades of each other. They are both symbols of a male-centric system where relations between men are mediated through women. Woman is imputed with male values without thought to the possibility of female autonomy and difference. Whether she is constructed as a lack or an ideal, her prescribed role is to reassure male power. The narrator describes her as an infinite cosmic principle whose power cannot be contained by the body. She realizes she is neither able to end her life nor free herself of her female embodiment:

> From the way the two men looked at her, Gauri gradually began to understand what had first puzzled her. She was, after all, a very young woman, perhaps not quite twenty. Both the older man and the younger one seemed to merge as they reached out to her, across the difference in their age. The evil aspect that had been shadowing her since that morning was now taking many forms. First, he was an old man, her husband. Then he assumed youth in order to jump aboard a moving train and to come and sit in front of her. Perhaps the ill-luck that had ruled her life since birth was contained in her own female form. But it was not possible for her to hold on to life and yet rid herself of the body that contained it.... Then a certain strength took hold of her mind, her face became radiant with a new look of clarity. Perhaps, she was a reflection of the infinite form of that female principle that embraces the

> whole world.... Her normally mobile beauty had assumed a set expression. Must men's lives be like that of moths, always circling the lamp until they are destroyed? How was a woman to keep herself from appearing attractive to the men who drew close to her? Can darkness become the light that it draws from the lamp? Gauri castigated herself.... (1997: 79)

The blurring of the male characters points to a fluid and unsubstantial notion of the self. All the three characters seem to renounce the necessity of action through an imagination of cosmic or eternal time where everything is predestined to happen. Gauri comforts herself by believing in the inexorable force of destiny. The husband at various points in the story betrays his belief in predestination and forswears responsibility because of his age and failing memory. He recognizes his own youth in the younger Subbayya and urges the latter to take a photograph of himself to freeze time as it were. Again, agency is suspended between a language of predestination or eternal time and self-consciousness. All the characters strive to transcend their embodied lives by relinquishing their agency to the workings of a cosmic time. As the husband recreates a mythical narrative of the clash between the god of creation Brahma and the god of destruction Shiva, he tells the young man, Kaliyuga or the age they live in has already been predetermined by the agonistic forces of creation and destruction, 'What sort of creatures are we, we the creatures of Kaliyuga? We are only dancing puppets. The tussle between the gods has left us helpless, without vitality. Our lives are a meaningless charade' (1997: 83).

Let us move on to another pair of interconnected stories, '*Niṉaivu Cuvaṭu*' (Memory's Imprint: 1948) and '*Uṟavu Pantam Pācam*' (Kinships, Bonds, Affections: 1968). Although the stories were written and published 20 years apart, they share certain thematic continuities. Both the stories focus on unconventional relationships outside the fold of marriage. These relationships are transient and subsist in brief conversations that evoke memories of a past intimacy. Both the stories focus on the male character's past relationship with an idealized devadasi. '*Niṉaivu Cuvaṭu*' focuses on briefly renewed intimacies that are again severed by loss and separation. Sundaram, the narrator of the story, accidentally meets Sekar, his friend from college while taking a walk along the beach one evening. Mauni often sets his stories at dusk, when there is a possibility of misrecognition. Through this device Mauni conveys an elastic and fragmentary notion of the self through mistaken identities or close resemblances. Sundaram is struck by the fact that Sekar has not changed even after 20 years. While they are sitting on the beach, they notice a group of young women sitting before them, and. when they leave, Sekar asks Sundaram to leave with him. Sundaram realizes that Sekar is following one of the young women. He appears to be mesmerized, involuntarily following her to her house. He seems to realize it, and shaken, stops at a small cigarette store to collect himself. As they walk past the woman's house, they hear a female voice entreating Sekar to come in. Sundaram finds himself following Sekar into the house, which belongs to a devadasi named Susila, who once had a relationship with Sekar. The woman who Sekar followed, mistaking her for Susila, turns out to be their daughter Kanta. Sekar is briefly reunited with Susila and silently embraces his daughter for the first and last time before he disappears in self-hatred.

As Sundaram is reduced to the status of an absent witness to Sekar and Susila's reunion, his gaze registers the affective transformations in their faces and bodies. To Sundaram, Susila seems enchanted by Sekar's unexpected arrival and the fact that he has not changed. Although Sekar is now older and married, no time seems to have lapsed since they were last together, but for their 20-year old daughter Kanta, who is a constant reminder of their past intimacy. In their joyful reunion, Susila's face seems to have acquired an ageless and alluring beauty like Sekar's that transcends time, 'She was very beautiful. An alluring quality, an unfading luster where the very thought of determining her age did not arise, had entered her face' (1997: 259). Their reunion freezes them in an eternal bond that excludes the ones around them. She appears aged when she looks at Kanta, but regains her youth when she looks at Sekar (1997: 260). Sundaram, who is clearly excluded in their presence, silently expresses his contempt of prostitutes for their utter lack of attachment or loyalty. As they are leaving, Kanta entreats Sekar to stay back for her sake. At the sight of his daughter, Sekar's face seems to betray his self-hatred: 'The youthful luster in his face was destroyed in a second' (1997: 264). To Sekar, the presence of his daughter Kanta taints his idealized memory of his relationship with Susila by sexualizing it.

'*Uṟavu Pantam Pācam*' reads like a sequel to the previous story. The anonymous narrator returns home after several years and discovers to his shock, a rapidly urbanizing town. As he walks through the town, he recognizes the devadasi's house that he and his friend used to frequent. He decides to meet his friend, but learns that he sold his property and left the town soon after his own departure. This is probably an allusion to Sekar's disappearance in '*Niṉaivu Cuvaṭu*'. He visits the old temple town that is now in ruins, where he finds Gauri, the woman who lived with his friend for many years. Gauri and the other devadasis now live in a ruined part of the town. Gauri seems to exhibit greater inner complexity than Mauni's other female characters. She seems to accept the impermanence of the world, which includes the friend's disappearance and the town's transformation. Her acceptance enables her to be free of all attachment. She tries to disillusion the narrator's nostalgia for the town of their youth:

Even though you see the old story die away before your very eyes like a dream, you still seem to be seduced by it.... How can you look for completion in that which is transient? Doesn't the shadow of the past always mingle mysteriously with the uncertainty of what is to come? [Narrator] You seem to have an odd philosophy, don't you, Gauri? [Gauri] Oh yes, all of you think of me as only a *tēvatāci*, a mere woman. Ask the pillar where you are leaning against, it might tell you why your friend left.... (1997: 133–4; italics mine)

The narrator, of course, like Sundaram in the previous story, interprets Gauri's detachment as a sign of indifference expected in a devadasi. She makes mocking guesses about the friend's whereabouts, and conjectures that he may have renounced worldly life to become an ascetic, or gone in search of the wife who left him. When she asks the narrator about his family, he is surprised that she is unaware that neither he nor his friend ever married. She cynically realizes that his friend had never explicitly told her, but also recalls that they had shared confidences in their relationship. Gauri's disaffection with relationships reflects a fundamental difference in the way men and women are constructed and socialized into conforming to their gender roles.

It seemed to her that the nature of men was not reflected rightly by any single person nor in any particular aspect. And the whole world continued to misunderstand the difference between man and woman. The entire nature of duty, order, dharma, seemed to be destroyed, and all kinships, bonds and affections rendered futile. She was floundering in her mind, not sure whom to blame, and for what. (1997: 136)

While men can be married and have extramarital affairs, women are unable to do so without being stigmatized. The social position of the devadasi is even more tenuous, as she is considered a prostitutes or loose woman owing to her relationships with male patrons, without the security of marriage. Gauri argues that women may lose their sense of self to men or marriage. She upholds the power and authenticity of women that lies in their longing for the other:

Ayya [sir] I'm a woman and a tēvatāci. You know about tēvatācis perhaps, but do you know about women? You are a man who did not marry. And it is right, in a way, which you did not. Suppose there had been a woman who lost her virtue to you simply because she was your wife.... We are women; we are tēvatācis. In one sense, we are married women. You could even describe us as wives. Ayya, often my state is that of a woman who has forgotten at what point she went away from her husband and is looking for him everywhere. Men can live without marriage. But women are not able to—doesn't our Hindu dharma say so? One should not live as a virgin; indeed one cannot. Even Kanyakumari, while remaining virgin forever, yearns constantly for the Other. Can a woman, beginning her married life, believe that her sacred self will never be invaded by her husband? If she is robbed of her wholeness by him, then can't she consider that she has lost her chastity to him? Perhaps men like you would make unique husbands, but you chose not to marry. *He* who created women, did not forget the nature of women.... You must certainly go in search of your friend. He understood this. (1997: 137)

'*Pirakñai Veḷiyil*' (Beyond Perception: 1960), written along the lines of '*Uṟavu Pantam Pācam*', equates romantic longing with feminine freedom and authenticity. Here, like in some of Mauni's other stories, love is a fiction that can only be experienced in absence or separation. The story is again set at a beach where Sekaran and Kittu, two childhood friends, meet after several years. Sekaran—unlike a few of Mauni's other male protagonists who resort to the countryside to avoid urbanization—visits an unknown town to escape the tedium of life in the village. The friends spot three young women sitting before them, one of whom is an indescribable beauty. While Kittu is mesmerized by Susila's beauty, which 'reflect[s] whatever mood or expression the spectator [chooses],' Sekaran is reminded of an inscrutable ideal of womanhood, whose awesome and fear-inspiring strength is suppressed by man:

Just look at her. How bravely her beauty ventures out to strike you! She is a young girl, as yet unmarried. She appears to be womanhood itself. Do you know what fearful strength womanhood possesses? But, a woman, by the very fact of being so, must become a man's wife. And a husband tries to confine this huge notion of womanhood within the tight frame of a child's slate, and gives himself the pleasure of drawing a picture there, which he calls *Wife*. As for seeking the womanhood in her, that is a terrifying thing.... Well Kittu, do you ever feel afraid when you look at your wife? (1997: 100–1; italics in the original)

There is an impulse to essentialize women in Mauni's stories, identifying them as incarnations of an essential feminine power that cannot be contained by their relationships with men. But there is also something unsettling about unravelling this mysterious power that does not in reality possess an essential truth. Sekaran identifies his wife, also called Susila, with this power that is both alluring and intimidating. The Susila he meets in the town appears a refreshing alternative to his tedious marriage, but over the course of the story, the two women become indistinguishable. When the time arrives for his return, Sekaran is torn between the two Susilas. The urban Susila begins to sympathize with the rural Susila and resents Sekaran for neglecting his wife. She begins to reflect on the ethical paradoxes of a life where the meaning of morality and accountability is contingent not on human actions but on circumstances. She realizes that she is indirectly responsible for keeping Sekaran from his wife because she shares the same name. But then she begins to identify with the wife who is possibly longing for her husband to the point that she begins to identify Sekaran with the absent wife. On the one hand, she trivializes the promiscuity of men like Sekaran, suggesting the insecurity that characterizes their masculinity; on the other hand, her desire for and identification with the longing wife's desiring self is mediated through Sekaran, the object of her desire. Susila tells her friend Bhanu:

It strikes me I didn't consider Sekaran as a man at first.... I understand very well what men are and what masculinity is supposed to be about. Men are like roosters, flapping their wings and crowing at the threshold, while the backyard door is left open so that they can slip away. But masculinity is like a plucked hen. I think, after all, I regarded Sekaran as a woman, and spoke to him in that way. Can a woman discern the power of womanhood in a man? Is it possible? Is that the reason why I both like and dislike him? He has a wife who has the same name as I. Is it she I am looking for in him? Has he claimed her womanhood and made her helpless? ... [Narrator] Perhaps Susila was thinking of the extent to which any man repels a woman by his antics and his words. How could a woman bear to spend a lifetime with a man, as his wife.... How can such an experience be described as a pleasure, or be called 'love'? ... In order to live one's life in a decent way, how many subterfuges one had to use! Perhaps it was only when their husbands were out of sight and elsewhere, that women got some sort of pleasure in waiting for their return. Susila had begun to think that Sekaran's wife's life was profoundly dependent on her own existence.... Suddenly she realized that what she had thought of before as a cruel tendency in herself, to which her mind would not agree, could now be seen differently. (1997: 107–8)

Sekaran's unexpected death in an accident collapses the two Susilas into one. If waiting for someone implies his return, Sekaran's final departure reduces Susila to a 'nameless form' that has again become 'a void' (1997: 109). In her imagination, she 'search[es] for her selfhood' until she discovers herself in Sekaran's wife who is now suspended, forever awaiting his return.

Were the distressed soul to be overwhelmed by sorrow, then at least it can look forward to dreams of joy. Perhaps life is nothing except the pleasure of pain.... Young Susila stood by her window, becoming the wife who awaited her husband's return and his passionate 'love'. In that case, a woman 'in love' is an unmarried widow—an absurdity! (1997: 110–11)

The female protagonist of '*Kuṭai Niḻal*' (The Umbrella's Shelter: 1959), Jones, is by far the most subtle and complex female character of Mauni's stories. The story consists of three encounters between Jones, a prostitute, and Sundaram, the male character. Here too, love is seen as an ideal that can never be realized in a relationship. Sundaram encounters Jones by the railway station, where he is searching for a friend. He is instantly drawn to Jones, a young Anglo-Indian woman, and when it starts to rain, shelters her under his umbrella and offers to walk her home. He cannot believe his luck at the thought of flirting and walking with a young woman at night. It is only when he drops her at a brothel that he realizes she is a prostitute. What is interesting is Sundaram's changing perception of Jones, which imputes her with qualities or values that would reassure his own masculinity even before he discovers she is a prostitute. She initially looks like 'an orphan who longs for protection,' but then there is no 'self-pity in her voice' (1997: 88). Once he discovers her identity, he imputes her with virtue, which elicits sympathy and an impulse to rescue her from her disreputable profession. The eyes that apparently sought his protection 'look away in boredom' (1997: 89). Then there is something hidden beneath her sorrowful eyes that may be 'the purity of her heart' (1997: 89).

The relationship between a prostitute and her client is an imaginary structure of desire and identification where the other is a reflection of the self. As Jones tells Sundaram, 'You must, after all, always think those thoughts of me that I myself have given to you and which you reflect back to me' (1997: 89). She realizes that her identity as a prostitute may make him contemptuous of her, or encourage him to realize his desirable values in and through her. To Jones, Sundaram may not have realized she is a prostitute, but he is still a typical man who sees her purely as a woman who is meant to be exclusively possessed. Indeed, for Sundaram 'there was no joy in speaking to someone who belonged to no one directly, but belonged to everyone equally' (1997: 90) For Jones, whose identity as a prostitute condemns her to perpetual loneliness, Sundaram remains a mere fantasy lover, 'you are the man who has appeared a thousand times in [my] daydreams' (1997: 89). The rest of the time they spend together is only an elaboration of an imaginary intimacy that is already rife with isolation. While she proclaims her love for him, he cannot stop himself from being deceived by her. He is filled with compassion and yet 'her words and her manner of speaking did not seem to belong to someone such as she. Was it his own extreme youth and inexperience that made him think so?' (1997: 91). That Sundaram pays her before leaving without having sexual intercourse may be an act of compassion, but it reinforces the impossibility of a romantic relationship that is not mystified by monetary exchange. If Jones is devalued by her fetishized status as a commodity, Sundaram is also devalued by becoming a substitutable object of her 'desire' that is indistinguishable from her mercenary aims.

During their second encounter, Jones, despite herself, is briefly moved to happiness by the compassion in Sundaram's eyes. When she considers the possibility of a love that is unsullied by money, he is unable to reciprocate her sincerity, 'Jones, let us go outside and walk about a little.... Why, and how did you get involved in this work?' (1997: 93). That he reduces Jones to her profession reinstates Jones's belief that she will always remain a false ideal. Only death, she says, can perfect human life. She believes only her dreams will survive even after her death. She dreams of her death when Sundaram visits her the third time and she tells him she is unable to remember her 'strange and happy' dream (1997: 95). She appears happy and carefree to Sundaram, as if she were already free of her existence. She no longer desires to see Sundaram and disappears and when Sundaram visits her again, he meets another woman. He gives her the money he was supposed to give Jones.

Mauni was preoccupied with disappointed desires and loves that are neither consummated in the body nor sublimated in a higher cultural aim. A sexual or romantic relationship, let alone marriage, is a mythic ideal that nevertheless animates his characters' orientation towards others. But in Mauni's fictional world, where recognition and identity can never be attained, there is always an irresolvable discordance between perception and reality. Even the oneiric structures of his stories are merely imaginary scenarios of self-realization, constituted by alienation and loss. His characters remain estranged from their own selves and from the world at large, and for some, death is the only way to attain freedom and perfection.

If the writers discussed so far have spiritualized desire, the next two chapters on Dandapani Jeyakantan and Tanjai Prakash, affirm the potential of desire or love to bind marginalized subjects and provide collective forms of self-realization. There is a transition in Jeyakantan from representing death as a way of purifying sexual abjection and attaining an imaginary sense of wholeness, to imagining the possibility of male–female companionships as the basis and instrument of social reform. In Prakash, the impossibility of a sexual relationship that promises identity necessitates the sublimation of desire in labour to reconfigure marginalized subjects and provide collective forms of self-realization.

Notes

1. See Jeyamokan on Mauni in *Kaṉavukaḷ Ilaṭciyaṅkaḷ* (2003a), where, referring to M.V. Venkatram's *Eṉ Ilakkiya Naṇparkaḷ* (My Literary Friends), he says B.S. Ramiah collected fragments of Mauni's stories and published them in *Tēṉī*.
2. Tirumular is one of the 63 Tamil Shaiva saints. Known for his work *Tirumantiram,* he is said to have used his yogic powers to transmigrate into the body of a cowherd named Mulan.
3. Translation of the 1997 title *Fictions: Mauni* is by Lakshmi Holmström.
4. Yāḻi is a mythical animal with the face of a lion and the trunk and tusks of an elephant.

5

Dandapani Jeyakantan

Loving Outcastes, Spirituality, and Reformation

Dandapani Jeyakantan (1934–2015) was born in Cuddalore, in the North Arcot district of the Madras Presidency to a family of wealthy Veḷḷāḷars, a landed agricultural caste. His father was a spendthrift and abandoned the family to live with another woman when Jeyakantan was young. Jeyakantan grew up under the care of his maternal grandfather who was first a nationalist and then a supporter of E.V. Ramasami Naiker's *Tirāviṭa Kaḻakam* party. Two of his uncles were supporters of the Communist Party, and another uncle supported Gandhi's satyagraha and introduced Jeyakantan to Subramania Barati's songs. But it was his uncles' communist affiliations that would have the greatest impact on Jeyakantan's literary career.

Jeyakantan left home when he was 12, unable to study or bear the cruelty of his school teachers. He moved to Vilupuram, where one of his uncles was a full-time member of the Communist Party, and then to Madras, where another uncle got him a job at the *Janasakti* press, the official Tamil paper of the Communist Party. He was later trained to work as a letter press compositor and sold copies of the paper. He lived and worked at the office, where he forged lasting friendships with other members of the commune, including some prominent leaders of the Communist Party—P. Jeevanandam, Mohan Kumaramangalam, P. Ramamurthy, A.S.K. Iyenger, M.R. Venkatragavan, Ismat Pasha, and Baladhandayudham. Jeyakantan was not admitted as a full-time member of the Communist Party till he turned 18. But by then his job was uncertain, with Sardar Vallabhbhai Patel's attempts to suppress the communists for their apparent opposition to the Quit India Movement and the general integration of the state. P.C. Joshi, who was dubbed a reformist, was replaced in 1949 by the more radical B.T. Ranadive as the new general secretary of the Communist Party of India (CPI). Many of the communist leaders went underground.

The temporary eclipse of the Communist Party witnessed the rise of the Dravida Kazhagam (DK) and Dravida Munnetra Kazhagam (DMK) parties. When C. Rajagopalachari was elected the first Congress chief minister of the Madras Presidency, he directed his efforts against the communists, dubbing them enemies of the state. With the help of the DK and the DMK the Communist Party was further suppressed. In 1957, Rajagopalachari was succeeded by K. Kamaraj Nadar, who came to power with the support of E.V. Ramasami Naiker and the DMK. Jeyakantan was always critical of DMK and the 'fascism' of the Dravidian cause that they espoused. Unlike his fellow writers, he was openly critical of E.V. Ramasami Naiker and his exclusionary view of Brahmanism. He distanced himself from the Communist Party that had failed to evaluate the evils of the DMK and was beset with rifts. He was labelled a deviant by the party when he moved to Madurai and later to Kumbakonam. There he wrote for Ismat Pasha, the founder-editor of the journal *Samaran*, but the Communist Party sabotaged the distribution networks of the journal. This led Jeyakantan to conclude that the CPI did not value individual opinion and suppressed anyone who did not conform to the party line. He declared his support for the lower-caste politician Kamaraj Nadar and his populist measures to reform caste and class inequalities. These opinions are seen in his political autobiography *Oru Ilakkiyavātiyiṉ Araciyal Aṉupavaṅkaḷ* (A Litterateur's Political

Experiences: 1974). From then on, for most of his life, Jeyakantan remained an independent writer without affiliations to any party.

Jeyakantan began his writing career in 1953, writing for prominent Marxist journals like *Carasvati, Tāmarai, Maṉitaṉ, Cānti, Kirāma Uḻiyaṉ*, and later *Āṉanta Vikaṭaṉ*. He also edited political journals like *Jeya Pērikai, Jeyakkoṭi*, and *Navacakti* that leaned towards Congress party philosophy. Like K.P. Rajagopalan earlier and many of his contemporaries as well, he read the Russian writers Leo Tolstoy and Maxim Gorky and wrote admiringly of them. He was invited as a state guest by Russia and was also given the Soviet Land Nehru Award (1978). As an independent and self-styled Marxist, many of Jeyakantan's writings feature socially and economically marginalized individuals and their attempt to resist exploitation. He did not restrict himself to purely economic issues, but often interwove them with the psychological workings of the inner mind. Thus, many of his working-class characters cannot be reduced to their working-class bodies or their identification with a working class force or union. They are described in all their human potential. This often places them at odds with the rest of their peers and society. In fact, many of Jeyakantan's novellas and stories address the idea of love between outcastes, which enables them to traverse social and sexual hierarchies. This elicited criticism from his readers, many of whom accused him of obscenity. In some prefaces to his works, Jeyakantan defends himself against these charges accusing his readers of hypocrisy. He affirms the creative freedom of the writer and the autonomy of the fictional text, neither of which are obliged to cater to the reader's preferences.[1]

In the works of Jeyakantan, a new form of love between equally marginalized men and women is seen that is based on the mutual recognition of abjection. This recognition is an empowering basis for a bond that is the only source of sustenance in the face of ostracism, violence, poverty, and exploitation. The love between several male and female characters, many of whom are outcastes or orphans, is characterized by a sense of care and responsibility that proves to be mutually redemptive and self-renewing. Drawing from the scholarship of certain feminist theorists of love like bell hooks, Shulamith Firestone, Carol Gilligan, and Mary Evans, care and responsibility can be seen as feminine modes of relating that have the power to resist sexual domination and reconfigure sexual norms. Without conflating the feminine with the female, my reading of Jeyakantan acknowledges the social potential of vulnerability to form the basis of collaborative bonds of compassion and empathy. It is crucial to resist the prevalent identification of vulnerability with weakness in popular culture, or even much feminist scholarship. Jeyakantan's narratives offer two ways of addressing abjection: one is the sexual reformation of male–female relationships where desire is renounced for asceticism and spirituality, and the other is the sublimation of desire in altruism. If desire is associated with an abject existence, it has to be abrogated or channelized towards a humanitarian spirit that imagines the marginalized not as lesser individuals but as social relationalities capable of reconfiguring norms and practices.

There are few women in Jeyakantan's fiction whose lives are not touched by sexual abjection. Considering that chastity or *kaṟpu* has been the reigning female virtue in the history of Tamil culture, the possibility of female desire without marriage is perceived as a threat to familial reputation. The metonymic relationship between female chastity and family thus renders the question of female sexual consent immaterial. The woman is, therefore, not a desiring subject but an object of exchange between families. One of the primary concerns of this chapter is to address the inescapable fact of sexual abjection that structures female subjectivity. Drawing from Julia Kristeva's conceptualization of abjection, I understand it as a structural form of marginality that both constitutes and potentially threatens or reconfigures normative sexual identity. In the texts discussed here, the only option available to the abject woman is to embrace her abjection in order to exercise the little agency or power possible within the structural constraints that both constitute and limit such agency. The act of internalizing abjection within the embodied self has to be understood not merely as a reinstatement of a constrained sexual agency, or even the subject's complicity in her own victimhood, but as enabling a parodic form of power that at once incorporates and destabilizes regulatory norms of sexuality. This chapter engages with the abject woman as a rhetorical figure that is invested with a particularly counterintuitive form of sexual power—parody. Following scholarly accounts of parody in literature, I argue that the mode of parody is never openly hostile but is a strategic form of ambivalence that simultaneously reinstates and subverts dominant constructions of sexuality to reveal the fundamental instability of sexual identity.[2] In the following texts, the parodic power of the abject woman lies in her ability to manipulate structural determinations of female sexual consent through her desire for a man outside the institution of marriage. That she ultimately never marries this man upsets the cultural equation between female virginity and marriage, and opens up the possibility of resistance to abjection.[3]

At the outset, I would like to make a distinction between two registers, that of the ongoing process of female subjectivization always already produced within social structures of power and consent, and that of subjection; of the power or resistance wielded by the subject in negotiating with these very structures.[4] Although these two registers are correlated, they never exactly coincide; there is always a slippage that produces agency and suggests that the subject is an effect of power, without ever being completely reducible to it. The protagonist's abject position and her evolving desire for an equally abject man outside marriage enable her to both uphold and interrupt the structures of consent where marriage is equated with perpetual female consent. Thus, abjection, I suggest, functions as a parodic, and, therefore, a powerful source of desire and pleasure enabling the protagonist to subvert the equation between female desire and marriage.

In the first part of the chapter, I examine the trilogy by Jeyakantan that disturbs cultural valorizations of the female body and sexuality as indices of familial honour: the short story '*Akni Piravēcam*' (Trial by Fire: 2001), and the novels *Cila Nēraṅkaḷil Cila Maṉitarkaḷ* (Some People in Some Situations: 1970) and *Kaṅkai Eṅkē Pōkiṟāḷ?* (Where is Ganga Going?: 1978). The narratives of the first two texts plot the psychological vicissitudes of the female protagonist's illicit desire for a man, which increasingly dissociate her desire from her concern for her virginity and reputation. The story describes the woman's sense of sexual novelty in the act and the ensuing regret. Although the first novel is set after the protagonist's first sexual experience, it opens with an allusion to it, thereby re-sexualizing her memory of the incident. This becomes a pretext to elaborate the vicissitudes of her illicit desire as it both conforms to and upsets formal structures of consent. In '*Akṉi Piravēcam*', the protagonist's confession of 'spoilage' ultimately wins her mother's forgiveness and sympathy, but in *Cila Nēraṅkaḷil Cila Maṉitarkaḷ*, the protagonist Ganga is condemned and ostracized following her confession. In the social worlds of both the texts, the possibility of female sexual consent without marriage is never a matter of significance, the emphasis being more on the loss of familial reputation. *Kaṅkai Eṅkē Pōkiṟāḷ?* hints at a new, spiritual form of love. This love is premised on the mutual recognition of abjection that enables the possibility of renouncing desire and the body, which comes to be associated with an abject existence. This relationship, which represents the possibility of care and responsibility, renounces sexual and familial ties and purports to improve the world. I elaborate this point later. The second half of this chapter is a reading of Jeyakantan's 1971 novel *Oru Naṭikai Nāṭakam Pārkkiṟāḷ* (An Actress Watches a Play). Here, love between outcastes reforms a heterosexist marriage and represents the idealized possibilities of an equal companionship.

'*Akṉi Piravēcam*' (Trial by Fire: 2001)

Let us read closely a description of the sexual encounter between the male and the female character.

The young woman ... is initially fascinated by a beautiful white car that brushes past her as she stands alone ... waiting for the rain to subside. Any man would want to possess the young woman's innocent, unblemished and precious beauty. Then the car suddenly stops and slowly backs up. A stylish young man with a captivating smile leans over ... to open the door for her to get in. He offers to drop her ... but she refuses. When she tries to shut the open door she feels his hand on hers. Flustered, she withdraws her hand and looks at him laughing.... Then the young man gets out of the car, walks around ... to where she is and asks her to get in.... She sees him getting wet in the rain and gets in unable to refuse him. She feels he has imprisoned her when he shuts the door.... The spaciousness of the car amazes her.... She ... feels unrefined and places the books she has been hugging ... beside her ... and sits more comfortably.... He looks at her in the rear mirror and smiles. As she curses herself for wearing a transparent davani [a half-sari] that ... is accidentally torn, the man hands her a towel to wipe herself. She loves the fragrance of the towel and buries her face in it. She suddenly realizes the car is not taking her home and asks the man ... but he remains indifferent to her mild protest. She smiles politely to suppress her anxiety lest he grows impatient and abandons her. He drives her to an isolated place.... She is alarmed to see the car has stopped. In the dim light of the radio in the car she silently admires his beauty.... She is as attracted as she is intimidated by the light in his eyes and his eyebrows that have an air of determination. He ... then gets out of the car and gets in through the rear door. He sits close to her and confesses ... his car has been following her for the past two years. He asks her if she likes him and she quietly says yes. She says she is scared because she is new to this experience. As he tries to comfort her he seduces her; her protests gradually relent to her desire for him. But later when she realizes she has been spoiled she angrily and desperately begs him to take her home. The man ... regrets having seduced her even as he silently rebukes her for misleading him.... (Jeyakantan 2001: 1189; italics mine)

The sheer novelty of an anonymous sexual encounter draws and intimidates the sexually inexperienced young woman, as well as her fascination with the young man's rather suave sex appeal. She is anxious to appear relaxed, confident, and refined even as she berates herself for having been careless. Although she is initially nervous and scared, she acquiesces to the man's sexual advances, but not before informing him of her virginity, that, I suggest, is an internalized sign of her desirability. That the man's desire is indifferent to her claim to virginity only encourages her to overcome her own anxiety over preserving her sexual integrity. She is scared and ashamed of her uncertain reaction to the sexual experience when she anticipates her mother's angry reaction and struggles to reconcile the pleasure she experienced with the social stigma and humiliation sure to follow. The man, meanwhile, is clearly confused by her visible pleasure and her dismay.

In her confession to her mother, the woman does not describe her sexual encounter as a violation. She uses the Tamil verb *keṭu* or 'spoil' when she confesses to her mother that *she* is spoiled. By presenting herself as the subject and not the object of spoilage, she takes responsibility for her actions. Her rhetoric enables her to negotiate with the regulatory norms of sexuality by stigmatizing her compromised sexual status without necessarily pre-empting the possibility of her desire. So her rhetoric of spoilage captures the shame and guilt of lost reputation rather than presenting it as a clear act of sexual violation. Her confession is an attempt to gain her family's sympathy and, crucially, conceal her inadmissible desire for the man. Her confession wins her mother's forgiveness and sympathy; she protects her daughter's privacy, dignity, and reputation by not lamenting her daughter's fate to a suspicious female neighbour. She then bathes her daughter in a symbolic act of purification that seemingly redeems her daughter's compromised integrity. The moral closure of the story thus preserves the structures of consent by suppressing the woman's desire and secretly renewing, as it were, her lost virginity, a necessary prerequisite for marriage.

Cila Nēraṅkaḷil Cila Maṉitarkaḷ (Some People in Some Situations: 1970)

The early part of *Cila Nēraṅkaḷil Cila Maṉitarkaḷ* elaborates the protagonist Ganga's inner conflict with guilt and shame over the loss of her reputation, which has resulted in a lack of faith in the world *and* in herself. The novel begins years after the sexual encounter, but its effects are implied in the opening chapter, that describes Ganga's acute discomfort and indignation as she travels to work in a crowded city bus. Her heightened alertness to the danger around her that is always sexualized, and her silent determination never to trust men are, I suggest, a compensatory reaction to the loss of her virginity and reputation. Her inability to assess her sexual vulnerability from any real threat of molestation is implied by her uncertainty of the sexual innocence of a male co-passenger's touch. Even the attempt to defend herself against the constant threat of a potential assault is precluded by the fear of undermining her sexual integrity. She suspects her very attempts to appear plain and inconspicuous are precisely what attract male sexual attention. Her potential victimhood structures her very existence by suspecting every man's sexual intentions; she is convinced that even her brother Ganeshan would have expressed his desire for her had they not been siblings. She realizes in impotent rage that sexual molestation and assaults are unfortunate but necessary costs of female independence.

In her introspections, Ganeshan emerges as a disembodied voice of patriarchal authority (who considers her a disgrace to the family's honour) that she both internalizes and rejects. Ganga recalls his familiar accusations of her sexual affairs with random men on the bus, linking her financial independence and professional reputation to her apparent sexual insolence. Ganga is convinced that her brother's suspicion betrays his jealousy and frustration with his own wretched existence. Equally, she believes that her sister-in-law's worry about people's opinion of her (her sexual indulgence), and its effect on Ganeshan's reputation, stems from a jealousy of Ganga's financial independence.

Ganga is, irrespective of her sexual consent, stigmatized for the loss of her virginity that I suggest, marks her diminished, 'public' womanhood—a stigma that is only entrenched and seemingly legitimized by her working life. In public spaces like the city bus, her financial independence and her appearance, which betrays no visible sign of marriage, are interpreted by men as a mark of her single—and, therefore, sexually available status. Her family perceives the attendant sexual risks of a working life not as a threat to her bodily integrity and being, but as opportunities for sexual indulgence. Presumably, Ganga seeks and deserves sexual assaults as punishment for her past sexual experience, which is at once a perpetual and recurring marker of her fallen status. The mythical status of virginity is suggested by her family's perception of Ganga's 'lost' virginity that serves as a permanent and potentially recurrent index of her sexual (dis)repute. Thus, virginity, as an imaginary construct, can be lost once and for all, and yet be lost again and again irrespective of the possibility of sexual intercourse. The phantasmatic idea of virginity as an ideal female virtue allows the possibility of its own destabilization that reveals the essentially contingent construction of the female body as (male) property.

In *Cila Nēraṅkaḷil Cila Maṉitarkaḷ*, parody is an inter and intra-textual device used for evoking female desire and pleasure that enables Ganga to embrace her abjection. Ganga's reaction to the fictional allusion to her first sexual experience, which is also the partial quotation of Jeyakantan's earlier story '*Akṉi Piravēcam*', enables her to reaffirm her desire and consent to validate her hitherto abject past. The act of incorporating a sexual narrative makes it possible for Ganga to affirm her desire over her guilt. Based on the quote from '*Akṉi Piravēcam*', I suggest a correlation between reading, narrative, and desire. In *Cila Nēraṅkaḷil Cila Maṉitarkaḷ*, reading operates at two narrative levels, one framed within the other: the reader reading Ganga's seductive story frames the inner narrative of Ganga reading the fictional allusion to her sexual encounter. Another relationship between reader and text is based on the reader's prior knowledge of Ganga's sexual experience that, independent of Ganga's and our own (re)reading of the story, is intertextually recalled and framed by the novel. These three levels of reading recall textual and readerly memories of female desire, crucially allowing Ganga to validate and resist her own abjection.

Cila Nēraṅkaḷil Cila Maṉitarkaḷ begins with Ganga reading the fictional allusion to her sexual encounter. What follows Ganga's sexual encounter is revealed when Ganga asks her mother Kanakam to read the story. The story shares a similar redemptive closure to the second novel *Kaṅkai Eṅkē Pōkiṟāḷ?* but crucially diverges from the novel in its exploration of the social and psychological implications of the sexual experience. In the story and the novel, the female protagonists are ritually purified of their stigma—in the story, the mother forgives the daughter's confession of spoilage and bathes her in a symbolic act of purification, and, in the novel, Ganga seeks sacred redemption by 'accidentally' drowning in the holy waters of the river Ganga. But unlike the mother in the story, who trusts her daughter and protects her dignity and reputation by keeping the illicit sexual encounter a secret, in the novel, Kanakam laments Ganga's 'spoilage' to Ganeshan's family and the neighbours who immediately ostracize the mother and the daughter. Ganga later regrets not safeguarding her reputation by preserving the secrecy of the sexual experience. Her confession of spoilage is again the only available means of disavowing her inadmissible desire for the man and possibly winning her family's sympathy. However, she later realizes that the loss of her reputation is independent of her sexual consent. She is trapped in a deadlock between being potentially temporarily stigmatized and being stigmatized forever. The undesirable publicity of the illicit encounter constitutes her forever fallen status and transforms the secret event into a social reality that upsets the value placed on female virginity. Ganga is held responsible for the supposedly irrevocable loss of her virginity that now forever signifies her sexuality depravity and perpetual consent. But as I argued earlier, this is contradicted by the mythical construction of virginity that once lost is still a recurrent threat to familial reputation.[5]

Unlike Ganeshan's overt patriarchal authority, Ganga's uncle Venku manipulates and eroticizes the ideological contradictions inherent in normative constructions of female sexuality that enable the possibility of their own undermining. Femininity has to reflect male desire but is also equated with the lack thereof. Ganga is thus perceived at once as a woman lacking consent and as a desiring, agential woman whose illicit sexuality is interpreted as an eroticized bearer of masculinity. On the one hand, Venku, a lawyer by profession, exploits the moral and legal authority that he represents by trying to convince Ganga of the irrelevance of her sexual consent by referring to religious/moral valorizations of female virginity that precondition wifely loyalty. Although the psychological narrative is ambiguous about Ganga's status as an adult and resists formal structures of female consent, Venku resorts to legal stipulations of statutory rape that eliminate the possibility of a minor woman's consent to a sexual act. Thus Ganga's stipulated status as a minor precludes the possibility of consent and deprives her of any claim to her own desire and body. Venku preserves the structures of consent by equating marriage with sexual intercourse and consent with non-consent. By encouraging Ganga to marry Prabhu, even though he does not want it, he effectively demands Ganga's retrospective consent to legitimize an act of sexual violation, which is really an illicit, but consensual sexual act. An illicit sexual act is thus collapsed with rape and then reduced to the status of a myth by its absorption by marriage. But on the other hand, Venku tries to further his secret desire for Ganga by preventing the possibility of her marriage under the pretext of upholding the sanctity of virginity and marriage. He urges Ganga to get married to Prabhu even as he tries to convince her that Prabhu will assume she is loose and never trust her honourable intentions of marrying him. His apparently indignant response to RKV's story that desecrates marriage by encouraging respectable women to become sexually promiscuous prostitutes barely conceals his pleasure of discovering the story's allusion to Ganga's potential desire for Prabhu. His attempts to extract an affirmation of her desire are evident through Ganga's memories of her conversations with Venku who constantly steers their conversations to the sexual encounter and obsessively questions her true feelings for Prabhu.

[He asked her] So you got into the car as soon as he asked you? [Ganga] I said no first. [Venku] Were you really willing or were you not serious? [Ganga] I was scared that's why I said no. [Venku] Then how did that fear disappear? [Ganga] I got in feeling scared. [Venku] Did you also like him? [Ganga] Nothing like that. [Venku] Then why were you scared? [Ganga] It was raining. [Venku] Was it raining heavily? Were you dripping wet? Was it cold? Did you feel like (here Venku lowers his voice and secretively asks with a smile on his face.... He winks and tightens his hold on my shoulder. I feel like crying but I am scared) you could have hugged someone in the cold? Tell me, you liked it too didn't you? [Ganga] No I didn't like it. [Venku] Don't lie, if you hadn't liked it this wouldn't have happened. (Jeyakantan 1970: 1217–18)

Ganga is rendered helpless by her filial gratitude to Venku, who rescues her and her mother when they are disowned by Ganeshan. When Venku tries to take sexual advantage of her vulnerability, she realizes she had rather be 'spoiled' by a man than pretend to be affectionate to a lascivious old uncle. Ganga realizes her internalization of Venku's sexual imperatives is responsible for the loss of faith in herself and in all other men and silently curses her uncle in indignant rage:

Women who are trapped by womanizers like you cease to find anything desirable that suits their hearts. When you who are old enough to die can assume that I would find you desirable, wouldn't he [Prabhu] at his age, not have felt desire? It is because you believe that I can make myself like you that you think I must have liked him. Even if I desired him I don't desire you. (1970: 1219)

The seductive power of the fictional allusion to Ganga's sexual experience enables her to affirm her desire, which triggers feelings that oscillate between shame and sexual affirmation, and whose temporal vicissitudes result in ever new and shifting interpretations of the sexual experience. Her decision to find Prabhu suddenly gives her lonely and austere life as a shamed woman a new sense of purpose. She believes her decision is not a sign of her restored trust in or love for Prabhu but the only available means of avoiding her uncle's predatory desire for her. But her re-encounter with Prabhu actually turns out to have a mutually redemptive effect that ultimately enables the possibility of Ganga's spiritual freedom from abjection. Although she is initially angry and bitter after her first telephonic conversation with a completely oblivious and shocked Prabhu, during their re-encounter, Ganga evokes his guilt and wins his sympathy by describing her past misery and humiliation. Prabhu remorsefully confesses he misunderstood her apparent consent. His perceived worthlessness and intellectual inferiority rouses her sympathy, and she decides not to deceive him when she discovers he actually trusts her. He says:

> You have a lot to say. I am good for nothing. You say you are educated; I don't even have the right to sit next to you. You probably wonder how I can speak in English. I studied it. I studied in a convent before high school. But what's the point? Now I can neither speak fluently in Tamil or English. That's why I am scared to speak sometimes. (1970: 1221)

Ganga tries to seduce him by alluding to his past indifference to her virginity. For Prabhu the secret loss of Ganga's virginity is not an impediment for marriage, although marriage is still the only means of redeeming himself and her. Ganga evades his attempts to get her married as she feels that would threaten her desire for him. She tries to win his sympathy for suffering a life of austerity and solitude to atone the loss of her virginity. When Prabhu assumes she is a married woman who wants to renew their acquaintance, Ganga sarcastically says, 'Oh! So there are married women who call you up and meet you like this?' To this Prabhu indifferently replies, 'What's not there in this world? But as far as I know you are the only woman in this world who wastes her entire life.' Ganga protests, 'How is that possible? Set aside my conscience. Who would want to marry a spoiled woman whose lost virginity has been openly discovered?' Prabhu then dismisses her:

> What are you talking? You keep saying, 'spoiled woman'! I've seen many instances of women who get divorced and marry again. Did everyone watch you lose your virginity? There has to be some use to our meeting now ... I want to see you married. Really! It's not right to see a woman waste her life like this! I will find you a top class man myself, just watch! I will bring you a

man who is beyond all this nonsense about being spoiled. What do you say to that? (1970: 1303–4)

Prabhu's indifference to her virginity and her desire for his reassuring and protective presence enables Ganga's self-affirmation. She exercises her agency by parodying the inherent contradictions of a patriarchal order that at once precludes the possibility of female desire and requires women to reflect male desire.[6] Ganga assimilates even as she subverts patriarchal oppositions to female sexuality and sexual consent by setting up and strategically manipulating an opposition between two representatives, Prabhu and Venku, of a fallible patriarchal order. She tries to simulate an (extra)marital relationship with Prabhu by asking him to pretend she is his concubine: 'I'm not asking you to marry me or accept me as your concubine, just pretend I'm your concubine'. She expresses her desire to be his concubine 'only in name' (1970: 1307). By simulating an (extra)marital relationship that does not amount to marriage, Ganga threatens the patriarchal equation of female sexuality with marriage and exposes the mythical status of virginity whose loss is both a singular and recurrent event. We see parody functioning here as a de-realizing strategy that apparently affirms Ganga's sexual experience and agency even at the risk of incurring social censure. She attempts to make agential what was once passively received as sexual abjection. She is determined to 'change people's naive impression of her as a sexually innocent fool by pretending to lose her virginity (again)' (1970: 1309–10). She feels secretly vindicated and triumphant whenever her rides back home in Prabhu's car eliciting her neighbours' disapproving stares and her mother's shame. She later toys with the possibility of having a surrogate child to redeem her boring and lonely life but dismisses it convinced her family will suspect the child is Prabhu's.

Prabhu's sense of degradation and estrangement partly redeems Ganga's fallen stature. In their conversations, Prabhu emerges as a model of abject masculinity characterized by sexual abuse, alcoholism, and sexual promiscuity. He confesses he was robbed of his sexual innocence when at the age of 12 he was raped by his nanny. He describes himself as the disenfranchised son of a wealthy businessman who bequeathed all his property to his wife Padma, empowering her to control Prabhu's debauchery. Prabhu confesses alcohol is the only means of mitigating his oppressive subordination to his wife and his shameful failure as a son and father. Padma refuses to indulge his alcoholism when she discovers his secret visits to prostitutes. Prabhu claims no woman, including his wife, has ever loved him; every woman he had a sexual relationship with deceived him by getting married to someone else (1970: 1313).

Prabhu feels unworthy of Ganga's potential friendship. Her self-esteem grows once she realizes she is no longer intimidated by Prabhu's suave masculinity. She 'even [forgets she] is sitting next to a man in the car' and 'realizes how much stronger she is than he ever was'. Prabhu's now diminished masculinity reduces him to 'a small child who hasn't changed since the rape'. She discovers she may have come to terms with her past now that she has lost her earlier 'naïveté and innocence that made her sacrifice herself to a fool like Prabhu'. She is amazed at how much she has changed in these years to even notice such a difference in herself. She is emboldened and amused by Prabhu's perception of himself as someone who has been cruelly wronged by the world. She ridicules his urbane masculinity, 'Did you really expect every woman on the street to fall in love with you just because you are smartly dressed and wear perfume?' (1970: 1313–14).

Ganga's anger and bitterness give way to sympathy and concern and a determination to reform his debauched life. She experiences a motherly sense of purpose and responsibility for Prabhu's welfare and perceives him as 'Padma's spoilt child' who needs to be disciplined and nurtured lest 'he spoil the other sons' (1970: 1330). Although she tries to have an ostensible affair with Prabhu to defy her family and protect herself from Venku's sexual advances, she is seduced by her own sexual pretence when she is compelled to acknowledge her desire for Prabhu. The seductive power of her desire is complete once it gives way to the hyperreality of desire that can no longer be distinguished from its simulation. She hopes Prabhu's 'concern, respect and sense of responsibility' actually insinuate his desire and love for her (1970: 1336). She jealously perceives his secret visits to prostitutes as an impediment to an exclusive relationship. She struggles to repress her feelings for Prabhu by being falsely concerned with the possibility of Manju and Padma mistaking their 'friendship' for a sexual relationship. She realizes she is 'trapped' in her 'fake' concern for their opinions when she is actually unable to admit her 'desire to be raped' by Prabhu (1970: 1336). She feels his rape 'that violated her privacy entitles [her] to have an intimate and honest relationship with him' (1970: 1338). She assumes the redemptive possibilities of their 'friendship' are an exclusive privilege that empowers her over his wife (1970: 1340). But Prabhu's refusal to take sexual liberties with her only provokes her scorn for his hypocritical respect and concern. She confesses she has lost faith in herself and fears she will succumb to any man's desire to rape her. She seeks his protection and confesses she had rather be raped by Prabhu than by any other man if she is destined to be raped. When Prabhu angrily dismisses Ganga's fears, she silently rebukes him for his inability to take sexual advantage of her vulnerability.

By couching her possessive desire for Prabhu in a rhetoric of rape, Ganga again parodies the very structures of consent that equate all forms of female sexuality with sexual passivity and marriage. She initiates the possibility of a sexually exclusive relationship that is apparently characterized by the irreversible and violent sexual domination of women by men and which is compensated by and entails the man's responsibility for the woman's security. For Ganga, rape becomes the only available and fetishized expression of this relationship. Ganga offers Prabhu exclusive sexual entitlement to her body—a privilege she thinks he deserves for appropriating her virginity—in exchange for protection from potential threats of rape. That Ganga never allows Prabhu to forget their sexual experience becomes the defining act of their relationship; her indifferent and insistent thrusting of her fallen status upon Prabhu and her attempts to win his sympathy and protection by expressing her vulnerability reflects Ganga's sexual agency that is constituted by her negotiations with a patriarchal system. Unlike the adolescent Ganga who was seduced by the novelty of sexual experience and rendered vulnerable by its estranging consequences, the adult Ganga perceives herself as an informed and agential woman who takes responsibility for the estranging consequences of satisfying her desire for Prabhu. By 'consenting to be raped' again by Prabhu, Ganga trades off the appropriation of her body in exchange for power via male protection. Assuming the identity of 'wife' even if it is fictive, and violently constituted, guarantees Ganga a pre-emptive zone of relative future safety and power. Wife/concubine, consent/rape, public/private, protection/autonomy or empowerment are reversible states and identities that Ganga upholds and collapses as circumstances warrant, with the dual goals of the survival of her protective sexual relationship with Prabhu and the critique of the sexual regulations of patriarchal kinship.

In her defence against his determination to get her married, Ganga upholds the ideological status of virginity whose loss pre-empts her marriage to other men. Her attempt to seduce Prabhu is hindered by his self-deprecatory guilt. Prabhu wearily absolves himself of all responsibility for his worthless past now that he no longer has his reputation at stake. His resignation only makes Ganga uneasy and desperate and strengthens her resolve to similarly absolve herself of responsibility for her lost virginity and reputation, her family's tainted honour, and even her desire for him. Having nothing at stake only urges her to pursue her desire for Prabhu as the only available means of redeeming her abject status. Ganga's defiant affirmation of her abject status is undefeated by her family's disapproval. Her widowed mother Kanakam—a hypocritical embodiment of female sexual morality, who, until Ganga's mocking retort, flouts sartorial prescriptions for orthodox Hindu Brahman widows—is dismayed and disgusted by her daughter's transformation from the austere woman she admired and even sympathized with to a heavily made-up and well-dressed woman. When Kanakam chastises Ganga for her illicit relationship with Prabhu, Ganga declares that she and Prabhu 'have surpassed the possibility of being a couple since Prabhu already has a family ... Prabhu will henceforth be [her] support' (1970: 1326). Kanakam abuses Ganga for ruining the family's reputation and accuses her of being a whore, 'from your very dressing up the world knows you know the world' (1970: 1326–7). Ganga acknowledges and comes to terms with her sexual vulnerability when she spurns Venku's final desperate attempt to seduce her. She feels she has managed to overcome her fear of being 'spoilt' by men. She realizes people like Venku 'are responsible for women's internalizations of certain notions of feminine modesty that make them avoid men so that when they reach adolescence they can no longer inhibit their sexual desires. Men mistake their shy modesty for love that they then exploit to their sexual advantage' (1970: 1471).

Ganga attributes her newly discovered power to her intimate relationship with Prabhu, which, she realizes, is the only significant relationship she has ever had; a sure sign of their intimacy lies in the security of his presence that seems to deflect male attention. But until the very end of the novel, Ganga is unable to differentiate this reassuring sense of security and concern from the love that it seemingly presupposes. She wonders if they are in love with each other when she discovers she 'always thinks of his body, his mind and his life with a lot of concern' just as 'he always thinks of her with such devotion'. She notices that unlike most romantic relationships that begin 'with a sublime, poetic and seductive notion of love and ends in sex', their relationship began with 'cheap, frenzied and animal-like sex like an accident' and ends with 'a sense of duty, an honourable friendship, affection and love'. Ganga feels their relationship has progressively matured from a vulgar sexual experience that was entirely accidental to an 'honorable friendship and love' based on mutual concern and respect, and presumably no longer merely premised on sexual attraction (1970: 1446–7).

Ganga's growing concern for Prabhu's well-being is no longer driven by sexual desire but by care and responsibility. As Carol Gilligan argues in *In a Different Voice* (1982), Ganga's empathy represents a particularly feminine form of morality that is constituted by compassion and obligation. The feminine should not be conflated with female but understood as a form of interrelatedness that is based on the mutual recognition of vulnerability. Gilligan opposes this form of morality to a masculine notion of morality that is located in a discourse of justice and fairness that sees every individual as an isolated and autonomous subject invested with rights and acting within certain rules. What has been taken as a sign of underdevelopment and weakness in women (or men for that matter) by psychoanalytic and sociological discourses, Gilligan argues, is paradoxically also their unacknowledged strength, namely, their ability to empathize and compromise their own rights and well-being for the sake of the other. This feminine comportment towards the world affirms the ability of pain and suffering to resist masculine structures of power without furthering violence. Ganga's new-found concern for Prabhu's welfare is not grounded in revenge or punishment but in the empathetic recognition of their shared abjection that in *Kaṅkai Eṅkē Pōkiṟāḷ?* forms the basis of a spiritual love that renounces desire, the body, and, for Ganga, life itself.

Cila Nēraṅkaḷil Cila Maṉitarkaḷ ends on a note of worldly renunciation. Prabhu decides to renounce the moral degradation and meaninglessness of urban life and retire to the idealized redemptive purity of the countryside. He is determined to atone for his past 'sins' by leading a solitary life of hard labour. At Ganeshan's behest, he threatens to sever ties with Ganga if she refuses a marriage offer. The possibility of never seeing Prabhu threatens her desire and compels the desperate profession of her exclusive love for him. She is determined to marry him, although she confesses she had 'lied' earlier about the impossibility of their love (1970: 1502). But her inability to convince Prabhu of her exclusive love and his subsequent loss/disappearance initiates Ganga's mournful descent into alcoholism in open defiance of her family.

Kaṅkai Eṅkē Pōkiṟāḷ? (Where Is Ganga Going?: 1978)

In his prefaces to *Cila Nēraṅkaḷil Cila Maṉitarkaḷ*, the previous novel, Jeyakantan addresses his readers' dissatisfaction with the epilogue of the novel. He suggests his readers' uncritical hatred or love for his characters is only a disavowal of the representative relationship between life and fiction. Fiction is neither a true nor a false reflection of life but offers an infinite array of narrative possibilities that blur the very distinction between truth and falsity. The creative autonomy of the writer and the text, Jeyakantan says, cannot be reduced to his readers' personal preferences and prejudices. To betray sorrow or wish for a happy ending only suggests the readers' naïve attitude to life, where sorrow has to be embraced to broaden the human mind. The literary merit of a text, he further argues, cannot be reduced to his readers' likes or dislikes without promoting an intellectual form of dictatorship. The very function of the literary text is to bring about change by transgressing and reformulating social norms. The very fact that the working title of *Cila Nēraṅkaḷil Cila Maṉitarkaḷ* and *Kālaṅkaḷ Māṟum* (Times Will Change), suggests this. For Jeyakantan, Ganga is an example of the tension between social change and individual transformation, 'Even if many transformations in social life are new, the transformations in individual lives are outdated and appear lifeless as permanent images of disappointment' (Jeyakantan 1978: ix). If changes in individual lives do not correspond to social change, the individual may be punished and cast out of society for her transgression.

In his preface to the sequel *Kaṅkai Eṅkē Pōkiṟāḷ?* Jeyakantan, like his readers, refuses to accept Ganga's bitter end. Thinking about his novels and characters as a larger reflection on life, he is filled with compassion for Ganga, who has become a part of his life. He believes that life should not end with bitterness, and to embrace pain and sorrow would be its ethical affirmation. *Kaṅkai Eṅkē Pōkiṟāḷ?* is Jeyakantan's attempt to attribute Ganga's character with a sense of wholeness and completion that culminates in her ambiguous freedom from an abject existence. The novel suggests two inter-generational possibilities of addressing sexual abjection—one is the spiritual redemption of an abject existence through love and death and the other, the renunciation and sublimation of desire in humanitarianism. While Venku, Ganga, and Prabhu seek purification and transcendence by embracing death, the younger generation, that includes Prabhu's daughter Manju, Ganga's niece Vasantha, and her orphaned doctor friend Arjun, represents the idealized possibilities of an altruistic friendship that reforms sexuality and aims to better the world.

The novel traces Ganga's affirmative transformation from a sexually disgraced alcoholic mourning a lost love to a woman whose growing independence and impunity is a function of her newfound financial authority. She gradually emerges from alcoholism when her relationship with Prabhu is accidentally renewed. When Prabhu decides to redeem his debauched life by retiring to a village, Ganga also decides to renounce her present life to share a life of asceticism with him. But her desire to renounce worldly life is temporarily frustrated by her sudden responsibility to rescue her debt-ridden family. She inherits Venku's house—an expiatory act from a remorseful uncle who tries to redeem his guilt by retiring to the holy city of Varanasi where he dies a painful and lonely death. Before he dies he requests Ganga to take care of his wife Ambujam, who is later discovered to be a victim of his sexual and physical abuse. Ganga's new inheritance, and Ganeshan's unexpected sickness that reduces his family to penury, enable her empowerment over the family. Ganga redeems Ganeshan's debts and rescues him from bankruptcy. She becomes responsible for her brother's family and their mother. Despite this, the family's perception of Ganga doesn't alter, although they express their gratitude. The novel ends with Prabhu and Ganga's worldly renunciation and her final spiritual liberation and death by drowning in the holy waters of the river Ganga.

When Ganga accidentally reencounters Prabhu she realizes they have exchanged fortunes: while Ganga is now the alcoholic who has been reunited with her family, Prabhu has become the solitary outcast disowned by his family. Prabhu's guilt, his miserable estrangement, and his gratitude for Ganga's friendship reassure her growing sense of maturity and emotional independence. Although she is initially overjoyed to meet Prabhu, she feels cheated by his indifference. She bitterly remembers the moments when she yearned for his presence. She clarifies that she only wants 'his friendship, his company' and not 'a sexual or romantic relationship'. She is convinced that neither of their lives can be changed and that 'advising each other is futile' (1978: 1657). She discovers she is no longer tormented by Prabhu's frequent long absences, and her familial responsibilities make her life more purposeful.

Kaṅkai Eṅkē Pōkiṟāḷ? like *Cila Nēraṅkaḷil Cila Maṉitarkaḷ* is a self-referential narrative—it frames an inner narrative that thematizes the metanarrative. The framed story embedded in this novel has a narrative and didactic function that alludes to Prabhu's redemption. When Prabhu disappears for a year, Ganga hopes for his return. During this time she discovers another story by RKV that alludes to Prabhu's attempt to commit suicide, which is stalled by an act of compassion that results in his spiritual rebirth. The story describes a wealthy youth whose father wills his property to his daughter-in-law to prevent the son from squandering his wealth on alcohol and women. The man feels betrayed by his father. When the wife's attempts to reform her husband fail, she asks him to leave the house. The man shamefully leaves the house in the middle of the night and bitterly warns the older servants in the house to leave before his wife drives them away. As he is leaving, he swears to return a rich man. But he is so ashamed of himself that he is determined to commit suicide. He drives aimlessly along a cliff and just as he is about to fall off the precipice, an old woman appears in the middle of the road gesturing him to stop. They do not speak the same language, but from her gestures he realizes she has a pregnant daughter who has to be rushed to the nearest government hospital some miles away. When he sees the pregnant woman, the man is filled with a new sense of purpose. He feels needed and this incident makes him realize that his life is worthless if he cannot help people in their time of need. The sight of the newborn baby and the old woman's gratitude and blessings fill him with a sense of hope and affirmation. He feels happy when he sees himself surrounded by poor people. He wonders if their happiness lies in their simplicity. He feels his own life is much happier now that he has renounced his wealth.

The moral didacticism of RKV's story is unmistakable; it traces the character's—and by extension, Prabhu's—spiritual transformation through an act of compassion. His compassion is also correlated to the natural environment of rural life, which is valorized over the moral corruption of the city. The potential of the natural environment to heal and liberate is further reinforced through Ganga's desire to renounce her disgraced life in the city. She is amazed at the sight of Prabhu's idyllic world as a mechanic, which comprises of other mechanics, a poultry farm, and an adopted son. The redemptive potential of Prabhu's rural existence lies in the ethics of work and labour that constitute his self-realization. His new sense of freedom from urban degradation lies in his labouring body that embodies his struggle against class privilege. He feels he has redeemed his abject past by becoming a self-reliant worker 'whose sweat drips on the land'. He tells his daughter Manju that 'her [old] father ... is dead' and that a new father 'has been resurrected' in the style of the Russian writers' idealization of land and labour. Listening to Prabhu reminds Ganga of Leo Tolstoy's novel *Resurrection*. Prabhu feels 'alienated from them and their class' for he 'now belongs to the working class'; the new world he has fashioned 'has no room for marriage or family' (1978: 1731). He says his assistants at the workshop are his friends and family. He is amused at the thought of having a young son without a wife.

Prabhu's self-fashioning as a worker free of worldly distinctions can be read as an attempt to challenge and opt out of the institutional inequities of class, patriarchal marriage, and family. What is also suggested is an alternative, fictive image of the family that excludes women; an exclusion that is premised on Prabhu's assumption that women, unlike men, have to be married; an assumption that is challenged only towards the end of the novel by Ganga's niece, Vasantha.

Vasantha and Manju belong to a new generation of independent young women who equate marriage with the patriarchal enslavement of women. Marriage for them is an institution that cannot be redeemed without being discarded. Both of them represent the idealized possibilities of cross-gender friendship that is indifferent to desire and sexual and social differences. While Manju extols the virtues of friendship to win her mother's trust when she is suspected of an affair with a classmate, Vasantha, despite Ganga's entreaties, refuses marriage as a means to avoid social disgrace and humiliation. Marriage, Vasantha says, merely 'preserves female sexual honor' by inscribing women as wives. She calls marriage a form of female enslavement; 'an aggressive yoke that insults, enslaves and vulgarizes women'. She questions the hypocrisy of women like her mother and grandmother who praise the 'heavenly' virtues of marriage when they have had unhappy marriages. She even objects to Ganga's devotion for Prabhu and suggests her faith in marriage is only a reflection of her naiveté. While Vasantha expresses her admiration for Ganga's independence as a working woman, she interprets Ganga's desire to get her married as a sign of her 'naive misrecognition' of patriarchy. She condemns all those Tamil writers and poets who have sung songs and composed poems that advocate gender equality when it is clearly 'a man's world' (1978: 1749–50).

At Manju's wedding, Ganga and Prabhu argue about her marriage. Vasantha supports Ganga's decision not to marry, which Prabhu interprets as hypocrisy; a 'middle-class, Puranic, Vedic, feudal mentality that she tries to disguise beneath a veneer of western cultural refinement' (1978: 1760). Prabhu accuses Ganga of embodying the unchanging hypocrisy of middle-class values that, unlike the rural, working-class world, is ridden with social distinctions. He claims his growing faith in himself enabled him to belong to a world that welcomes everyone irrespective of their social class. Ganga is determined to renounce worldly comforts for a life of asceticism. When Prabhu insists on her getting married, Vasantha argues with

Prabhu about the misogynistic implications of marriage. Vasantha questions the institution of marriage, which she implicitly associates with heterosexuality. She claims to be neither a man-hater nor against married couples, but the very institution of marriage that guarantees a life of slavery for women. She clearly stigmatizes sexuality, for she urges men and women to relate as friends without having any sexual relationships. Sexual desire has to be repressed and sublimated to forge philanthropic friendships between men and women driven by the noble purpose of bettering the world, 'men and women should volunteer to collaborate to serve the world ... and not renounce the world without a social purpose just to escape or avoid social misery....' She expresses her contempt for people who ridicule the body by merely perceiving it as an object of pleasure when an artist or an aspiring doctor like her would respect and worship the body (1978: 1763–4). Her friendship with an orphaned classmate from another province embodies the noble ideal of altruism that affirms life.

Ganga decides to retire from the world to live the rest of her life with Prabhu and relinquishes her property to Vasantha. She admires Vasantha, Arjun, and Prabhu, to whom 'asceticism comes naturally ... not in renouncing the world but devoting their lives to bettering it; serving it' (1978: 1808). Unlike her brother, her sister-in-law, and mother, they think of the world with 'a sense of duty; they have even turned their private affairs into a general dharma and have become images of sacrifice for the people of this earth to have better lives' (1978: 1810). Prabhu weeps helplessly to see her 'accidentally' drowning in the powerful currents of the river as she slips. The narrative voice captures Ganga's purification in the holy waters of the river she was named after. The description of her experience of death suggests her absolution from shame and abjection, and freedom from all human ties. Death is a self-divesting moment that erases distinctions between the past, the present, and the future as she becomes part of an internally undifferentiated whole beyond existence and meaning. But the transcendental experience of death is not without irony. It is the ultimate form of sexual liberation that comes with renouncing desire and patriarchy even as its religious and redemptive significance implicitly reinstates social ideals of female sexual virtue. Thus, even if sexuality is oriented towards death, which marks both the ultimate pleasure (of bodily freedom) and the cessation of all pleasure as Freud (1955, 1950) has argued, its purifying function reinforces sexual norms.[7]

Oru Naṭikai Nāṭakam Pārkkiṟāḷ (An Actress Watches a Play: 1971)

In my reading of Jeyakantan's earlier works, I explored the renewing and empowering possibilities of intimacy between outcaste men and women. These texts also suggested the possibility of friendships among men and women who sought to reform the world. *Oru Naṭikai Nāṭakam Pārkkiṟāḷ* similarly underlines the potential of love and care in dismantling sexual domination within the confines of marriage. Again, the protagonists of the novel are marginalized for different reasons, but the novel does not idealize the love between outcastes who are, initially at least, still within the folds of a heterosexist marriage. The novel dramatizes the clash between two gendered understandings of love that are embodied by the characters. One is a masculine notion of love as sacrifice that demands the reassurance and possession of the beloved, and the other is a feminine one that equates love with freedom and unconditional care. Love is represented as a dialectical struggle between autonomy and possession, or between identity and difference that can only end in a crisis. The end of the novel sees the birth of a new understanding of love that involves an exchange of selves and binds the protagonists without promising identity. In the preface to this novel, Jeyakantan argues that violence is an innate quality that characterizes all life. If violence is inevitable, love is no exception to it. Violence, he believes, constitutes love, which is nothing but an ideological form of intolerance and exploitation.

> Love is an oppressive ideology like politics, aesthetics or religion that is exploited to sometimes unconsciously inflict one's ambitions, opinions, and preferences on others ... even those who love us exploit us in the name of love to make others conform to their opinions ... aggression committed in the name of love is a form of mental rape or violation ... people ... who either openly curse life or are inwardly conflicted and broken within are left with no self confidence; with hollow love; with reduced affection, and affected devotion. (Jeyakantan 1971: 2400–3)

In the novel, violence operates at the inter and intra-subjective level and is portrayed as a symptom of the insecurity of the male subject as he appropriates and seeks the assurances of the feminine other. But in the dialectic between the self and the other, a violent appropriation of the other pre-empts the possibility of attaining the other's recognition and identity. Thus, violence, as Jeyakantan suggests, is the condition of its own possibility even as it poses its own limits, 'Our aggression only finds satisfaction in seeing our enemy maimed and physically disabled. Only such a fatal crisis can elicit sympathy and satisfaction' (1971: 2405). If violence is a sign of male impotence, care, and responsibility are valorized as specifically feminine modes of relationality that have to constantly negotiate with difference and conflict. The wisdom of human nature, Jeyakantan argues, lies in withdrawing from cruelty rather than trying to get rid of it. Renouncing life or denying cruelty or confronting it with love, he says, may reflect our sense of justice, but is not a solution to our individualistic lives (1971: 2404). For Jeyakantan, peace and reconciliation are really a suspension or avoidance of conflict and not a permanent solution to wars and enmity. If lasting peace is an ideal, it can be potentially attained through the cultivation of a love that negotiates difference. In the novel, Kalyani embodies such an ideal, while her husband Ranga mistakes her equanimity and unconditional love for arrogance and indifference. His aggressive impulse to subordinate her troubles him more than it does Kalyani as 'it gives him a false sense of victory and joy' (1971: 2405), and he imputes to Kalyani his own insecurity and intolerance. It is her close encounter with death that compels Kalyani to confront her own vulnerability and dependence, enabling the remodelling of their love on the ethics of mutual care and responsibility. While Ranga realizes the selfishness of his demands, Kalyani admits her failure to assure him of her attachment.

Ranga is an erstwhile political journalist and critic known for his controversial criticism of theatre. He first encounters Kalyani, a theatre actress at a playhouse where one of her plays is being performed. From the moment they meet, Kalyani appreciates their differences. She secretly admires his criticism and his political and aesthetic sensibilities even though she does not entirely agree with them. She develops an unacknowledged affection for him and writes him an anonymous letter asking him to meet her. Ranga recognizes her letter and decides to meet her on the pretext of interviewing her for the newspaper where he writes. The interview functions as a formal device that legitimizes Kalyani's encounter with Ranga and enables them to discover their love for each other. Through the course of the interview, Ranga discovers, to his surprise and admiration, that Kalyani is a 'noble and genuine' woman who alleviates his contempt for the deceptive lives of actresses (1971: 2409). Like Janakiraman's women characters, whose moral integrity is untainted by their sexual engagements, Kalyani is one among many of Jeyakantan's female characters who retains her moral essence despite the stigma of being an actress. When he asks her if she aspires to become a cinema actress, she expresses her indifference to the wealth and fame of cinema and privileges theatre for its respectability and creative freedom, 'I respect drama and don't aspire to become a cinema actress ...' and is anxious about the possibility of 'losing her soul ... of becoming morally bankrupt in a world that requires sexual favors in return for progress' (1971: 2410). For Ranga, Kalyani marks a clear distinction between the private and the public woman whose authentic private self is separate from and untainted by her public life, unlike most cinema actresses whose avowedly private selves cannot be distinguished from their public performances.

> [An actress] was society's open book ... to even think she possessed a private self is a pretense that is an independent delusion ... [he knew] that once her private self has been disclosed, the actress has to believe her fame has grown to the extent that those who have nothing to do with her life imagine she possesses the private selves she doesn't have. (1971: 2449)

For Kalyani, however, her life as an actress is not a self-estranging life but something that enables her to take care of herself, '[I] admire [my] own beauty and love wearing makeup' (1971: 2469). In fact, and this becomes clear later in the novel, it is Kalyani's ability to love and take care of herself that enables her to take care of others. Her life as an actress constitutes her very identity. Kalyani's integrity and reputation is tied to her stigmatized birth as the illegitimate daughter of a clerk and a devadasi. As the disenfranchised product of an inter-caste sexual affair, her life as a theatre actress enables her self-realization. She is grateful to her father's boss Annasami for supporting her and nurturing her career by inducting her into his own troupe. During the interview, she clearly refuses to sacrifice her profession for other 'ordinary' joys like marriage and family. When she tells Annasami of her decision to marry Ranga, she reassures his anxiety with her determination to never sacrifice theatre, which she believes constitutes her 'self-expression' (1971: 2468).

The possibility of losing Kalyani to Ranga compels Annasami to acknowledge his own love for her. The novel implicitly idealizes Annasami's love, which later becomes a model for Ranga's own love for Kalyani. Annasami is a sensitive man rendered vulnerable by his love for Kalyani. As the husband of a jealous wife who suspects his emotional bonds with his fellow actors, Annasami seeks Kalyani's presence to mitigate his loneliness. His love is irreducible to sexual attraction and is premised on care and responsibility. It is a form of love that is made compatible by shared intellectual and aesthetic interests.

Annasami continued to speak with greater intimacy, 'While others keep talking seriously about this relationship, why should we deceive each other by denying it? After all, my wife is not in any way more attached to me than you. Kalyani, do you understand what I'm saying? I have no one but you in my life.' His voice turned hoarse with emotion. Kalyani could understand his thoughts and distress. It did not surprise her—she felt no sadness, no irritation. She thought about the context and the rationale of his feelings. She wondered why this understanding had eluded her all this while. She knew it was too late for such understanding and did not know how to make him understand. It was clear to her that Annasami's attraction was no infatuation. She knew the regard he had for her, the hopes he had pinned on her talent, his sensitive appreciation of her beauty and acting abilities, his involvement in her growth and his deep interest in her well-being and future—all these had contributed to his love for her. She had a sympathetic understanding of his feelings.... 'If only he had expressed his feelings to me before I met Ranga, before I thought of writing that unsigned letter to him, I well might have happily clasped his hands and expressed my consent,' she thought ... she was surprised she had never imagined Annasami could be nursing such feelings for her. Even at this stage, she was not prepared to assume any ulterior motive behind all the help he had given her or his concern for her ... the more she thought of him the more she sympathized with his situation. She thought of his family members who totally despised his qualities, his nature and his involvement in his arts. She could understand the inclination of such people to forge a relationship more in agreement with their own qualities and attitudes. (1971: 2476–8)

The novel's valorization of a selfless love is reflected in Kalyani's evaluation of the possibility of a particularly ideal marriage that would redeem her 'lonely and meaningless life' (1971: 2479) and grant her the domestic joys of family and motherhood without compromising her professional or sexual integrity. In a world that is susceptible to the corrupting effects of sex and money, Annasami's honourable love promises Kalyani the respectability and security of marriage; a privilege that she has never had. Far from being the self-sufficient woman that Ranga takes her to be, Kalyani longs to share her life with someone who would rescue her from loneliness and spiritual decadence. For Kalyani, Annasami is the ideal man who would be above the temptations of money and sex.

> [She could no longer] take the emptiness of a lonely life ... anyone who established a life-long relationship with her could be poor, earning just a hundred rupees a month or be a lowly clerk somewhere. She wanted him to respect her, love her, and be a noble person. She feared she would destroy her soul and devastate her personal life by becoming the concubine of womanizers, rich and greedy men, or film producers and acquiring any amount of material and financial comforts would have provided her with considerable wealth and material comforts ... but she feared that in due course it would. (1971: 2479)

It is remarkable that Kalyani chooses Ranga over someone as compatible as Annasami. The novel implicitly valorizes Kalyani's steadfast love for Ranga but at a more significant level, her choice corroborates a popular understanding of love as a complementary relationship between opposites. Their love proves to be a mutually transformative experience that has to negotiate with difference—without ever promising identity. That the possibility of having a secure, romantic relationship with Annasami never occurred to Kalyani only reinforces this transformative notion of love that contrasts Rajagopalan's ideal love or even a contractual notion of love that emerges later in the novel. Kalyani and Ranga embody contradictions constitutive of their ideological positions on aesthetics and love. While Kalyani embodies aestheticism, Ranga's socialism identifies aesthetics with elitism and sexual indulgence. It is Kalyani's honourability rather than her aesthetic sensibilities that evoke Ranga's love, although his initial impulse is to dismiss love as a 'cheap fantasy'. He believes poetry, drama, and art and aesthetics are the 'perverse creations of rich people to waste their lives' (1971: 2465). He is anxious that he 'may end up being seduced by cinema actors, imitating them like the naive urban poor in his locality' (1971: 2465). He is clearly conflicted by his love for Kalyani's authenticity and his ideological disregard for the duplicitous and immoral world of theatre and cinema. For Ranga, art has to have a social value that lies in its ability to serve the interests of the poor. He even belongs to a locality populated by mill workers, coolies, and the poor who are united by caste but divided along lines of class (1971: 2538). He perceives Kalyani's preoccupation with flowering plants as an ostentatious 'bourgeois' hobby that is ultimately useless in satisfying hunger. He exhorts her on the benefits of growing food grains and vegetables in a country that is ridden by starvation and poverty. Kalyani, on the other hand, upholds the freedom of artistic expression that is founded on a general attitude of care towards the world and is not necessarily determined by social interests. Her life is devoted to the cultivated performance and nurturing of beauty whose value does not have to be legitimized by its social function. Her care is extended to her selfless and almost maternal love for Ranga through her acts of bathing and feeding him. When Ranga accuses her of indulgence, Kalyani retorts that reducing every human activity to its social value or worth makes all kinds of creative expression superfluous (1971: 2597).

Kalyani and Ranga have contrasting opinions of love. Unlike the ideal romantic roles she essays as an actress, Kalyani has a detached and pragmatic response to love that can never be privileged at the cost of life. This is evident when Kalyani's cousin Pattu threatens to commit suicide if her mother does not allow her to marry her lover. While Ranga sees Pattu's love in her willingness to sacrifice her own life, Kalyani dismisses her self-sacrificing love as an act of cowardice that is only suitable for the theatre. Ranga, who is otherwise the rational critic, is, to Kalyani's amazement, irrational when it comes to love, 'He is a sterile politico who sees only vanity and snobbery in growing flowers and lovingly fondling a pet dog. It's strange that he sees nobility in the mushy sentimentality of love' (1971: 2602). Kalyani's belief that sacrificial love only leads to enslavement is reaffirmed when Pattu's marriage fails. Kalyani's own unconditional love for the world is premised on the affirmation of life. But to Ranga it is precisely the unconditional and detached nature of her love that makes it look like indifference and egotism. His initial understanding of love subsists in sacrifice, in erasing difference, and fashioning the other in one's own image. Like Kalyani, Ranga has also lost his parents in his youth, and severs ties with his caste neighbourhood that disapproves of his marriage to an actress. Although he is contemptuous of his unrefined and illiterate neighbours and relatives, he idealizes their poor but industrious lives and their sacrifices to their husbands that make Kalyani's love seem selfish. He expects Kalyani to be grateful for his act of sacrifice, but her selfless devotion elicits his dissatisfaction. Unlike Ranga's notion of love that is tied to sacrifice and possession, Kalyani's love connotes freedom as it is devoid of any expectation. The reason for their estrangement lies in the perceived hierarchy of their love—as a recipient of Kalyani's unconditional love, Ranga has to occupy a position of indebtedness. Following their marriage, he refuses to live in her house and as per Kalyani's suggestion decides to rent an apartment at his own expense. He interprets her financial independence as an affront to his masculinity. Kalyani interprets Ranga's insecurity for dignity positively, as a sign of his prudence and concern for their future, now that he has been disowned by his caste community.

The crisis in their marriage occurs when Kalyani refuses to sacrifice her career or be grateful for his voluntary sacrifices. She even questions his hypocrisy when he refuses to marry his dead wife's sister who is willing to sacrifice her happiness by marrying him and adopting his child. Love for Kalyani has to be a voluntary and unconditional surrender of the self to the other, as 'unwilling sacrifices to satisfy the demands of a loved one only promises dissatisfaction and loss and ensures a never ending life of slavery' (1971: 2660). While Ranga believes marriage entails compulsory sacrifice and perfect identity, Kalyani believes love is indifferent to marriage, which is only a ritual acknowledgement of love. Kalyani and Ranga occupy two extreme understandings of love: one believes in absolute autonomy and detached care, and the other in absolute dependence and possession. Ranga is unable to differentiate Kalyani's detachment from egotism, 'Can a woman establish a human relationship only for her own pleasure, only to satisfy her desires and treat it like the objects and things that she owns?' (1971: 2605). He believes she has reduced their marriage to a contract devoid of emotional significance, but she dismisses his selfish understanding of love as a fictional ideal undesirable for life:

> [T]his 'love' you keep talking about is not essential for life ... sincerity, honesty, compassion these are essential in life ... the word love means different things to different people. That is why I say it may be essential for stories and plays. Life is different.... I recall you telling me on one occasion that we are not teenagers. You are not the first man in my life and I am not the first woman in your life either. Let us be sincere, honest and compassionate to each other. If this is not love, let that exalted love remain on its lofty perch. Nothing will be lost. (1971: 2654)

By the end of the novel, Ranga distances himself from Kalyani, unable to reconcile to the unfairness of asking her to sacrifice her career for his happiness. They decide to apply for a divorce on the grounds of a lack of love, but his lawyer says their divorce will be granted only if they can prove their incompatibility by living apart for a year. As the lawyer suggests, love is indifferent, if not antithetical, to the law and 'never a sufficient condition for enabling or ending a marriage ...' (1971: 2665–6). If the law invests the individual with rights and duties that are enforceable, love is a voluntary surrender of rights in the process of caring for the other. Every romantic relationship is a process of negotiation that sets up its own set of variable 'rules' that may not conform to legal or contractual definitions of marriage. In the end, their estrangement and separation proves to be redemptive: Ranga admits his insecurities and Kalyani's moral superiority. When Kalyani suddenly succumbs to a life-threatening disease, Ranga selflessly nurses her back to health. Through this crisis, a new kind of love, one that no longer relies on its reciprocation, is realized. The hostility of the law to love becomes evident to Ranga as he reflects on the cruel irony of the law, which deems health and happiness as sufficient conditions for marriage, but entitles people to seek divorces when they fall sick and need support (1971: 2609). Kalyani also realizes that she could have prevented their estrangement and assures Ranga of her commitment to him. While Ranga admits his possessiveness destroyed their marriage, Kalyani refuses to get divorced and acknowledges her exclusive love for Ranga. This new form of love is a redemptive one that heals the characters but also involves the exchange of selves. This love negotiates difference and is valorized above an ideal or contractual notion of love as marriage.

Thus, Jeyakantan's narratives underscore the importance of love as care and responsibility in forging cross-gender bonds and reconfiguring normative constructions of gender and sexuality. As seen in the first set of narratives, female desire negotiates and resists social structures of consent, where female sexual consent is equated with marriage. The texts draw attention to the parodic powers of the female protagonist, who imitates and yet displaces these very structures to reveal their contingent nature. By not reducing heterosexuality to sexual violence or marriage, and by enabling the female protagonist to openly affirm her own desire and being, these novels imagine the creative possibilities of female sexual autonomy. Equally important are the empowering empathetic bonds between equally marginalized men and women that, however, do not erase sexual difference or hierarchy. These bonds represent the possibilities of renouncing an abject existence in pursuit of spiritual redemption. In other cases, these bonds serve to reform sexuality and sublimate desire in the service of the world. In the last novel, the bond between the male and female character rests on an ideal of care that reworks the unequal terms of conjugality. All of these stories emphasize the importance of the marginal in negotiating and traversing social and sexual hierarchies. My next chapter on Tanjai Prakash extends and complicates this engagement with marginality through the figure of the working-class woman. If Jeyakantan's narratives highlight the transformative potential of intimacies between marginalized men and women, female desire, in Prakash, becomes a historical agent when it is sublimated in labour. The reorientation of female desire in labour remakes the self, enabling individual and collective forms of self-realization.

Notes

1. For a discussion of Jeyakantan's reception, see Vallikannan (1986). From Jeyakantan's responses to his readers' letters, it is evident that his readers are not clear about what they consider obscene. Anything from prostitution to the sight of a mother nursing her child is deemed vulgar.

2. See Rose (1979) and Dentith (2000) for discussions on parody in literature.
3. See Kalpana Kannabiran and Vasanth Kannabiran (2002) for a discussion on the cultural and legal politics of rape and sexual consent in India. Rape, according to Kannabiran, is an ideological concept that divides women into spheres of consent according to the indices of their relationship to men. Thus, an identical act of sexual violence is seen as rape in the case of unmarried virgins, and as consensual sex in the case of wives and prostitutes. These distinctions, however, are effectively collapsed, because the woman's consent and body are never of any significance: once her virginity is lost, her reputation, and consequently that of her family is ruined.
4. See Judith Butler (1997) for a discussion of power, resistance, and subjection.
5. Following Emmanuel Levinas's *Of Escape*, which attempts to free the analysis of shame from a frame of moral culpability, Giorgio Agamben sees in the experience of shame a convergence of de-identification and inescapability. 'In shame,' Agamben says, 'the subject ... has no other content than its own de-subjectification; it becomes witness to its own disorder, its own oblivion as a subject. This double movement, which is both subjectification and de-subjectification, is shame' (1999: 106).
6. In the essay 'The Signification of the Phallus', Lacan (2002) argues that woman has to both reflect masculinity and symbolize lack.
7. See Sigmund Freud, *Beyond the Pleasure Principle* (1955) and *Civilization and its Discontents* (1950). Freud suggests that sexual instincts orient the living subject towards death, which is paradoxically the ultimate pleasure and the cessation of all pleasure, as it spells a return to an original state of inorganicity. In *The Ego and the Id* (1962), he extends this argument to suggest that human civilization rests on the repression of man's aggressive instincts.

6

Tanjai Prakash

Between Desire and Labour

Born Mark Lionel Prakash, Tanjai Prakash (1943–2000) in his brief writing career published three novels, a collection each of essays and short stories, two biographies, and a compilation of folk stories from the Tanjavur district of Tamil Nadu. Not much is known about his life or the reception of his writings, which is partly because Prakash never published his own works in a disciplined fashion, being more keen on reading and promoting other writers. Most of his writings were published by his wife only after his death. The introduction to his collection of essays by his wife suggests his knowledge of several Indian languages and his father's role in introducing him to art and literature. He was impressed by the stories of his aunt and grandmothers, and this led him to publish an anthology of folk tales rich with the history and culture of the Tanjavur district. Not having completed his education, Prakash was unable to find a stable job and spent his life in various parts of the then Madras Presidency. He was involved in many literary activities, that included setting up a publishing house in Madurai and Tanjavur, editing a Tamil journal called *Pālam* (Bridge), organizing several literary meets where he introduced many upcoming artists and writers to the Tamil literary world, and founding a literary 'movement' in the 1980s in Tanjavur that focused on the art of storytelling and the narrative.

As we have seen already, the Tanjavur and Kumbakonam districts have produced some of the finest modern Tamil writers of sexuality, from K.P. Rajagopalan to Mauni, T. Janakiraman, L.S. Ramamirtham, and Karichan Kunju. Tanjai Prakash's writings were to a large extent inspired by the depiction of sensuality in these earlier writers, for whom desire in all its sensual possibilities was a lens to explore embodied subjectivity. Another similarity is the way desire is neither limited to nor exhausted by the sexual act. While the earlier writers spiritualized desire and love by divorcing them from the body, desire in Prakash's novels has an ontological function to discover alterity as a reflection of the self. I argue that the repeated failure of desire to attain recognition and identity in these narratives forms the very basis of the social contract as it reconfigures the relationality between the self and the other. For Prakash, the transformative potential of desire is revealed when it is deceived and sublimated in labour, for it then acquires the ability to blur the very distinctions that make power, meaning, and subjectivity possible.[1]

I read Tanjai Prakash as a historical novelist whose narratives historicize human subjectivity as a dialectical process. His novels take the subject not as a stable essence but as a temporal category that is always in the making. The self is constituted through a process of identification through and with the other, a process that is, however, always contingent and incomplete. The act of identification occurs through the medium of desire whose ultimate goal is the other's desire and recognition. Thus, desire has a reflexive function of affirming the self through the other.[2] Since perfect identity is a much-longed-for but imaginary ideal, the reflexive structure of desire is necessarily constituted by deception. Prakash's characters embody a fundamental human desire to attain recognition and identity through the body; a desire that is invariably betrayed and disappointed. But the repeated deception of this desire is precisely what urges the subject towards identity, enabling the possibility of self-transcendence. In the novels discussed here, the sexual disappointments of the characters reveal the irredeemable lack that structures and perpetuates desire and subjectivity. The fact that desire can neither be eliminated nor entirely satisfied makes it the very medium and instrument of transformation and freedom.

Prakash's novels dramatize a particular scenario of desire where the male protagonist renounces the inauthenticity of his privileged existence in search of authenticity. He is drawn to an abject working-class woman whose body indexes her apparent authenticity. But the disillusionment of his desire compels him to recognize the true object of desire, which is not the body, but the other's desire and recognition. The protagonist is transformed by his attempts to attain recognition and identity, which is ultimately never accomplished. The protagonist further deploys seduction to repeatedly evoke and betray the desires of other abject women for him, and consequently for the other women he supposedly desires. By the end of the stories, there is a group of women whose desires for one another and for the male protagonist are mediated by the male protagonist. The women's internalization of the unattainable protagonist serves as a creative force that propels them to sublimate their frustrated desires in creative labour, which offers objective validations of their abject status. The male protagonist thus functions as a creative principle in a regime of productive labour that sublimates female desire into action thereby re-centring the female body as the very medium of self-transformation and historical progress. What indicates an implicit shift in this androcentric economy is when the internalized protagonist is rendered dispensable by women belonging to different castes whose labour is an instrument of the self and collective remaking. Despite this, Prakash's creative universe is based on an androcentric economy of desire and labour where the male protagonist is a circulating meta-signifier that enables the very articulation of female desire and agency. There is no room in these texts to destabilize the heterosexual male centre and reconfigure this economy around women or intimacies among men.

Kaḷḷam (Deception: 1994)

Prakash's novels privilege the labouring body over the sexual body. The sexual body, here mostly the female body, is inextricably embedded in ideological structures of social power where any form of resistance only reinforces subordination. Prakash seems to suggest that any attempt to sexually empower oneself through one's body is an illusion that reinstates hierarchy and oppression. In other words, there is no scope for transformation within these structures unless one recognizes the fact that the desiring subject is structured by an insatiable, albeit, creative lack. It is only when desire is channelized in the creative enactments of the labouring body that it reconfigures the very distinction between power and subordination. Only creative activity, Prakash suggests, offers the possibility of recognition and self-transcendence. The betrayal and disappointment of desire and the sublimation of desire in labour is a persistent theme that unites Prakash's novels. For the purpose of this chapter, I restrict my analysis to his first two novels.

The central motif of Prakash's first novel *Kaḷḷam*, like all his other novels, is change. The opening scene describes the transition from a traditional past to a modern anachronistic present; a transition that interplays sameness and difference, the old and the new. The following passage correlates a glorious past of Maratha rule with the vital possibilities of a decadent present.

> It was morning, it was Tanjavur; it was the palace; everything was old and dusty ... centuries old ... everything crumbling.... The smell of bat droppings that could not be seen seemed to pervade the place ... moss that from the rain had spread over the solid four foot tall, century old, crumbling slake lime walls, had now faded and blackened, and had again reemerged because of the rain and spread like a green pillow over the walls and crevices. (Prakash 1994: 25)

What is also suggested is the male protagonist Paranthamaraju's uncertain appraisal of ancestral art on the walls of the royal palace—he is awed by its original value and is aware of its present state of disuse. The description of his filthy and unkempt body lying in a drunken stupor in one of the dark hollows of the palace is continuous with the general mood of abject loss and destruction invoked by the palace. Although he is nostalgic for the irretrievable loss of an artistic world, he rejects its outmoded aesthetic values. His repudiation of the past is conditioned and confirmed by his disparaging dismissal of his father Minakshiraju's paintings, which no longer reflect the originality of his ancestral heritage. During an argument, he confronts Minakshiraju with the synthetic value of his art that is neither original nor reflective of the social exigencies of the contemporary world. He accuses his father of producing imitative art, although he is unable to offer an alternative to counter his father's charge of hypocrisy.

[Paranthamaraju] '... You cannot even draw a line by yourself. The one who drew [jewelry] for the Sita you draw was your grandfather Sitaraju ... finally my father Minakshiraju sells the painting in a crafts exhibition in France for five or ten hundred thousand....' His father replies, 'Stop it! You don't have the guts to earn your own money ... let's see you draw a painting.... I'm the artist, the extractor of money. What have you achieved? ... Your challenges ring hollow ... is there a town I haven't been to or artists I haven't seen ... and you're asking me to draw a line. Hey I'll throw a mirror before you. Let's see you take the pieces of glass and stick them together to form a figure....' Paranthamaraju says, 'Why this unnecessary talk? ... You don't have to accept me as an artist. You be the artist. That's enough. But the things you take abroad: Rama's corpse, Sita's corpse, Alilai Kannan's corpse.... For how long do you think they will continue buying these dead corpses? ... You may think you have deceived the foreigner ... it isn't as though they don't know that your paintings are merely glass pieces stuck together. It's all craftwork. You asked me to stick glass; I can do that in poetry, father. Do you know poetry? ... Who besides me can tell you your mistakes? Who is there to show you the errors of your tradition and age? ... Your unoriginal art, your soulless music, your disfigured sculptures; the painting that does not reflect your age will gather like a heap at your feet. You will not be there to see that disgrace, we will....' His father says, '... [I]f you can earn for yourself that's enough for me ... I know someone everywhere. I said I would somehow make you a collector.... But you refused. I asked you to become a doctor ... but you said no. You said you would finish your BA but it ended up with no use and you refused to find a job ... finally you said you would paint. You said you would join a painting school but.... You ran away in the third year. Then you scribbled some modern art and had an exhibition.... Create modern art, I'm not saying no. Let's see you sell your art. Okay, you don't have to sell your paintings. Can people at least appreciate your work? Do those people understand your work? You just scribble a drawing and some poetry in a large canvas and ... If asked you say it's existentialism or some nonsense....' (1994: 89–90)

Paranthamaraju's argument with his father challenges a fetishized notion of tradition that constitutes its apparent self-identity by excluding other artistic possibilities. Paranthamaraju's rejection of his father's art poses a threat to a linear narrative of traditional art that has hitherto posited its own telos. For Paranthamaraju, the future existence of his father's paintings is threatened by their inherent lack of value; they are lifeless imitations of their ancestral precursors whose value has been lost by commodification. Their indifference to the contemporary world threatens their end but their synthetic status is precisely what conditions the possibility of producing new forms of art that will challenge their fetishized authority. Paranthamaraju insinuates—and this becomes significant later in my discussion of the novel—the contemporary reinvention of traditional art and aesthetics to symbolize the existential dimensions of the very sources of abjection that otherwise resist representation: hunger, longing, disease, poverty, and death. The aestheticization of abjection, I suggest, produces new works of art inasmuch as it reconfigures marginalized female subjects in the act of creation. Later in the novel, when Paranthamaraju trains a group of women flower sellers to reclaim their artistic heritage, they are transformed by their creations that provide objective validations of their abject status. Their shared recognition and validation is what enables the possibility of self-remodelling.

Ideas of Desire and Deception

Prakash describes encounters between male and female characters as struggles for recognition and identity. He privileges the perspectives of his male protagonists who seek—and invariably fail—to obtain absolute recognition from their female counterparts.[3] Every encounter, instead of promising absolute self-knowledge and identity, ends up being a misrecognition that exposes the equally contingent and fragile nature of being male or female. Paranthamaraju's failure to attain full self-consciousness through a series of encounters with women ends up blurring the very distinction or hierarchy between male subjectivity and female objectivity. For instance, his experience of two seemingly autonomous women, Sarala and Babi, confronts him with his own opacity.

Minakshiraju's artifice is not limited to his artwork but includes the refashioning of his secretary Sarala, once a poor, emaciated woman from his caste who 'suddenly descended like a sculpted statue in a temple hall' (1994: 45). She is transformed, to Paranthamaraju's contempt, into a deracinated 'body' whose suave and sexy self-fashioning is just another one of his father's synthetic creations and a mere advertisement for his art in international markets.

> She who had [first] come clad in a thin, coarse cotton sari was now refined, travelling abroad with his father. She had cut her hair and taken hot steam baths in beauty parlors abroad, she had her hair styled, had body massages and developed greater self-confidence that had made her body all the more curved and muscular giving it a look of suave indifference and complacence. Whiskey, pork, beef and foreign mushrooms had transformed her tastes ... *Paranthamaraju knew she had discarded her bodily needs before working there.* Sarala was a man among men and a man among women; she wore a skirt and a sleeveless vest as she sweated exercising with her maid servants on the terrace at dawn; she swam in the evenings, did some gardening, bred fish and as if that weren't enough, owned several domestic cats. She did *poojas.* She called Brahmans and conducted *homas*. Without skipping any religious festival she observed fasts, rituals and so on. The only thing she never did was to get intimate with Minakshiraju or Paranthamaraju. (1994: 69–70; italics mine)

Paranthamaraju perceives Sarala's virile self-disciplining as a lack of authenticity. Here authenticity has to be understood as a consciousness of the self as a lacking, and, therefore, a desiring being. Paranthamaraju resorts to sexual slander and assaults to compel Sarala to acknowledge her abject past, which is suppressed by her disciplined body. In an attempt to expose her dissimulation, he insults her derivative authority when Minakshiraju entrusts her with Paranthamaraju's finances. Paranthamaraju is initially unable to make them recognize the deception that structures their relationship; the 'falsity of their relationship', which is 'the very reason for their relationship ...' (1994: 89). His taunts to make Sarala confirm the truth of his sexual allegations elicit, to his initial shock, her defiant affirmation, 'I'm his kept woman ... just as you and your father are my kept men' (1994: 90). But the apparent truth of Sarala's confession actually confirms the fictional status of absolute identity that can never be achieved. Paranthamaraju's incredulous laughter renders Sarala vulnerable at the thought of being 'easily stripped naked' by the exclusive power of 'his rapid paintbrush', an anticipation of his ability to enable women to attain self-knowledge through artistic labour (1994: 75). For Paranthamaraju, Sarala's emotional outburst only reiterates the synthetic status of female sexual embodiment that does not possess the truth of self-knowledge. He says:

Sarala, how will I make you understand that you aren't merely a woman? Are you going to prove that you're a woman too by crying? She could've defeated you earlier, father! You could have handed over your business to her earlier like the way you chose her for your work. How many disguises! How many masks! What's all this? A pretense to deceive me? (1994: 89)

When Sarala turns to Paranthamaraju for recognition, she is inexorably fascinated by his spectacular and defiled presence that, I argue, embodies the authenticating desire for self-recognition. He spells the potential dissolution of her artifice, and indeed, her very self. She literally embraces her own loss by embracing Paranthamaraju, an apparently primordial act that captures the suspension of time as it were and the erasure of the spatial limits of their bodies. That 'purificatory' moment involves the temporary erasure of difference and the exchange of selves. While Sarala discovers her sense of self in and through Paranthamaraju, he is confronted by self-estrangement. Through their encounter, he admits his longing to discover the truth of his own being.

That which she had *anticipated* for twenty years now stood before her, terrifying. That which had weakly hit her and fallen a little earlier; that which she had *for so many years* indifferently trampled and pushed far away; that with which she had become familiar now overturned on her like a massive form; a huge Meru. She struggled to rise. She wasn't prepared to fall and cry and slide again and again ... the merciful darkness that had fallen on her; the smell of alcohol, the stench of sweat, dirt; *Paranthamaraju who lived in that moment*; she rose to push and turn him away with disgust ... how did that happen? *She spewed that desire and became purified* ... how did her fragrantly perfumed body sink in that sewage? How did she swallow the dirty ball that she has pushed away? How did her feet, her arms, her sari, her breath and her life betray her? Sarala, how did you cut and sacrifice yourself? ... Who was defeated in those three minutes? Who knows? He did not expect her to rise and embrace him tightly. It was a blinding moment that everyone experiences—*when these shes who could vanquish everything were unable to defeat themselves.... Will it never happen to me?* ... He emerged as he was reminded of Sarala's sweat impressed on his chest and dirty hands. He had to separate Sarala's hands from his and separate her from him ... the dust of the red earth from his body defined her face, breasts and shoulders as though her skin had been cut and molded. (1994: 91–2; italics mine)

Paranthamaraju has a similar encounter with Babi, the prostitute he accidentally meets in the ruined palace. He associates Babi's sexual artifice with his father's synthetic art. To him, Babi embodies the sexual pretence of (prostitutional) femininity whose apparent integrity is undermined by its constitutive historicity. When he first sees Babi, he traces the unfortunate historical demise of her ancestors—a lineage of courtesan-dancers who danced for the Nayaka rulers and fled the Konkan following the defeat of the Vijayanagara empire—to Babi's sexual decadence. There is a clear disjunction between his perception of Babi's adorned body that, like the paintings on the broken palace walls, conjures an idealized and seemingly organic royal world and her sexual indulgence that infuses this ideal with sexual artifice. The narrator echoes Paranthamaraju's disparagement of Babi's self-indulgence that suppresses her victimhood at the hands of a violent husband. Her courage and resilience, the narrator remarks, is forgotten once she comes to Tanjavur to earn her living as a prostitute. Female self-consciousness is, in other words, tied to an awareness of fear and vulnerability that conditions the possibility of sublimating desire in creative labour. Like Sarala earlier, the narrator betrays his contempt for Babi's putative integrity that undermines his implicit admiration for her former fearlessness and pride.

A couple of glasses of foreign whiskey helped her [tolerate] the actions of two effeminate politician thugs tugging at her blouse and skirt all night long before putting them back on ... men were not new to Babi. She [knew] the scents of different kinds of men over the past ten years. First Maratha, then Brahmanan, then Tamil, and then someone else—it was just this arrogance that was left. (1994: 25–7)

When Babi discovers Paranthamaraju is the son of an internationally renowned and wealthy painter, she tries to seduce him. But he interprets her attempt as a dissembling and corrupting sign of greed and insults her beauty before dismissing her. Later in the novel, we see a more explicit dramatization of Babi's attempt to seduce Paranthamaraju that becomes a violent struggle to achieve recognition by overcoming the other; a struggle that confirms the impossibility of a sexual relationship that is based on a necessary but imaginary notion of sexual identity. Desire constitutes the split between the mind and the body that undoes any notion of a stable self, although

Paranthamaraju tries to resist Babi's sexual advances, he is betrayed by irrepressible signs of bodily pleasure. He perceives his inability to control his body as a sign of self-estrangement, 'He saw a long milky white stain run down his trousers ... [He wonders] if he is deceiving himself when he is repelled by Babi's stinking body when his own body is defiled' (1994: 108). Babi's inability to sexually overpower Paranthamaraju marks her failed femininity. This is contrasted to her servant Jamna's ability to seduce Paranthamaraju without 'stripping naked or making sexual advances' (1994: 110).

Paranthamaraju is confronted by his own opacity through his experience of Sarala and Babi's apparent integrity. His dead mother Lochana represents the fantasy of the abject mother who constitutes an elusive sense of wholeness; of absolute knowledge that determines and sustains his longing for self-recognition and identity. He laments his inability to dispel Babi's sexual artifice to his dead mother, 'Lochana! The mother who gave birth to me! I'm unable to unearth and give you what women like you are waiting to get from my body ...' [4] (1994: 74). Later in the novel, Paranthamaraju admits to Sarala, it is his mother's 'impossible love' that 'made him desire every woman that is something he cannot make anyone else understand' (1994: 200). The ultimate joy of his love for his mother is an ideal that cannot be matched through his sensuous encounters with Sarala or Babi. Jamna's abject body, on the other hand, is perceived as an indeterminate metonym for his mother. She ostensibly incarnates both the ideal of absolute identity and a lack that falls short of it, or indeed like Paranthamaraju, the very desire for recognition that can only be attained through labour.

> Her peaceful, sympathetic and fearless face.... *She could be two years younger than Babi*. But she was a servant. She worked in the Tanjavur palace. His eyes dulled in tears; *she looked ten years older* than Babi; with her hair slightly graying and her breasts hanging, she looked like an unwed old woman who served royalty; a poor woman; some kind of a slave. Woman has always been subordinate. *In any country. In any age*. Paranthamaraju *didn't need to know Jamna's history* ... he stared at her. The several crumpled folds of her black skirt that spoke to him *for centuries*; the old floral printed cotton sari stained with dirt; the end of her sari that veiled her face; her fingernails all dirty. The smell of cloves from her body and her arms and feet that had paled with work. For no reason his eyes moistened ... he finally made a mistake—he tightly embraced

Jamna to his chest, leaned her against the wall—his head burned—*without any reason or interest*—all unkempt—he kissed her in several places ... was this Paranthamaraju's first experience of a woman? With a dirty servant woman? This isn't experiencing a woman. She could appear worse than Babi or Lallu. Or she may have a vital pulse that is clearer than Jamna's. Jamna! *Which century do you belong to?* Aah.... *It seems Jamna and my mother, were among the many dissembling women from any century.* It's disgusting. A beastly union that disturbs the relationship between man and woman, which has been shaved bare, completely stripped naked. Jamna doesn't have Babi's happiness, her tricks, her commerce. *But the prostitute called life had sucked Paranthamaraju dry. Paranthamaraju looked at his body in disgust* ... when he hugged Jamna, her sweat, the fragrance of cloves and the body that had hardened with work and was prepared to do anything was missing in her breasts. *When he embraced her, her breasts were cold and hanging emptinesses making him shrink. What provoked him to hug her and kiss her? He had never kissed anyone else except his mother, which is why Jamna was bitter.* (1994: 44–50; italics mine)

Paranthamaraju's perception of Jamna betrays a tension between her sexual and her labouring body; between a deceptive sense of identity and the authenticity of self-recognition. Unlike Sarala's disciplined body or Babi's synthetic beauty, Jamna's labouring body embodies dialectical change: for, like the Tanjavur palace, it correlates sinewy vitality and old age, identity and difference, authenticity and deception. Jamna is as located in her historical particularity as she transcends time and history to invoke a disembodied and indeterminate sense of universality. She, I argue, embodies the dialectical rhythms of desire, which is a desire to overcome the ontological disparity between the self and the other. The desire for identity has to be mediated through the body, although it can never be fulfilled. It is evident from the above description that the desirability of her body is elusive; her touch at once evokes and exorcises his desire that, in retrospect, is not directed at her body. Over the course of the novel, Jamna's body becomes a seductive fantasy that repeatedly evokes and disillusions Paranthamaraju's desire for her desire and recognition. Jamna's body is, in other words, the very potential of desire to affect self-transcendence and create history.

Prakash's novels dramatize the dialectics of the desire for recognition that progresses through a series of deceptive misrecognitions. To Paranthamaraju, Jamna appears as an irresistible fantasy of perfect recognition. Although he is suspicious of her deception, he surrenders to the pleasurable sensuality of her selfless devotion. Her touch conveys her apparent authenticity, which is ostensibly confirmed by her sexual victimhood at the hands of violent male clients. Paranthamaraju associates Jamna's abject body with visions of ancestral poverty, ignominy, and death following the defeat of the Vijayanagara empire to the Bahmani sultans. The intoxicating *paayas* (rice pudding) Jamna feeds him at the palace and the sound of female workers speaking his mother tongue, Telugu, trigger delirious fantasies of his mother's abject life, first, as the daughter of a sculptor who was one of the many ancestors who died of disease, and then as a poor, subordinate palace worker. Jamna's presence invokes the irredeemable destruction and loss of a royal world in the form of an imagined painting, 'Tanjavur's Serfoji Maharaja, Jamna's mother, grandmother, *tabla, sarangi,* that age, a century' (1994: 106; italics mine). Like Jamna, the ruined palace walls symbolize an abject past that threatens the disillusionment of all desire, meaning, and identity for Paranthamaraju. Yet the possibility of possessing Jamna again confronts him with his own inscrutability.

That wall called out to him cruelly. The cushioned wall exposed to heat and covered with moss seemed to open its mouth wide open and its thickness stirred within him a cloud of sorrow and pain. He clearly saw in triangles, the world's stupidity, which had been deceived by man about the meaning of life; *his stupidity that had deceived Jamna* and pushed and rolled her aside. (1994: 107; italics mine)

Jamna, unlike Babi, wields a seductive power over Paranthamaraju that is encoded by her willed enactments of powerlessness. She secretly witnesses Babi's attempt to overpower Paranthamaraju and the involuntary loss of his self-control. She undermines his apparent integrity and abstinence by ostensibly surrendering as a 'faithful subordinate *tāci*' (1994: 124). Her servility wins his faith and seems to reassure the loss of his integrity with apparent pleasure, 'Who said you're useless? *Maharaj*, when you kicked me today it hurt for three hours, do you know? How amazing, when you pull my hand the pain just disappears. *I know, don't deceive me*' (1994: 125; italics mine). She is certain of securing with his protection, her freedom from Babi in exchange for her own body. Her seductive attempts to pleasure him, 'the smell of her body that smells of cloves, sweat and dirt' and 'her faint voice asking him to be sympathetic to her' arouse and sustain his violent passion (1994: 128). His desire is only intensified by her apparent protests that suggest her potential freedom lies in her body's ability to work and labour, 'Leave me. I'm a prostitute. I have no one—I'm an orphan. Anyone can do anything to me. I have to work to survive, if I lose my hands and legs it doesn't matter. Don't do anything to me Maharaj. Babi is standing at the staircase, leave me' (1994: 126–7). She seemingly relinquishes her body to his violent desire even as she claims her body is her only means of survival. Her labouring body that signifies enslavement now becomes the instrument of potential freedom.

The repeated evocations and betrayals of Paranthamaraju's desire compel him to realize that all individuals are as interrelated as they are different. Jamna's apparent impotence and transparency both reassures and undermines Paranthamaraju's desire and integrity. He is suddenly seized by an impotent impulse to destroy the dissimulation of the world to discover 'the truth'. In his 'fury, anger and helplessness', he is determined to 'break the painting'; dispel the 'conspiracy of this age' by 'tearing Jamna, break Babi's triangle, crush Sarala's essence, and remove Lallu's phlegm ... crush and carve out father's, god's and his own essence' (1994: 106–7). The following quote reiterates Paranthamaraju's faith in the ability of art to represent the ultimate truth: that human beings are as divided as they are interrelated. Therefore, self-recognition cannot be an individual achievement that only results in the violent extermination of the other, but is an understanding of the self gained through the other.

> How many triangles are burning in Sri Lanka, Angola, Nagasaki, East Berlin, Pretoria and Congo? How many helmets cover the overturned milestones? How many crosses on the side? A heap of crosses that cannot be buried. Like ants, like germs, how many triangles of corpses? Am I Paranthamaraju? I have to say all this in my paintings! Oh Man of tomorrow! Why do you hide your selfishness? You know where your heart is. You have more reasons to die than live. I today experience the sorrowful pains of your age that take me ahead. Do you think my inert sorrow will not reach you? My voice will sound throughout the ages. My art will sing of this. My poem's poverty will reflect this. My disguise will prove this. I'm not a body. I'm not a mind. That reason. An only soul. Don't tease me. Don't threaten me with hunger. Don't kick me with food. *I and you are one in any age. One within one. One mixed with the other. When separated we are within each other.* Just a palace. Fearful poverty.... (1994: 100; italics mine)

The artistic representation of destruction and renewal resists meaning or interpretation. Paranthamaraju's artistic creations share an obsession with the triangle that symbolizes the recursive regeneration of the world; the constant renewal of self and meaning to undo their fictional identity. With a nail, he draws on the wall '... White, brilliant, long triangles on the mossy wall that transcend time ... his aggressive lines and furious meanings spread over the ages as echoes in triangles of the questions of humankind that repeatedly died and birthed' (1994: 108).

Paranthamaraju's attempt to recast ancestral art initially emerges as a reaction against traditional aesthetics' exclusive engagement with mythical and immortal subjects (Hindu deities and mythological figures in different postures) that are apparently resistant to change. But a more positive formulation of a contemporary form of art emerges first in the form of Paranthamaraju's abstract paintings and poetry that suggest that the deception of desire is necessary to reveal the lack that reconfigures meaning and subjectivity. His poem engages with adultery as a formal expression of the inherently social and mediated nature of human desire that does away with the hypocrisy of monogamy. In his poem Paranthamaraju embodies the deceptive identity of a prostitute who seduces the world by simulating and disappointing the social values she is imputed with to rid the world of deception.

My job isn't to write poetry.
Adultery.
Days of adultery.
What else?
I don't have the seductive ways of the living world.
The subtle waves and tunes of poetry are not in my heart.
I am always a stranger to
The brilliant light of the dream.
The talent of writing.
I don't have the skills of sculpture making.
That drains the imagination.
Conquers dreams and achieves grace.
To live and work.
To work and live.
The law of the world is for me something insignificant.
Even then
Sticking to the world

Leaking,
As a licking dog
As a burdened mule
Every day I sell myself,
I'm not ashamed of being the deceptive prostitute of the street who sells her body,
Because today in this society no job can exceed or redeem this standard.
My job,
Yes!
Poetry, Adultery. (1994: 200–2; italics mine)

In the latter half of the novel, Jamna and Paranthamaraju move to a locality of poor flower sellers where their abstinence enables self-realization. Paranthamaraju eschews alcohol and food in order to constantly experience lack; a lack that Jamna symbolizes. He is unable to renounce his desire for Jamna 'whose thought is intoxicating ...' because she '*is* his hunger, his fasting, his food' (1994: 227; italics mine). Through his experience of abstinence he realizes the possibility of remaking an abject world characterized by poverty and starvation through art. When a poor artist discovers he is Minakshiraju's estranged son and refuses his offer to make a cut glass painting of the goddess Kali, Paranthamaraju, who has been struggling to survive, welcomes this disappointment as an opportunity to renounce his hitherto privileged existence. He affirms the potential of hunger to reconfigure an abject world.

No use. Nobody gave him anything. It had become dark. Hunger ... starvation ... ate yesterday. What an ordeal? He laughed. What's a bigger ordeal than this? *Hunger ... he really needed this. He clearly knew his father was the reason for the life he lived until today. I cannot live anymore because of him.* I should not. His eyes darkened. He discovered an ordeal through Jamna. The next thing was not the dust of his body. *The body had to be split. Its cloud had to be split. The reason for living had to be discovered and torn in another way. If that wasn't possible, a new meaning for life should be created.* Or it should be buried in absence. *Everything has been created out of nothing after all. There is nothing that has been created from the beginning. Something can be scientifically created from something else. Something cannot be created isn't it?* Hunger ... darkening eyes ... so many hundreds of thousands of starvation deaths in our country ... on the African coast, how many black children from how many countries in skin and bones stretching their arms to the sky.... (1994: 146; italics mine)

In his interpretation of one of his paintings, Paranthamaraju expresses his anxious hope that humanity is never deprived of the self-transformative power of desire to create history. To attain a state of desirelessness would put an end to all forms of life. His enormous glass painting depicts an all-powerful demon representing the world-consuming, regenerative power of human hunger, which can neither be entirely gratified nor destroyed. The ultimate truth of existence is the irredeemable lack that structures and perpetuates desire, meaning, and subjectivity. The ultimate desire is thus the desire to keep desiring. In the following quote, Paranthamaraju affirms the power of desire to repeatedly undo a stable notion of being, so that nothing in the world possesses an essential truth. Only the submission to desire and its transmutation in labour enables self-transcendence, which is something the women flower sellers enact through their labour.

The guardian of the world that constantly dies and is reborn ... the guardian of birth! The guardian of destruction! ... He was a symbol of the poor people who are living now ... it's not just hunger. The destruction of hunger lies in its subduing. The suffering of desire only fades with the subduing away of the demon. *Devi Mahamayi stays within us in the form of desire, in the form of hunger; oh hunger! Never recede. Oh poverty! I have not come to defeat you.* The demon flies with outspread hands and legs because poverty can no more be destroyed as the engagements of these superstitious people who cannot know my knowledge and the affection in my heart. A million universes—ending swirling ignorance—how many differences? All forms of hunger. Moving motion—hunger ... I salute you always. *Burn in me always everywhere and remove my ignorance.* Oh demon! I stopped in search of god ... I touched Shiva ... everything, a dream. The ocean of erotic desire swelled into the cauldron of sewage. When women opened their cauldrons to me I drowned in my cauldron.... Jagadeeswari your hips aren't enough for me ... your erotic desire isn't sufficient to suppress me ... my lust is sewage ... a fecal heap ... *when they are hungry and have nothing to eat ... they sleep with their husbands or with their neighbors or with someone they don't know ... without any desire, they knowingly or unknowingly stoke the fire of their desires.* A mouthful of food is enough. The next day another mouthful or even half of that is enough, no morality for them. If this day passes they are supremely happy. *The only difference between me and them–I understand these things but still wander while they wander without understanding this. Is it good for them to understand this? Or is it good not to understand this? 'Being-Nothingness'—this is the eternal tune....* (1994: 184–5; italics mine)

Desire shifts from its operation within a dyadic structure to acquire the status of a social and political agent that binds working-class women. Paranthamaraju deploys 'seduction' (Baudrillard, 1990) to evoke and betray the flower sellers' desires for him. According to Baudrillard, seduction belongs to the domain of irreducible irony that resists the masculine world of power, meaning, and production. Seduction blurs and renders ever reversible the distinctions that are necessary for power, meaning, and representation. There is no truth to seduction that transmutes meaning into ironic signs that resist interpretation. Thus, the boundaries between power and oppression, the repressed and the liberated body, are blurred. Desire can no longer be distinguished from its representation and loses its reality, as it becomes an ironic interplay of signs. In the realm of seduction, the body loses value and meaning becoming instead an ironic and indeterminate object of desire. Sexual identity can then only be a seductive ideal that can never be realized. So, for instance, on one of his trips back from selling paintings, Paranthamaraju is accompanied by two flower sellers who secretly long to bear his child. But he disappoints them and reveals the essentially deceptive nature of the body and desire that can never affect absolute identity without reinstating fragmentation. Sexual relationships and procreation, Paranthamaraju suggests, only reinstate the impossibility of absolute identity. Only abstinence and a sexual fantasy of union can 'fulfil' all desires and liberate one from the marital and filial ties of monogamy and motherhood.

'You're beautiful now. You play with me. If you have a child all this will disappear. It's a disguise. It's a disguise everyone puts on ... you know the happiness that is got from a man and a woman sleeping together is all a disguise. The moment the disguise is removed they separate and hunger on their own ... all the women say you are my kept woman....' [Sippi Vellai says] 'It's alright if you don't marry me. But if you leave me I'll die. I'm a low caste dog, a stinking prostitute....' Paranthamaraju hugged her and wiping her eyes, with a shaky voice said in her ears, 'I'm keeping you, you dog! ... But I cannot keep you like this forever, not just you ... but all those who wished to be kept by me ... they all want me for themselves and are stripping and dragging me to a dark corner ... it will take me just ten minutes to lie and roll with you in bed. But I've already stripped you completely. Everyone may not understand this like you ... *it's enough if you think I can give you anything you ask for ...*

having a child is just an identification mark ... the disguises will all disappear one by one in thin air ...' [Paranthamaraju quickly kisses Sippi Vellai in the crowded bus before anyone can notice them] ... [Sippi Vellai realizes the truth of Paranthamaraju's words as she thinks of all the men in her life who desire her] Marriage, children, desire, love—these were only suited to cinema. (1994: 236–8; italics mine)

The generalized simulation of Paranthamaraju's desire for all the women including Jamna reduces them to substitutable objects of his hypothetical desire. A symptom of their frustrated desire for Paranthamaraju is his substitution of the other women he (apparently) desires. As Lacan argues in his essay 'The Subversion of the Subject And the Dialectic of Desire in the Freudian Unconscious', 'To desire an other's desire is to substitute the desiring subject for the value desired by this desire so that the value that the subject represents becomes what the other desires' (2002: 112). The flower sellers' longing for Paranthamaraju undergoes a transformation as they begin to desire his desire for the other women, so that by the end of the novel Paranthamaraju mediates the desires of all the women for him and for one another. A criss-crossing network of frustrated female desires that reflect and mediate each other blurs the distinction between subjectivity and objectivity, thus becoming the social basis of a labouring community of women. Paranthamaraju is the enabling factor in a regime of artistic activity that relies on the sublimation of betrayed female desire into creative action. Their artistic labour entails a reclamation of their traditional artistic heritage.

With the wetness of Sarala's lips still on his [Paranthamaraju] lips, he slipped near Ramalakshmi and, touching her lips with his, sucked her saliva as though he were sucking her breath and life. Although that insolent act enraged Ramalakshmi, his lips that smelled of the morning's meat crushed her anger like small sour grapes. Although Sarala's betrayal shocked Ramalakshmi, Raja Paranthamaraju had from the very beginning imprisoned her.... Although he had said he would give her a child some day, there were no signs of it. *He is deceiving everyone. But still no one could stop getting deceived.* Because everything that those women were supposed to get in ... their life had been denied. The women there had no faith in their men.... He provoked the feelings of all the women. He confronted them separately and troubled and provoked their femininity that had been rendered lifeless by poverty, hunger, disease, social control. Of the upper caste Maratha women he had seen at the Tanjavur palace—their artistic sensibility—*the lust that naturally rises in the blood of every subordinate caste—had not been expressed as artistic sensibility.* Paranthamaraju isn't merely an expert at painting. He isn't a womanizer. No one in any age will ever understand that *he has created them by ... using their sexual desires as a means of expressing the ancient, aggressive but wonderful art that they don't know is in their blood.* Everyone including Sarala was scared of him but could not know him. Paranthamaraju was like a snake in a pit when it came to revealing himself. Because she knew this, Jamna is never trapped by him ... that the women's provoked lust was the reason for their new art that shattered old, ancient traditions and customs was unknown to the French, German and English critics who praised their art to the skies ... if one looked up at the ceiling [of the temple] one would be aroused by the apparent feeling of being embraced by a woman. But if one looked close, one would realize from the strips of blue and red glass pieces that the woman one saw isn't a *gopi* [but] Krishna himself ... signs of very modern art like the sight of every woman entering Krishna and countless overlapping *yonis*, would remind one of the problems of the modern age. The deep red coloured and hairy testicles of masculinity made of dark black glass prevented them from being discovered easily. (1994: 245–6; italics mine)

Paranthamaraju is internalized as a creative force that mediates the women's mutual intimacies and enables them to sublimate their longing in artistic labour. In the process, the very distinction between subject and object, identity and difference, power and oppression is rendered reversible. Two of the flower sellers, Sippi Vellai and Ramalakshmi, for instance, are unable to avoid Paranthamaraju, who overworks them 'like slaves'. Ramalakshmi claims he is her saviour who 'bought her freedom' from a cruel man (1994: 259). It is her internalization of 'Paranthamaraju's virility' that enables her to construct a statue of Valmuni, one of their gods, which leads to a rediscovery of their 'forgotten mythology ... their inherent, forgotten artistry'. The massive statue of the deity with a tall horn on his head reaching the sky seems to suggest 'the liberation of her mind' (1994: 260). Their artistic creations offer recognition and the possibility of self-transcendence.

If the earlier writers privileged mind over body, Prakash centres the labouring body at the dialectics between desire and politics. The labouring body becomes the only means of negotiating the relationship between the self and the other, the individual and the collective. For the flower sellers including Jamna, labour enables the possibility of transcending desire and the gendered body. The equally deceived Jamna incorporates Paranthamaraju and immerses herself in the self-divesting rhythms of labour to overcome her longing for him. Her liberation from bodily existence is, paradoxically, possible when she sublimates her desire in the embodied rhythms of work. She tries to excise her femininity by 'sleeping on her chest' to 'destroy her breasts' until she could 'remove them from her body.... She achieves liberation [even as she is] subordinated' by her body (1994: 217).

> The happiness of being consumed and possessed by him is not to be got from the body ... although Paranthamaraju's nerves could give her the demonic strength and this happiness only through the body that was under his control ... [she is] happy like him with his careless, effortless, meaningless sorrow like a bird wandering the town; the danger of all women desiring him, the asceticism of speaking about everything with everyone or saying nothing at all; his needless lamentations; his hunger, starvation.... (1994: 189–90)

For Paranthamaraju, the possibility of a free and authentic life lies in enduring desire and renouncing the longing for self-identity. Since perfect self-identity is impossible without impeding one's immediate awareness of existence, the quest for perfect self-identity is a ceaseless striving that ends only with death. He realizes that true autonomy lies in realizing the interrelatedness between individuals that never promises absolute identity. Paranthamaraju furthers suggests that the quest to become one with the world ultimately becomes a strictly individual journey to an undeterminable destination (non-existence/death?) that can only be facilitated by artistic creativity. Artistic creativity, I argue, has to be understood here not merely as constitutive of an object of art but as a practice that is equally constitutive of subjectivity. If the process of artistic creation blurs and reconfigures the distinction between subject and object, it enables the possibilities of remaking the abject self. Paranthamaraju believes women can never escape their sexual embodiment but can instrumentalize the very bodies that are the source of their oppression to attain potential freedom through creative work. Productive labour, Paranthamaraju suggests is the only means of reconstituting and possibly redeeming an abject world ridden with poverty, disease, and hunger. By the end of the novel, Sarala and Jamna set up an art school where they dedicate themselves to teaching art to children. Before Paranthamaraju leaves for an unknown destination, he tells Sarala,

> Sarala.... This world isn't enough for me. I don't have enough time not just to know, learn and experience but to also transform this world into art and fully embrace it. Happiness isn't important for me. Peace isn't necessary.... I don't want answers to questions.... I don't want to even understand anything. It's enough if I turn into 'that'. 'I' has to become 'that'. Is it possible to mix into everything and become everything? This entire struggle is only to discover a way to do that.... In short, every man has to discover and experience anything on his own. I think it was a mistake to have brought all of you through my way. But I will bring those who are still buried beneath the ground. I will bring them to my painting and with their hands, can and will arrive at a new world.... But I still cannot teach you. I cannot show you the place we are going to. You have to go on your own.... When I searched for someone for that I found Jamna ... now even Jamna is beyond me.... You women cannot get rid of your chastity and go with a man or live with him. I see nature's deceit as an artistic creation. A woman can never escape from herself. Will a man let her be? But I let go of Jamna ... from now on if Jamna wants me I can't go in search of someone for myself.... I can't tell Jamna this ... Jamna escaped with me because she was disgusted by men. I have leaped at her yoni like a womanizer. Unable to bear my own absurdity, I've ... subjugated myself by ... staying hungry. I saw my own form only in hunger. By hunger I don't mean starving. I learnt that it was fasting from desire.... No one can escape from this ... the body will overpower man at every stage. It will defeat you in different ways at every age. The only way I had of escaping from this was fasting ... Jamna! It's your patience that constantly transformed me.... But you're a woman. Yoni-womb—you are an animal that cannot be liberated. But I've still freed you.... I got all my freedom from you. I created a life for you that a woman would desire.... I have drawn your postures into a means.... Women will ... now ... be my noble friends. I'm not going to discover and bring up any more Jamnas. They will liberate themselves. My bits of glass, lime and glue are enough for that.... (1994: 279–83)

Karamuṇṭār Vūṭu (Karamuntar House: 1998)

A Brief History of Caste Violence in the 1990s Tamil Nadu

Prakash's second novel *Karamuṇṭār Vūṭu* emerged in the wake of renewed violence against Paḷḷars, a Dalit caste group found predominantly in the southern districts of Tamil Nadu. This violence needs to be placed against a long history of anti-Paḷḷar violence and exploitation. The southern districts have witnessed a series of incidents of inter-caste violence over the past century. This violence is a product of a whole host of social and economic factors that are both an effect of the structural oppression of certain Dalit communities and their attempt to resist such oppression. The Paḷḷars, who form the largest percentage of Dalit caste groups in these districts, have suffered economic and social injustice at the hands of other backward caste groups including Thevars (which include Kaḷḷars and Maravars, and Agamudaiyars), Nadars, and Vanniyars. Paḷḷars have historically been landless and exploited agricultural labourers working in the fields of their Thevar landlords. One of the root causes for the violent clashes between Paḷḷars and Thevars has been over the fact that Paḷḷars have long been underpaid or paid less-than-minimum wages. Beginning with the 1990s, there was a violent backlash against the growing political and economic autonomy of the Paḷḷars. In the mid-1990s, when they began to support a new political leadership in the form of two independent movements: the Dalit Panthers of India, Tamil Nadu, and the Devendra Kula Vellalar Federation led by Dr K. Krishnasamy, a member of the Tamil Nadu legislative assembly, which became the political party Pudiya Tamilagam in 1998. These new political forces resisted untouchability in its many forms such as the maintenance of separate glasses at tea stalls, condemning the Paḷḷars to their ritually demeaning roles in funerals, and demanded greater access to shared public resources including land and water, greater and equal participation in temple festivals, and so on. The social mobility and political empowerment of Dalits from the early 1990s in terms of the political parties they have formed or the concessions they enjoy from the state through reservations in educational institutions, and the income they receive from relatives working abroad has made them less dependent on their Thevar landlords.[5] This has made them the object of Thevar rancour and violence.

The impunity of the Thevars has largely been attributed to the fact that they represent around 30 per cent of the state's police force. The support of the state police and district officials and the misuse of preventive detention with the Tamil Nadu Goondas Act and the National Security Act, 1980, to arrest Dalit youth has further entrenched their political power. The state itself has been complicit in perpetuating anti-Dalit sentiments by condoning officials guilty of casteism or abetting caste atrocities and by failing to implement anti-caste laws like the Schedule Caste and Scheduled Tribes (Prevention of Atrocities) Act, 1989, has ensured that Dalits never receive the benefits of state protection and justice. Often, Dalit women have been the scapegoats of inter-caste clashes between men over land and property. In fact, sexual assaults and custodial rapes and torture of Dalit women by upper-caste men and the police are intimately tied to Dalit demands over access to public spaces and resources like land and water. Another volatile context for inter-caste violence have been inter-caste affairs, particularly those between Paḷḷar men and women of other castes, which has led to mass killings of Paḷḷars and the destruction of their property. Many of these killings have been politicized by caste-based political parties like Pudiya Tamilagam, but in the process, the Paḷḷars have received little justice and security from the state government.

Since the annual celebration of B.V. Ambedkar's birth centenary celebrations in the early 1990s, there has been a rich plethora of Dalit writing ranging from poems to short stories, political commentaries, and (autobiographical) novels. Prakash's second novel *Karamuṇṭār Vūṭu* (Karamuntar House: 1998) follows a particular strand of Dalit fiction that foregrounds the fraught intersections of caste, gender, and sexuality. Prakash does not limit himself to these intersections, but goes on to explore the historical and social potential of desire to remake marginalized selves. If caste here is understood as an apparatus that regulates sexuality primarily through women's bodies, inter-caste sexual relations, particularly between upper-caste women and lower-caste men are interpreted as a violation of the sexual codes of caste. These illicit relationships have internecine consequences for two of the adversarial caste groups in the novel, the Kaḷḷars and the Paḷḷars. The later chapters of the novel stage an abject scene of massacre that nearly decimates all the men of the two castes, yet it also conditions the possibility of reconfiguring meaning and subjectivity. The novel further explores the rather transformative intimacies between the male Kaḷḷar protagonist and Paḷḷar women, as well as those among women of both castes. The focus lies in the power of the subaltern, here the (lower-caste) woman, to deploy seduction to repeatedly evoke and betray the desire of the upper-caste man, and, in the process, create a community of women predicated on mutual lack and longing. But this shared sense of lack possesses a generative power when it is transmuted or sublimated in acts of creative labour that produce objective validations of its marginalized makers. The emphasis here is on desire as a creative lack that constantly remakes human subjectivity as it strives, albeit unsuccessfully, to overcome the ontological disparity between the self and the other. The novel ends on a note of rebirth and progress: the survivors of the caste war are mostly women of both castes whose desires for one another and the male protagonist are betrayed and sublimated to serve the collective purpose of remaking their destroyed world through an act of land cultivation.

The novel poses the trope of change as a product of the dialectical relationship between a glorious past and imminent ruin. The novel is chiefly structured around two temporal metaphors that embody the dialectical possibilities of historical transformation: the female protagonist Kathayamba and her ancestral home Karamuntar House (that I shall henceforth call KH), a fortified mansion on the banks of the river Kaveri. Like Prakash's other novels, *Karamuṇṭār Vūṭu* begins on a note of decline: the mansion, once a symbol of Kaḷḷar identity and pride, conditions the possibility of its own end and with the inexorable passage of time has to give way to something new. A constellation of interrelated factors are responsible for the imminent destruction of the Karamuntar family and the village of Anjini that survives on the family's largesse. Kathayamba's father and patriarch of KH, Chandras Karamuntar, is an idle man whose extravagant expenditure on temples and political campaigns quickly depletes the ancestral wealth that was supposed to last generations. His generosity to the farmers and peasants of Anjini only precipitates the imminent bankruptcy of the Karamuntar family. The future of the Karamuntar family is also threatened by the absence of a male heir and Chandras lavishes money on countless religious rituals and sacrifices to be blessed with a son. The end of the Karamuntar lineage is anticipated in a flashback that recounts the encounter between Chandras's father, Raghunath Karamuntar's third wife Mangalam and Wesley, an Englishman who is struck by her exotic beauty. He takes a picture of her but when her photograph is later discovered by the family, which has never seen a camera, it taints her reputation forever. She drowns herself and her unborn child in Wesley's swimming pool while he is brutally murdered by Raghunath's Paḷḷar henchmen. The women of the family still mourn what could have potentially been a male heir. KH's imminent destruction is further literalized by its precarious location on the banks of the river Kaveri. We get a sense of KH's mythical glory through Kathayamba's grandmother Thorachiyappayi. Her memories of the house are laced with an unmistakable sense of pride and resolution that protected her family from the flooding waters of the Kaveri which apparently submerged the entire village. Her gratitude to the Paḷḷars (a largely landless agricultural caste of Dalits that have relied for generations on KH for their own survival) for rescuing the family's belongings from the rising waters of the river recalls a past that was also characterized by hierarchical but interdependent inter-caste relations. But the house's ruin is, as always, imminent, as her husband resists the government's threat of demolishing it if it is not relocated from the banks of the river, even as he fails to completely secure it with rocks.

There are internal fissures in the extended family that belie its apparent integrity—Chandras forbids his younger brothers' education lest they later threaten his financial authority. The frustrated brothers struggle to free themselves; while Ramu is rumoured to have an affair with a Paḷḷar woman, Subbu gambles at horse races. The women of the family helplessly turn to religious worship fearing the family's annihilation. But the greatest threat to KH's future existence is the double standard that governs inter-caste sexual relations: while the men of the family have illicit relationships with Paḷḷar women, the Kaḷḷar women are forbidden from straying from the household or their promiscuous husbands. They have to bear the burden of embodying the honour of the Karamuntar family. The crisis in male caste identity towards the end of the novel is a consequence of those Kaḷḷar women who undermine the sexual norms of caste and forge radical intimacies with lower-caste men and women. From these intimacies emerges the possibility of blurring social and sexual hierarchies, rendering them ever reversible.

Desire in Prakash's narratives is ultimately a metaphysical yearning to attain perfect identity. The inevitable failure of such a desire constantly reconfigures the dialectical process of identification to produce subjectivities that are always in the process of becoming. But unlike the Hegelian paradigm where the historical development of the human subject is a teleological one that leads to a totality, Prakash's novels are not oriented towards a totality. The emphasis seems to lie on the productive failure of desire to attain a perfect sense of identity, for it is in the very striving for identity that the transformation of the subject becomes possible. Like in Prakash's other novels, in *Karamuṇṭār Vūṭu* too, deception constitutes the structure of desire whose true object is not the body but the other's desire and recognition. So while desire is seemingly spontaneously directed towards the body, it is not directed towards any particular object, but is always already mediated by the other's desire. Desire here has to be understood as an ideology that moves between the material and the representational; the physical and the metaphysical. The repeated betrayal of desire by the body reveals the generative lack that structures and perpetuates desire and subjectivity. The social potential of desire lies in the shared recognition of this lack that can never promise stable identity or equality.

In Prakash's works, this network of intermediating desires begins and ends with the seductive power of the female body. The female body has to be thought of as a set of productive contradictions that serve the function of constantly remaking the self in relation to the other. The trope of the virile woman whose body signifies both enslavement and potential freedom is central to these narratives. The narrative reveals that Kathayamba's father raised her like a son and, by teaching her to swim in the Kaveri, transforms her into a virile representative of the Karamuntar clan. However, like the other women, she embodies the honour of her family with her piety and virginity. With the passage of time, even she betrays the fractures of self-estrangement as she struggles to break free of her integrity. This becomes evident in her ambiguous desire for her cousin Telakaraju and the impossibility of marrying him without threatening her family's future. Kathayamba was promised in marriage to him and over the years internalizes her family's imperative to marry him. She associates his youth with the pain and blood of sexual maturation, but when she meets him years later she rebukes his violent desire for her, 'Don't touch me Mama! Keep this for the Paḷḷar quarters!' (Prakash 1998: 90). She is unwilling to marry a man whose mother's demand for her share of the ancestral property further threatens the Karamuntar family's precarious existence. As for Telakaraju, he is initially transformed from an urbane and educated youth to a manly and provincial hero when, Kathayamba, to his shame, rescues him from drowning in the river. He is betrayed when Kathayamba spurns his aggressive measures to seek assurances of his masculinity. The early chapters of the novel dramatize the repeated betrayal of desire between these two apparently self-identified individuals. The gratification of desire is suspended in the impasse between identity and difference, autonomy and longing, in the process, compelling Telakaraju and Kathayamba to transcend themselves.

Radical Encounters

Kathayamba spends much of her youth trapped in her own body that later becomes her only means of freedom. She is initially incarcerated in a box used to store paddy following her possession by the goddess Mahamayi when she threatens to kill everyone with a sword. While the prison is initially an attempt to constrain Kathayamba's rebellion against caste, family, and her own uninhabitable body, it later turns into a voluntary refuge from these very strictures. In her solitude, her longing for Telakaraju undergoes a transformation when she substitutes him for the Paḷḷar women he desires. When Selli and Sevathe, two loyal Paḷḷar women who work at the KH, inform Kathayamba of Telakaraju's sexual affair with Selli's sister Manji, Kathayamba claims exclusive possession of Selli and Manji. She projects her imagination of his desire for the Paḷḷar women in her passionate and aggressive intimacy. Kathayamba is amazed by the 'firmness and silkiness' of Selli's 'bronze body' as she lies on her 'oil smeared body ... grasping and pulling her hair'. Selli is equally struck by Kathayamba's body that is 'shaped like a block of sandalwood' (1998: 90). For Kathayamba there is something authentic and authenticating about the resilience and creative potential of the Paḷḷar women's labouring bodies as they endure imprisonment and sexual violence. This becomes clear later when Kathayamba secures Sevathe and Selli from her uncle Ramu whose Paḷḷar henchmen had captured them when they were both trying to escape with Paḷḷar men. Ramu later imprisons Selli in a cell where she bears his illegitimate children until she, like Kathayamba, is possessed by Ayyanar, a local deity, and acquires the supernatural strength to terminate her third pregnancy. Selli's possessions gradually become less frequent before they are miraculously cured by Kathayamba's healing touch, 'she takes care of her like Ramu did when she was imprisoned in his cell' (1998: 91). Although Kathayamba embodies and openly praises the sexual integrity of Kaḷḷar femininity, she secretly envies and eroticizes the youthful and sinewy bodies of the Paḷḷar women, who appear relatively free of moral or social constraints. Their intermediating desires seem to both uphold and temporarily erase bodily markers of caste, reducing them to their bare human selves.

Kathayamba's first intimate experience with a woman is with her young aunt Uma. The neglected wife of a mostly absent husband, Uma disillusions the social stigma around sex, 'they had been deceived that (sex) was something dirty, sinful and bad' (1998: 92). Kathayamba is initially ashamed of having intimate relationships with women but later realizes that her body is not merely 'a mistake' or a hindrance to the possibility of freedom, but the only available means of liberation (1998: 153). In their passionate encounters, desire is understood as a creative need with the potential to reformulate the self in its relation to the other. Uma's 'masculine' seductions are mediated by her longing for her absent husband but in the rising pitch of their passion the husband becomes dispensable. For Kathayamba, Uma's body 'teaches her a way of discovering and domesticating her own body's pleasures' (1998: 92). The following description of their passion suggests the potential of desire to transform their shame and guilt into the empowering mutual recognition of marginality. They resist it even as they are consumed by an agonistic passion that enables them to create a new intersubjectivity although this is still couched in a heterosexual axis.

> Umamahesvari would embrace Kathayamba with her long whip like arms. Then it was an illusion ... it was as though the snake's venom had risen to her head, and gradually spread through her body, blue, to the tips of her fingers like drops and again entered Uma's body like fire. This was initially an enjoyable game! Then it was a hungry need. The two women twisted and turned like two snakes, like a man and woman, not like two snakes but like a snake and a cobra. Subba Karamuntar was no longer needed.... (1998: 152)

Ramu introduces the hitherto abstinent and sexually inexperienced Telakaraju to alcohol and encourages him to satisfy his sexual desires with his loyal Paḷḷar women now that he is destined to a married life without sexual pleasure. But Telakaraju's experience of Manji, one of Ramu's kept women, turns out to be one of a series of deceptive encounters that disillusion his ideal liberal notions of 'equal justice, socialism, gender equality, communism' that bear no resemblance to their lived reality (1998: 51–2). Manji's power over Telakaraju lies in her ability to ironize distinctions necessary for sexual meaning and subjectivity. Manji's seductive enactments of powerlessness both uphold and undermine Telakaraju's belief in equality. Her subservient appeals to his mercy and protection from Ramu who 'keeps her sister, her mother and her aunt' provoke his helpless indignation at an unjust world that inevitably implicates both of them (1998: 52). He is uncontrollably seduced by her professions of exclusive love and devotion even as he is struck by the absurdity of seeking exclusive assurances from a woman who is not sexually exclusive. Manji's assurances partially compensate for Kathayamba's apparent indifference, even as she swears her body and loyalty to Kathayamba and the Karamuntar household that fed her. Her seductive enactments of deference and powerlessness are self-divesting—Telakaraju realizes he is unable to resist his fascination for Manji's 'defiled and sensuous body' even at the risk of 'los[ing] his self' (1998: 55). Even as he feels he has been freed of his privileged caste status, Manji reinforces her apparent faith in a caste and sexual hierarchy. He is unsettled when she questions his sexual experience that reminds him of his failed attempts to sleep with prostitutes. She entitles him to exclusive ownership of her body to pre-empt the possibility of being approached by other Paḷḷar men even as she swears her loyalty to Ramu, 'Sempattu Pallan Kattiri kept pestering me to marry him. I didn't know a prince like you would come to take me away. My sister told me I would struggle if I married a Paḷḷar. I'm always a Kaḷḷar man's Paḷḷar woman' (1998: 52). His unsettling sexual encounter with Manji is compared to a historical act of creation that enables the exchange and dissolution of caste identities and the potential birth of a fundamental human self ostensibly beyond social definition. When Manji appeals to his protection, Telakaraju cries:

'You are my Paḷḷar woman. I will not leave you.' He cried, 'I'm your Paḷḷar' as he leaped and embraced her and slid down. For a long time ... a very long time ... *that Kaḷḷar woman and Paḷḷar man were man and woman, crumbled, and mixed in the event of creation that was centuries old.* Telakaraju grew scared. With what speed Manji had tossed and turned him. Manji had avenged the entire world. Even when Telakaraju was spent ... Manji did not leave him, 'What Karamuntare? Is that all?' ... which Kaḷḷaci will give me [him] this? Can they give him [such pleasure]? ... he turned the empty bottle upside down. 'Wait *ayya* [sir], I'm coming.' ... 'Manji!' '*ayya*' 'Don't call me *ayya*!' 'Then what shall I call you?' 'Say "hey fellow"' 'What *ayya*, are you drunk? I will not call you that.' 'I'm a coward' 'Who said? You're a hero! ...' 'I can't tie you a tali [marry you] *tevatiya*!' 'What are you saying?! You're my husband in this hut.' 'No one will accept it' 'Who has to accept it?' 'My caste people' 'You foolish man! That you say I'm your Paḷḷaci is enough. No fellow can do anything to me. This is above the tali. Just bravely say Manji is your Pallachi. All Kaḷḷar men visit the prostitutes' quarters. Who doesn't? But the Paḷḷaci's story is different! Paḷḷacis only go to Kaḷḷar men.' The world revolved above his head like an *appalam*. 'I studied! I competed with ten fellows. I earned a degree Manji. I had to compete there too. They said 'the Karamuntar woman was for you'. Again I had to compete with eight prospective grooms. That's the story everywhere. You say some fellow called Katiri is competing for you?! ... Can any Karamuntar woman accept me the way you have? Call that a house? Chey! ... Now I've to marry an Amman with sacred ash smeared on her forehead.... (1998: 55–7; italics mine)

Telakaraju has similar radical experiences with two other Paḷḷar women, Nachi and her daughter Sonai. Sonai and Nachi's passion undermine his sexual and political ideals that are a far cry from the reality of illicit intimacies and the greed for wealth and political power. Sonai mockingly compares his moral hypocrisy to the hypocritical claims of political parties that promise to destroy caste and class when they actually entrench social differences in exchange for power. She claims his moral indignation is a veil that conceals his insatiable sexual desire. He is overpowered and emasculated by Sonai's passionate intimacy, which frees him of his urbane trappings and undoes all his political knowledge, leaving him with a sense of nothingness. But it is precisely this experience of nothingness that conditions the possibility of renewing himself to strike a new ontological relationship with the world. Following his transformative experiences with the Paḷḷar women, he loses his faith in monogamy and marriage that interrupt the social potential of desire to alternately underscore and integrate individual differences in a collective. He realizes that Kathayamba, like her ancestral land, can never belong to anyone.

While Telakaraju imagines his transformative encounters with Manji, Nachi, and Sonai have erased the reality of caste; his argument with Kaliyan (Uma's secret Paḷḷar 'lover'), reinstates the explicit and insidious ways in which caste operates through political power and gender relations. By the end, Telakaraju is compelled to disown his privileged caste status; he feels he has been freed to become an 'ordinary' man of 'the earth' who 'has descended to breathe the air' (1998: 139). Kaliyan, the illegitimate son of Chandras's father and a Paḷḷar woman, represents a violation of the integrity of caste. The intimidating sight of Kaliyan's strong and muscular body that reminds Telakaraju of the bronze statues from the Chola period implies the potential of human labour to affect change. Unlike most of the other Paḷḷar men in the village, Kaliyan is an educated man and a member of one of the local political parties. Telakaraju notices his speech betrays no sign of his caste identity. While Telakaraju feels caste does not exist in Anjini, Kaliyan suggests Telakaraju's elite status affords him the privilege of being oblivious or immune to the unchanging reality of caste that structures the existence of KH and Anjini. Electoral politics, he argues, grants the lower castes suffrage and the freedom to speech without investing them with the political power to represent themselves. He berates Telakaraju for his naïve egalitarianism, which contradicts his informal manner of addressing Kaliyan and reinstates the structural hierarchy of caste and class that inevitably separates them.

For Telakaraju, Kaliyan's 'flawless' words and labouring body index his authenticity. He silently admires Kaliyan's affair with Uma, whose courage to pursue an illicit intimacy with a lower-caste man is similarly interpreted as a sign of her authenticity. Kaliyan is one of the few Paḷḷar men who no longer work for the Kaḷḷar families. He realizes that education will not guarantee him a job because of his low caste status. No one is willing to marry their daughter to him because of his political reputation of exhorting the Paḷḷars to rise above their hunger and corruption. He has no hope of an egalitarian future and he expresses his disillusionment at his earlier ideals of 'socialism, communism, the rule of the proletariat, food for everyone, everything for everyone ...' (1998: 132). Despite his mother's entreaties, he refuses to work for free for the Karamuntar family that disavows caste and prides its harmonious and supportive relationship with the

Paḷḷars while forgetting the legacy of its own ancestors' illicit affairs with Paḷḷar women.

For Telakaraju, Kaliyan and Uma's illicit relationship is a reflection of their authenticity but like all the relationships in Prakash's narratives, this one resists sexual definition. Kaliyan confesses they are not in love with each other and suggests their intimacy is really a mutual need for recognition that resists the double standards of caste, marriage, and family. When he rescues Uma from drowning herself, they instantly discover 'their need for each other regardless of their caste difference' (1998: 138). For Kaliyan, the Karamuntar family embodies the sexual hypocrisy of generations of Kaḷḷar men who have had illicit relationships with Paḷḷar women while expecting their wives to remain chaste. Kaliyan empathizes with Uma's loneliness and longing for a husband with whom she shares a comfortable but loveless life. And yet neither Kaliyan nor Uma want to or can escape their entrapped existence without running the risk of triggering a caste war and putting the lives of their people at risk. Kaliyan knows they have no hope of surviving outside Anjini without the support of KH. Uma had rather be discovered by her husband and murdered along with her unborn child. Even the city for Kaliyan is no escape, as its capitalism, by privileging the individual and family pre-empts the possibility of a socialist world.

Through his radical encounters with Manji and Kaliyan, Telakaraju is compelled to acknowledge the impossibility of attaining perfect recognition and identity. If he initially represents the privilege of upper-caste patriarchy, by the end of the novel he is completely disabused of all those binaries like 'man, woman, paḷḷar, kaḷḷar, I, he/she' that necessarily structure the self and meaning without ever guaranteeing identity (1998: 79). All the women around him, including Kathayamba and Manji, appear opaque and inscrutable, leaving him with a sense of self-estrangement. He is sensitized to the inequities that fragment the apparent integrity of KH, and Kathayamba's repeated betrayals only sustain his desire for recognition, ultimately enabling the emergence of a new social order. Telakaraju's transformation is evidenced by his encounter with Mayi, Kaliyan's schoolmate and lover who returns to Anjini after completing her education. She is determined to abolish casteism and make education accessible to everyone. When she sees Telakaraju's strong and unkempt body, she mistakes him for Kaliyan. Their passionate encounter turns into a violent but failed struggle for identity and recognition, a struggle that is likened to the struggle between Kaḷḷars and Paḷḷars. When she discovers Kaliyan's 'affair' with Uma, she substitutes him for Telakaraju. While Telakaraju is seduced by the transparency of her surrender, she is divested of her professional reputation, her political idealism, and her very self.

The climactic event that precipitates the destruction and rebirth of KH and Anjini's village is Kathayamba's 'kidnapping' by Kaliyan to avenge the rape and murder of Selli and Mayi by Ramu for their alleged escape with Telakaraju. Kaliyan kidnaps Kathayamba when she is hiding in the box and 'assaults' her in the very forest where Mangalam drowns herself in shame. Kathayamba is initially ashamed over the loss of her sexual reputation but later realizes she has been ironically freed of her status as a metonym for the Karamuntar family. She experiences the liberating loss of her own caste and sexual integrity when he 'spoils' her and when he reduces her to 'a Paḷḷaci', she 'understands the secret of the body, the death of caste' (1998: 189, 205). Kathayamba begins to enjoy his 'flawless strong body', his 'valor' that only a 'valorous woman' like her can enjoy (1998: 205). Their union mirrors Telakaraju's sexual encounters with the Paḷḷar women in the way it compels the temporary exchange and dissolution of caste identities and reduces them to their human selves. Kathayamba embraces her newfound Paḷḷar status and Kaliyan is transformed by the touch of her virgin body that dissolves their social difference and creates identity. She expresses her willingness to either be united with Kaliyan 'as a man and a woman' shorn of their caste identities or be killed by the Paḷḷar and Kaḷḷar men pursuing them (1998: 205).

Destruction and Rebirth

The internecine violence and destruction that follows Kathayamba's kidnapping is so chaotic and complete that it erases traces of its own origin. The original cause of the war remains shrouded in rumours that fuel an escalating spiral of violence and bloodshed. Paḷḷar and Kaḷḷar women kill themselves; the Brahmans migrate to Madras, while the Muslim businessmen who bought their houses are nowhere to be seen. The Paḷḷars who are divided by their loyalty to the

Kaḷḷar household are killed in their internal war. Paḷḷar and Paṟaiyar (another Dalit caste group) huts are burnt, and innumerable Paḷḷar and Kaḷḷar men of the Karamuntar family are massacred. Most of the survivors of the violence comprise Kaḷḷar and Paḷḷar women who take refuge in KH—the only mute and detached witness to the chaos and destruction of the war. Subbu discovers Uma's rumoured 'affair' with Kaliyan and tortures her to death. In the course of the war certain other inexplicable events occur that exacerbate the event—Chandras's disfigured body is discovered floating on the river, while his brother Ramu's dismembered body is retrieved by some Paḷḷar men. It is not clear whether Ramu's dismemberment is a response to the rape and murder of Selli and Mayi or to the mysterious dismemberment of a Paḷḷar woman. Chandras's dead body is reduced to an abject state; his wives are reluctant to touch him or organize his funeral rituals. His corpse is as neglected as his body was respected when he was alive. Anjini is incinerated by exploding tins of tar. In the bloody massacre and mayhem, bodily distinctions of caste no longer hold. But the abject dissolution of Anjini becomes necessary for its remaking. The destruction coincides with the birth of KH's male heir, as Radha, one of Ramu's wives, gives birth to a son.

The annihilating effect of the war erases any incriminating evidence even as several men and women confess to the killings, making it impossible for the police to identify the guilty. The Kaḷḷars, thanks to their upper-caste status, are never suspected, while the Paḷḷars and the Paṟaiyars are held as potential suspects. Although official reports of the massacre accuse Kaḷḷars of caste prejudice, the police are unable to prove any of the Kaḷḷars or Paḷḷars guilty. Multiple and contradictory interpretations of Chandras's and Ramu's murders emerge. No one confesses to murdering Chandras while his mother Thorachiappayi tells the police that Chandras murdered Ramu to uphold the pride and integrity of his Kaḷḷar ancestors. She is the only person who openly accuses Subbu of murdering Uma for having an affair with a Paḷḷar man. She challenges the police to find witnesses who would confirm charges of casteism. She blames the political parties for fuelling the destruction with their hypocrisy of preaching social equality while entrenching caste differences.

When the Paḷḷars attack Telakaraju, he swirls his knife to confront the men who are transformed into metaphors for social injustice 'he turned the society around him, the enemies around him into metaphors for the enemies to his thoughts ...' (1998: 233). When Sonai tries to warn him of the Paḷḷar men, he confesses to murdering Ramu. He now expresses his wish to be killed by the Paḷḷars to prove the hypocrisy of those who actually win political power and claim there is no caste. He is sure Ramu would have killed him if he had not. He interprets his murder as an act of liberation from his internalization of Ramu and from his Kaḷḷar identity. He is convinced that the Paḷḷar women do not desire him because he is of a higher caste. He does not believe Kathayamba eloped with Kaliyan or that she was kidnapped. There is a realization once the violence ends that this war erupted owing to a mistaken assumption of inter- and intra-caste enmity, which was collectively simulated by the two caste groups. Although the Kaḷḷars and the Paḷḷars accuse each other of casteism, they do not accuse anyone in particular. The internecine strife is mediated by political parties that preach caste equality.

Telakaraju affirms Kathayamba's decision to 'abandon' KH and see it as an opportunity for him to assume her status as an embodiment of its resilience. Telakaraju's dissatisfied desire for Kathayamba conditions the possibility of sublimating his desire towards the social reconstruction of Anjini and KH. Through his generalized simulation of desire for every woman, he provokes and betrays the desires of the Paḷḷar and Kaḷḷar women only to sublimate them towards the renewal of Anjini and KH. His vision of collective reconstructive labour unifies people across castes with the intention of dissolving social difference. Telakaraju is transformed into a hard-working man who labours with his Paḷḷar peasants. He is perceived as the saviour and god of KH and Anjini, as he incorporates the hopes, beliefs, and fears of their people. His scarred body embodies the hypocrisy of caste regulations. He fortifies the now disused mansion from the flooding waters of the Kaveri with a concrete wall. He claims he is no longer a free individual and represents the collective spirit of an abject community. But the last chapter of the novel also suggests that once the reconstruction of the village is underway, the women no longer need Telakaraju, who is then reduced to the status of a dispensable onlooker.

In both these novels, the male protagonist becomes a creative principle that is internalized by a group of women belonging to the

Paḷḷar and Kaḷḷar castes. Both male and female protagonists incarnate the power of desire to seek the other's desire and recognition. The repeated and unavoidable evocation and exorcism of this desire revealed the lack that structures and reproduced all forms of desire and subjectivity. It was in precisely in the striving for identity that the female characters were transformed. The sublimation of their betrayed desire to incorporate the man and his desires, that is, each other, in labour, offered a shared validation of their marginalized selves. This enabled them to potentially transcend themselves and create a new social order on the basis of female collective labour. While Prakash gestures at the empowering and creative bonds among women to the exclusion of the man, the male protagonist still retains the status of a creative principle that in the second novel may also revive a caste and sexual hierarchy. This, of course, leaves open the question of whether all kinds of sexual bonds (including those among men) were inherently inimical to the production of an equitable social order.

Notes

1. My argument draws from Frantz Fanon's understanding of labour in *The Wretched of the Earth* (1968) where labour is a revolutionary instrument that offers value and recognition to the devalued black subject and Alexandre Kojève's *Introduction to the Reading of Hegel: Lectures on the Phenomenology of the Spirit* (1980) where labour is an instrument of freedom and self-transcendence.
2. For a discussion of the desiring subject as a dialectical process, see Hegel (1977), and for desire and its correlate, deception, see Judith Butler (1997).
3. Woman occupies a paradoxical position in Lacan's phallogocentric schema of sexual difference where she has to reassure male integrity (be the phallus) and incarnate a lack in the symbolic order. The power of the woman lies precisely in this, that she can resist incorporation and expose the equally contingent and fragile position of being masculine/have the phallus. Psychoanalytic feminists like Juliet Mitchell, Teresa Brennan, and Toril Moi have critiqued Freud and Lacan's phallogocentrism by distinguishing sexual difference and gender, which has been rethought in and through the feminine, the maternal, and so on.
4. In his essay 'The Subversion of the Subject and the Dialectic of Desire in the Freudian Unconscious' (2002), Lacan gives a structural account of the loss of jouissance (roughly translated as transgressive, uninhibited

enjoyment) with the subject's entry into language. The subject's entry into the symbolic order presupposes the loss of full jouissance (castration) that constitutes him. Jouissance here refers to the subject's unbroken access to the Other, that is, the maternal body, which is lost and becomes impossible once he enters the phallic domain of language. He thus gives up his attempts to be the imaginary phallus for the mother. The possibility of attaining full satisfaction becomes a myth or an ideal whose pursuit keeps the psychic economy alive. If full satisfaction were to be attained, it would spell the subject's psychic death.

5. For a detailed analysis of this renewed culture of violence against Paḷḷar, see Christodas Gandhi (1999).

Conclusion

I began with an analysis of K.P. Rajagopalan's short stories where the segregation of unrelated men and women made the possibility of any form of intercourse suspect. The sensual relationships between men and women in some of his stories encapsulated a whole range of intimacies where it was not always possible to distinguish sexual from other forms of intimacy. The problem that Rajagopalan seems to pose is the possibility of sustaining a cross-gender relationship that resists sexual or romantic definition outside marriage without being stigmatized.

A recurrent trope that ties Rajagopalan to the later writers is triangular desire, where desire and love are mediated differently by one of the men or women characters. If the triangle comprises two men and a woman, there emerges a moral bifurcation where one of the men, invariably the woman's husband, is the 'bad' man and an explicit model of patriarchy, while the other is an intimate or sympathetic acquaintance who respects the woman's body and integrity. There are also instances where Rajagopalan's female characters are sexually assertive and violate sexual norms, even if this violation is a momentary sensual transgression. Power was wielded by these women in the way they both reassured and undermined male integrity.

Many of Rajagopalan's scenarios describe vivid memories of young love and the idealization of unfulfilled love in the lover's heart. Love, in Rajagopalan's stories, mostly remains a sensual or literary ideal that cannot be realized in marriage without transgressing social divisions. Some of the stories show lovers substituting one form of intimacy for another to sustain their relationship. For instance, lovers marry into the same family to exploit kinship as a protective guise, ensuring the possibility of physical proximity and conversational intimacy. Even in the stories where love ends in marriage, there is an attempt to ground this love in an unconditional and reciprocal sense of care that goes beyond (the imperfections of) the body. Blindness sometimes functions as a literal metaphor for this unconditional love.

Janakiraman extends Rajagopalan's scenarios of triangular desire within the space of the household. There is an attempt to blur or soften the moral bifurcation of women in his novels, where there is neither an unequivocal celebration of female chastity nor a condemnation of women who assert their desiring selves. If Janakiraman's male protagonists initially pre-empt the threat of female sexuality by idealizing women, the assertion of female desire de-idealizes women, compelling the protagonists to acknowledge their own desires. Thus, the narrator of *Mōkamuḷ* betrays sympathy for Thangammal, the lonely young wife who expresses her longing for Babu in a letter. Her idealization is lost once she asserts her desire for Babu and she eventually ends her life by drowning in the temple tank. Yamuna, too, is de-idealized when Babu consummates his desire for her and is disillusioned by a sexual act that he thought would bring him absolute recognition and identity. He is then compelled to partly displace his desire for Yamuna to music.

The protagonist of *Ammā Vantāḷ*, Appu, reciprocates the desire of Indu, the young Brahman widow, when the discovery of his mother's affair undermines his exalted perception of her. He is then able to displace his desire and devotion from his mother to Indu. Similarly, in *Cemparutti*, the protagonist Sattanathan is conflicted by his desire for Kunjammal, his widowed sister-in-law who he once thought he would marry, and a sense of familial responsibility. His wife Buvana initially understands Sattanathan's affections for Kunjammal and trusts his loyalty, but later suspects that the two are conspiring against her. She, too, loses her sacrality, and once Kunjammal leaves the family to live with her daughter, Sattanathan turns to socialist literature and social reform as a way of freeing himself of the restrictive ties of family. In *Marappacu,* the last novel by Janakiraman, the female protagonist Ammani embodies a tactile ideal of free love that idealizes touch as a way of transgressing and traversing social and sexual norms and (gender) boundaries. Like in *Cemparutti,* socialism and the working class represent the idealized possibilities of a righteous social order that can be established through touch and labour. Unlike the earlier novels, however, this novel is from the perspective of the female protagonist. Through Ammani, the novel erects and blurs a moral opposition between the male and female characters. Ammani's older lover Gopali is a renowned singer, whose voice initially embodies an ideal of subaltern love that unites women and other marginalized sections of society. Gopali loses his exalted status in Ammani's eyes when she discovers his sexual hypocrisy. He is possessive of her and suspects her of affairs with men even as he pursues affairs with other women. She displaces her exalted perception of him to his nephew Pattabi, who, for Ammani, represents the idealized self-sufficiency of the working-class male body. Ammani is finally disillusioned of her impulse to know and love the world through touch, through her encounters with Bruce, a Vietnam War veteran, and Maragatham, her domestic help. Ammani is impressed by Bruce's self-estranging experience of the war and his attachment to and longing for a sense of home and family. She also internalizes Maragatham, who is posited as an embodiment of domesticity and chastity. When Ammani discovers Gopali's sexual advances towards Maragatham, she feels she has to protect Maragatham and the security of domesticity that she embodies. Ammani realizes that security is possible in a stable and exclusive relationship within the security of the home but without the ritual tie of marriage. She ends up in a committed relationship with Pattabi, although she doesn't marry him.

In my next chapter on the works of Karichan Kunju and M.V. Venkatram, the imagined conflict between sexuality, religiosity, and spirituality is located in the diseased male body. For Kunju, the diseased male body represents sensual and ethical possibilities of being in the world. There is an extension of the idealization of touch from Janakiraman's *Marappacu* to Kunju's *Pacittamāṉiṭam,* where touch is valorized over sight as a reciprocal mode of sensuality that produces an ostensible sense of identity. Touch also has an ethical potential as a way of reaching out to other diseased and disabled outcastes. But ultimately, it neither promises Ganeshan, the protagonist, a sense of recognition, nor does it erase the class and sexual hierarchy that constitute the protagonist's sense of power and responsibility towards other, less-privileged outcastes. I also argued that Ganeshan's longing for spiritual transcendence is only a pretext for a desire for sexual recognition. The protagonist is left with no option but to suffer in the body in the hope of attaining spiritual transcendence.

There is no resolution to the perceived conflict between sexuality and religiosity in Venkatram's *Kātukaḷ*. While *Pacittamāṉiṭam* explored the sensual and ethical possibilities of a visible form of disease, leprosy, Venkatram's novel dramatizes the inner psychological conflict of the debt-ridden male protagonist. The male protagonist of Venkatram's novel is embattled by his illicit desire for various real and imaginary women and his religious devotion to Lord Murugan as well as other deities. The domains of sexuality and religiosity interpenetrate each other in the imaginary world of the protagonist, as the seductive women he supposedly desires merge with seductive goddesses who threaten his masculinity. Thus, signs of self-estrangement share a reversible relationship with signs of self-empowerment.

Mauni's short stories extend the earlier writers' engagement with triangular desires and the perception of the woman as an object of desire and devotion. I note a perceptible shift in the representation of women from his earlier stories, where they merely reassure and/or undermine masculinity, to more complex portrayals as subjects with interiority. Mauni was interested in the ability of the human imagination to produce dreamlike scenarios where desire and longing for a woman can be potentially realized. In his early works, women embody an elusive ideal of devotion that forever defers the fulfilment of the male protagonists' desire. Mauni presents these women as either abandoned by or separated from their husbands or a memory that animates the protagonist's imagination. In his later work, women are young wives of other men or virtuous devadasis who become objects of male desire. These women acquire a greater degree of complexity as they repeatedly evoke and disillusion male desire. But ultimately dissatisfied desire leaves Mauni's male characters feeling self-estranged.

Jeyakantan's works reiterate the possibility of spiritualizing bodily desire in an ascetic companionship between an outcaste man and woman that enables them to transgress and renounce marriage and family. By the end of his second novel *Kaṅkai Eṅkē Pōkiṟāḷ?*, there is an ambiguous reiteration of the social value of female chastity when the female character is purified of her sexual stigma by her 'accidental' drowning in the holy river she was named after. To redress this moral ambiguity, as it were, the second novel idealizes the possibility of partnerships between men and women that are driven by the purpose of reforming the world. Jeyakantan's third novel *Oru Naṭikai Nāṭakam Pārkkiṟāḷ*, tracks the reformation of conjugality through a domestic crisis that creates a form of love that goes beyond gendered and contractual notions of love embedded in marriage and entails the reciprocal exchange of selves. This is a form of love that is ideally characterized by commitment, selfless care, and compassion.

My last chapter on Tanjai Prakash stands out from the earlier writers in the way he depicts the transmutation of betrayed and unsatisfied desire into creative acts of labour and reconfigures marginalized working-class and lower-caste women. Here, desire becomes the instrument of self-transformation, with an emphasis on the female labouring body. Desire as labour enables both individual and collective forms of self-realization in Prakash's texts, thus refocusing attention on the labouring body. If the earlier writers focused on the mind as the site where sexual norms were both upheld and transgressed, Prakash's novels posit the female labouring body as the site of self-transformation.

This book explores a number of modern Tamil texts featuring men and women who do not always conform to established notions of masculinity and femininity. It also engages with the creative possibilities of a desire that is neither limited to nor exhausted by the sexual act. Some of the writers I discuss trace the partial sublimation of desire in spirituality, love, social reform, or acts of creativity that enable individual and collective forms of self-realization. In the extreme and unusual case of Mauni, the very insatiability of desire impels the characters to seek perfection in death. By not limiting desire to the body, these writers indicate the potential of desire to reconfigure meaning and subjectivity. What ties these writers together is that their narratives end in neither violence nor normative marriage, but in the mutual recognition of a lack that in some cases conditions the possibility of forging intimate bonds. Many of the men in the stories discussed are unable to live up to their gender roles because of their desire for more assertive female counterparts who defy sexual norms in the face of love and romantic loss. Further, many of the male protagonists are embattled by their illicit sexuality and their impulse to preserve their spiritual or aesthetic integrity. The women often affirm their sexuality or reorient their desires in love, spirituality, or labour. The accent of these writings thus lies in the reformation and redirection of desire in various sensual and non-sexual forms of activity that open up the possibility of remaking the self.

Historically, writers (male and female) of sexuality in Tamil have either idealized an asexual form of love as the basis for an equal society or renounced desire and marriage altogether. If male writers have valorized chaste women and stigmatized sexually assertive ones, female writers have similarly differentiated men and exhorted women to either forswear and sublimate desire or defy sexual norms. In either case, there has been a suggestion of compassionate bonds between men and women that form the basis for potential emancipation. Rajagopalan or Janakiraman, for instance, betray their sympathies for transgressive characters whose illicit sexuality is not reduced to a marker of their personhood. These transgressions take the form of sensual gestures that momentarily violate social and sexual norms. There is also an attempt in Janakiraman to avoid the moral bifurcation of women on the basis of the indices of their relationships to men as either whores or virtuous wives/virgins. In fact, there is a resemblance in *Cemparutti* between the wife and the other woman (Buvana and Andal) and a moral reversal between the wife and the other woman (Periyanni and Andal). But a common thread in most of these writers, except, possibly, Jeyakantan and Prakash, is the deification of the woman as a feminine essence, what Janakiraman and Mauni call *cakti* in their texts. This may be a reflection of the religious environments of their childhoods as Shaiva Smartha Brahmans literate in Sanskrit and English. Cakti in its form as Ambal is possibly imagined as the equal feminine counterpart of Siva, the two being co-constitutive. But as noted, this awesome conception of woman as cakti is a male projection that inspires the fear of being nothing but an empty ideal. This becomes clear in Mauni where woman is a source of fear and attraction; a seductive ideal that threatens to unsettle the apparent unity and autonomy of man with its own lack. Thus, the idealization of woman is a defence against the threat of being confronted with one's own inadequacy. Janakiraman to an extent succeeded in shedding the male idealization of women through his portrayal of women who desecrated the pieties of motherhood or marriage.

This book's focus on fringe masculinities does not include some of the more obviously marginalized figures of the homosexual or transgendered person. I have not included the memoirs and autobiographies by transgender women who have to engage with the fraught intersections of masculinity and femininity and hierarchies of class and caste. A. Revathi's *The Truth about Me* (2010) is a case in point, where the protagonist is never completely at ease with the male body she was born with or with the female body she later acquires. They both hold their own promises, risks, and disappointments. And the few narratives that feature same-sex male intimacies, including Ambai's short story 'One and Another' and S. Samuthiram's *Vāṭā Malli* (The Unfading Jasmine: 2007) tend to equate male homosexuality with effeminacy so that there is no real difference between homosexual men and (transgender) women. They both apparently face the same forms of oppression and are similarly disadvantaged. There is in other words, nothing 'unmanly' about the men in my book; it is the acknowledgement of their own vulnerability and their caring relationalities with women and other men that renders them unconventional. My attempt to salvage mainstream masculinity from its ideological moorings in violence and oppression emerges admittedly from my own position as a male researcher interpreting literary texts. This is not to say that I am blind to some of the gendered limitations of these texts that are, in the end, representative of their historical and social contexts. My criticism of these texts echoes some explicitly feminist strains of literary criticism in English and Tamil. The sexual valorization or demonization of women cannot go unquestioned, but it is also important to not characterize all men as equal beneficiaries of an androcentric system. If both men and women can be victims and perpetrators of patriarchy, any attempt to resist has to be a politically and culturally contingent strategy that does not perceive men and women as monolithic groups. Men and women can both be variously marginalized and derive different dividends from a patriarchal system. The only way that true emancipation is possible is, I believe, through love as care and vulnerability that can resist sexism and reconfigure gender and sexuality.

I end with a question that has been left unexplored. The idea of love that emerges in the above texts as something separate from desire and pleasure can appear as a patriarchal idea that reinforces the hierarchy of the mind to the body and its gendered implications. The possibility of redeeming the mind–body hierarchy through the transformative potentialities of the labouring body emerges only in the novels of Tanjai Prakash. Prakash fits in with a more widespread and consistent preoccupation with working-class and lower-caste characters post the 1980s. But Prakash is also unusual in the way he interlinks gender, sexuality, and labour to bind and remake marginalized female subjects. Many of his female characters seem to have intimate encounters that are still mediated by the internalized male protagonist and couched in an image of heterosexism. But eroticism still has to be channelized into a higher cultural aim or a productive regime of labour to become the basis of a transformed social order. This begs the question of whether erotics (within or without marriage) can be imagined as an ethical and inclusive basis for society and politics. What about the nature of a social or political order that, for instance, sanctions polyamory for all? Most of the writers I have engaged with betray a discomfort with marriage. Does this imply that marriage ought to be imagined as an irredeemable institution, or do certain kinds of intimacies within marriage have empowering possibilities? On the contrary, are intimacies outside marriage automatically emancipatory? This is clearly not the case in the texts I discuss where the reformation of desire in altruism, spirituality, or cross-gender companionships does not naturally erase sexual difference and hierarchy. What form an egalitarian world would assume in the face of changing articulations of resistance cannot be anticipated and will, of course, be contingent on social and political contexts.

Bibliography

Agamben, Giorgio. 1999. *Remnants of Auschwitz: The Witness and the Archive*, tr. Daniel Heller-Roazen. New York: Zone Books.

Anantha Raman, Sita. 2005. *A Madhaviah: A Biography*. New Delhi: Oxford University Press.

Arondekar, Anjali. 2009. *For the Record: On Sexuality and the Colonial Archive*. Durham: Duke University Press.

Barati, Subramania. 1981. *Peṇ Viṭutalai*. Erode: Nyanabarati.

Barnett, Marguerite Ross. 1976. *The Politics of Cultural Nationalism in South India*. Princeton: Princeton University Press.

Baudrillard, Jean. 1990. *Seduction*, tr. Brian Singer. New York: St. Martin's Press.

Beschi, Constanzo. 1999. *Paramārttakuruviṉ Kataikaḷ* (The Adventures of Guru Paramartha), tr. Bengamin G. Babington. New Delhi: Asian Educational Service.

Blackburn, Stuart. 2003. *Print, Folklore, and Nationalism in Colonial South India*. Delhi: Permanent Black.

Butler, Judith. 1993. *Bodies That Matter: On the Discursive Limits of "Sex"*. New York: Routledge.

———. 1997. *The Psychic Power of Life: Theories in Subjection*. Stanford: Stanford University Press.

Chakraborty, Chandrima. 2011. *Masculinity, Asceticism, Hinduism: Past and Present Imaginings of India*. Bengaluru: Permanent Black.

Chatterjee, Partha. 1990. 'The Nationalist Resolution of the Woman's Question', in Kumkum Sangari and Sudesh Vaid (eds), *Recasting Women: Essays in Indian Colonial History*. New Jersey: Rutgers University Press, pp. 233–53.

Chaudhuri, Maitrayee (ed.). 2005. *Feminism in India*. London and New York: Zed Books.

Chellappa, C.S. 2002 [1974]. *Tamiḻ Ciṟukatai Piṟakkiṟatu*. Chennai: Kalachuvadu Patippakam.

Chopra, Radhika (ed.). 2007. *Reframing Masculinities: Narrating the Supportive Practices of Men*. Hyderabad: Orient Longman.

Chopra, Radhika, Caroline Osella, and Filioppo Osella (eds). 2004. *South Asian Masculinities: Context of Change, Sites of Continuity*. New Delhi: Women Unlimited.

Chowdhury, Indira. 1998. *The Frail Hero and Virile History: Gender and the Politics of Culture in Colonial Bengal*. New Delhi: Oxford University Press.

Collier, Jane Fishburne and Sylvia Junko Yanagisako (eds). 1987. 'Introduction', in *Gender and Kinship: Essays towards a Unified Analysis*. Stanford: Stanford University Press, pp. 1–52.

Connell, R.W. 2005 [1995]. 'Introduction', in *Masculinities*. London and New York: University of California Press, pp. 1–25.

Dentith, Simon. 2000. *Parody*. New York: Routledge.

Derrett, J. and M. Duncan 1973. *Dharmashastra and Juridical Literature*. Wiesbaden: Harrassowitz Verlag.

Devika, J. 2007. 'Lust for Life: Desire in Lalithambika Antharjanam's Writings', in Nivedita Menon (ed.), *Sexualities*. New Delhi: Women Unlimited, pp. 236–54.

Ebeling, Sascha. 2010. *Colonizing the Realm of Words: The Transformation of Tamil Literature in Nineteenth-Century South India*. Albany: State University of New York Press.

Frantz, Fanon. 1967. *Black Skins, White Masks*. New York: Grove Press.

———. 1968 [1963]. *The Wretched of the Earth*. New York: Grove Press.

Fraser, Nancy. 1990. 'Rethinking the Public Sphere: A Contribution to the Critique of Actually Existing Democracy', *Social Text*, 25–6: 56–80.

Freud, Sigmund. 1955 [1915]. *Beyond the Pleasure Principle*. London: The Hogarth Press.

———. 1950. *Civilization and its Discontents*, tr. and ed by James Strachey. New York: W.W. Norton & Company.

———. 1962 [1923]. *The Ego and the Id*, tr. Joan Riviere. New York: W.W. Norton & Company.

———. 1966–74. *The Standard Edition of Complete Psychological Works of Sigmund Freud*, (ed.) James Strachey. London: The Hogarth Press.

Gandhi, Christodas. 1999. 'The Pattern of Abuse: Southern District Clashes in Tamil Nadu and the State's Response', available at www.hrw.org/reports/1999/india/India994-07.htm (accessed on 20 March 2016).

Geetha, V. 2005. 'Periyar, Women and an Ethic of Citizenship', in Anupama Rao (ed.), *Gender and Caste: Issues in Contemporary Indian Feminism*. London and New York: Zed Books, pp. 180–203.

Geetha, V. and S.V. Rajadurai. 1998. *Towards a Non-Brahmin Millennium: From Iyothee Thass to Periyar*. Kolkata: Samya Book Review Literary Trust.

Gilligan, Carol. 1982. *In a Different Voice: Psychological Theory and Women's Development*. Cambridge: Cambridge University Press.

Girard, Rene. 1965. *Desire, Deceit and the Novel: Self and Other in Literary Structure*. Baltimore: John Hopkins Press.

Gopal, Priyamvada. 2005. *Literary Radicalism in India: Gender, Nation and the Transition to Independence*. London and New York: Routledge.

Goux, Jean-Joseph. 1990. *Symbolic Economies: After Marx and Freud*, tr. Jennifer Curtiss Gage. New York: Cornell University Press.

Govind, Nikhil. 2014. *Between Love and Freedom: The Revolutionary in the Hindi Novel*. New Delhi: Routledge.

Grosz, Elizabeth A. 1990. *Jacques Lacan: A Feminist Introduction*. Abingdon: Routledge.

Hegel, G.W.F. 1977 [1807]. *The Phenomenology of the Spirit*, tr. A.V. Miller. Oxford: Clarendon Press.

Irschick, Eugene F. 1969. *Politics and Social Conflict in South India: The Non-Brahmin Movement and Tamil Separatism, 1916–1929*. Berkeley: University of California Press.

———. 1986. *Tamil Revivalism in the 1930s*. Chennai: Cre-A Publishing.

Iyer, Rajam. 1896. *Kamalāmpāḷ Carittiram*. Tiruchirapalli: Intira Patippakam.

Iyer, V.V.S. 1986 [1953]. *Maṅkaiyarkkariciyiṉ Kātal*. Chennai: Alliance Publishing Press.

Janakiraman, T. 1962. *Etaṟkāka Eḻutukiṟēṉ?*. Chennai: Elutu.

———. 1964. *Mōkamuḷ*. Chennai: Minatchi Puttakalayam.

———. 1966. *Ammā Vantāḷ*. Chennai: Minatchi Puttakalayam.

———. 1968. *Cemparutti*. Chennai: Minatchi Puttakalayam.

———. 1975. *Marappacu*. Chennai: Minatchi Puttakalayam.

Jeyakantan, Dandapani. 2001 [1969]. *'Akṉi Piravēcam'* in *Jeyakāntaṉ Ciṟukataikaḷ*. Chennai: Kavita Publications, pp. 1186–91.

———. 1970. *Cila Nēraṅkaḷil Cila Maṉitarkaḷ* in *Jeyakāntaṉ Nāvalkaḷ*. Madurai. Minatchi Puttakalayam.

———. 1971. *Oru Naṭikai Nāṭakam Pārkkiṟāḷ* in *Jeyakāntaṉ Nāvalkaḷ*. Madurai. Minatchi Puttakalayam.

———. 1974. *Oru Ilakkiyavātiyiṉ Araciyal Aṉupavaṅkaḷ* in *A Litterateur's Political Experiences*. Madurai. Minatchi Puttakalayam.

———. 1978. *Kaṅkai Eṅkē Pōkiṟāḷ?* in *Jeyakāntaṉ Nāvalkaḷ*. Madurai: Minatchi Puttakalayam, 187–9.

———. 2001a. *Jeyakāntaṉ Nāvalkaḷ*. Chennai: Computer Printers.

———. 2001b. *Jeyakantan Ciṟukataikaḷ*. Chennai: Kavita Publications.
Jeyamokan, B. 2003a. *Kaṉavukaḷ Ilaṭciyaṅkaḷ*. Chennai: Tamilini Books.
———. 2003b. *Mutal Cuvaṭu*. Chennai: Tamilini Books.
Kailasapathy, K. 1977. *Tamiḻ Nāval Ilakkiyam*. Chennai: Aintinai Patippagam.
Kannabiran, Kalpana and Vasanth Kannabiran. 2002. *De-Eroticizing Assault: Essays on Modesty, Honour and Power*. Kolkata: Stree.
———. 2005. 'Caste and Gender: Understanding Dynamics of Power and Violence', in Anupama Rao (ed.), *Gender and Caste: Issues in Contemporary Indian Feminism*. London: Zed Books, pp. 249–60.
Kojève, Alexandre. 1980 [1969]. *Introduction to the Reading of Hegel: Lectures on the Phenomenology of Spirit*, tr. James H. Nichols, Jr. Ithaca: Cornell University Press.
Krishnan, Rajam. 1973. *Rōjā Itaḻkaḷ*. Chennai: Pari Puttaka Pannai.
———. 1979. *Karippu Maṇikaḷ*. Chennai: Pari Puttaka Pannai.
———. 1982. *Cēṟṟil Maṉitarkaḷ*. Chennai: Pari Puttaka Pannai.
———. 1988. *Maṇṇakattu Pūntuḷikaḷ*. Chennai: Takam.
Kristeva, Julia. 1982. *The Powers of Horror: An Essay on Abjection*, tr. Leon S. Roudiez. New York: Columbia University Press.
Krithika. 1966. *Vācavēsvaram*. Chennai: Nulakam Publishers.
Kumar, Dilip. 1992. *Mauṉiyuṭaṉ Koñca Tūram*. Chennai: Vanati Patippagam.
Kunju, Karichan. 1978. *Pacittamāṉiṭam*. Chennai: Vanati Patippakam.
———. 1990. *Ku.Pa.Ra*. Chennai: Vanati Patippagam.
Lacan, Jacques. 1998. 'The Subject of the Unconscious', a seminar.
———. 2002. *Ecrits: A Selection*. New York: W.W. Norton & Company.
Levinas, Emmanuel. 2003. *On Escape*, tr. Bettina Bergo. Stanford: Stanford University Press.
Madhavaiya, A. 2002 [1898]. *Patmāvati Carittiram*, tr. Meenakshi Thyagarajan. New Delhi: Katha Books.
———. 2005. *Clarinda: A Historical Novel*. New Delhi: Sahitya Akademi.
Marikkar, Mukammatu Kacim Sitilevai. 1974. *Acan Pe Carittiram*. Tiruccirappalli: Jamal Mukamatu Kalluri.
Mauni. 1991. *Mauṉiyiṉ Kataikaḷ*. Chennai: Pikak Patippakam.
———. 1997. *Fictions: Mauni*, tr. Lakshmi Holmström. New Delhi: Katha Books.
Menon, Nivedita (ed.). 2007. *Sexualities*. New Delhi: Women Unlimited.
Merleau-Ponty, Maurice. 2012 [1962]. *Phenomenology of Perception*, tr. Donald A Landes. Abingdon: Routledge.
Mitchell, Juliet and Jacqueline Rose (eds). 1982. *Feminine Sexuality: Jacques Lacan and the école freudienne*, tr. Jacqueline Rose. New York: W.W. Norton & Co.
Murugan, Perumal (ed.). 2013. *Ku.Pa.Rā. Ciṟukataikaḷ*. Nagercoil: Kalachuvadu Publications.

Osella, Caroline and Filippo Osella. 2006. *Men and Masculinities in South India*. London and New York: Anthem Press.

Pillai, Samuel Vedanayakam. 1969 [1859]. *Nītinūl*. Chennai: Vurthamanatharunghini Press.

———. 1978 [1870]. *Peṇ Mati Mālai Peṇ Kalvi Peṇ Maṉam*. Tiruccirappalli: Vetanayakam Pillai Ninaivukkulu, Virpanai urimai, and Tamil Ilakkiya Kalakam.

———. 1991 [1879]. *Piratāpa Mutaliyār Carittiram*. Nakapattinam: Imaya Patippakkam.

Pillai, Saravanmuthu. 1902 [1895]. *Mōkaṉāṅki*. Chennai: V.N. Jubilee Press.

———. 1979. *Cukuṇā Cuntari*. Chennai: Vanavil Piracuram.

Prakash, Tanjai. 1994. *Kaḷḷam*. Chennai: South Asian Books.

———. 1998. *Karamuṇṭār Vūṭu*. Nakappattinam: Virpanai Urimai, Kumari Patippakam.

———. 2002. *Mīṉiṉ Ciṟakukaḷ*. Chennai: Kavya Publishing House.

———. 2003. *Tañcai Pirakāṣ Kaṭṭuraikaḷ*. Chennai: Kavya Publishing House.

———. 2004. *Tañcai Pirakāṣ Kataikaḷ*. Chennai: Kavya Publishing House.

Puri, Jyoti. 1999. *Woman, Body, Desire in Post-Colonial India: Narratives of Gender and Sexuality*. New York: Routledge.

Ragunatan, T.M.C and Ponneelan. 1994. *Muṟpōkku Ilakkiya Iyakkaṅkaḷ*. Chennai: NCBH.

Rajesh, V. 2014. *Manuscripts, Memory and History: Classical Tamil Literature in Colonial India*. Cambridge: Cambridge University Press.

Rajkautaman. 1992. *Eṇpatukaḷil Tamiḻ Kalāccāram*. Bengaluru. Kavya Publishing House.

Ramasami, I.V. Thanthai Periyar. 1981. *Collected Works of Thanthai Periyar E.V. Ramasami*. Chennai: Anaimuthu.

Ramaswamy, Sumathi. 1997. *Passions of the Tongue: Language Devotion in Tamil India 1891–1970*. Berkeley, California: University of California Press.

Ramiah, B.S. 1980. *Maṇikkoṭi Kālam*. Chennai: Manivacakar Nulagam.

Rao, Anupama. 2005. 'Understanding *Sirasgaon*: Notes towards Conceptualizing the Role of Law, Caste and Gender in a Case of "Atrocity"', in Anupama Rao (ed.), *Gender and Caste: Issues in Contemporary Indian Feminism*. London: Zed Books, pp. 276–309.

Revathi, A. 2010. *The Truth about Me*, tr. V. Geetha. New Delhi: Penguin Books.

Rose, Margaret A. 1979. *Parody/Meta-Fiction: An Analysis of Parody as a Critical Mirror to the Writing and Reception of Fiction*. London: Croom Helm.

Samuthiram, S. 2007. *Vāṭā Malli*. Chennai: Aruvi Publishers.

Sarma, C.V. *Gurusami*. 1893. *Pirēmakaḷāvatiyam*. Chennai: Vanavil Piracuram.

Sartre, Jean Paul. 2003 [1956]. *Being and Nothingness: An Essay on Phenomenological Ontology*, tr. Hazel E. Barns. London: Routledge.

Satish, V. (ed.). 2011. *Ku.Pa.Rā. Kaṭṭuraikaḷ*. Chennai: Adaiyalam Publishers.

Scott, Darieck. 2010. *Extravagant Abjection: Blackness, Power and Sexuality in the African American Literary Imagination*. New York: New York University Press.

Sedgwick, Eve. 1985. *Between Men: English Literature and Homosocial Desire*. New York: Columbia University Press.

Seshadri, K.G. 2007. *Kariccān Kuñcu*. New Delhi: Sahitya Akademi.

Shah, Nandita and Nandita Gandhi. 1992. *The Issues at Stake: Theory and Practice in the Contemporary Women's Movement in India*. New Delhi: Kali for Women.

Sinha, Mrinalini. 1995. *Colonial Masculinity: The 'Manly Englishmen' and the 'Effeminate Bengali' in the Late Nineteenth Century*. New York: Manchester University Press.

Srinivasan, Perundevi. 2014. 'Nationalist Fabric, Gendering Threads: Notes on Subramaniya Barati's Draupadi', *International Journal of Hindu Studies*, 18 (1): 1–31.

Subramanian, Narendra. 1999. *Ethnicity and Populist Mobilization: Political Parties, Citizens, and Democracy in South India*. Delhi and New York: Oxford University Press.

Thomas, Calvin. 2008. *Masculinity, Psychoanalysis, Straight Queer Theory: Essays on Abjection in Literature, Mass Culture, and Film*. New York: Palgrave Macmillan.

Trautmann, Thomas R. 2006. *Languages and Nations: The Dravidian Proof in Colonial Madras*. Berkeley: University of California Press.

Unknown. 1986. *Vacaṉa Campiratāya Katai*. *International Journal of Tamil Studies*, 30 (12): 1–14.

Vallikannan. 1986. *Sarasvati Kālam*. Chennai: New Century Book House.

Vanita, Ruth. 2005. *Gandhi's Tiger and Sita's Smile: Essays on Gender, Sexuality and Culture*. New Delhi: Yoda Press.

Vanita, Ruth and Salim Kidwai (eds). 2000. *Same-Sex Love in India: A Literary History*. New York: St. Martin's Press.

Venkatachalapathy, A.R. 2006. *In Those Days There Was No Coffee: Writings in Cultural History*. New Delhi: Yoda Press.

Venkatram, M.V. 1992. *Kātukaḷ*. Civakankai: Annam Publications.

Žižek, Slavoj. 2008 [1989]. *The Sublime Object of Ideology*. London: Verso.

Zvelebil, Kamil V. 1986. 'The First Six Novels in Tamil', *International Journal of Tamil Studies*, 30: 12.

Index

About the Author

Kiran Keshavamurthy is currently assistant professor of Cultural Studies at the Centre for Studies in Social Sciences, Calcutta. He completed his PhD in modern Tamil literature at the Department of South and Southeast Asian Studies at the University of California, Berkeley. His interests comprise modern Indian literature and caste and sexuality studies. His publications include 'Action, Habit and Literature: Sundara Ramasami's *J.J.: Some Jottings*' (*Jadavpur Journal of Comparative Literature*, 2014), 'Violence and the Dalit Woman' (*Journal of Tamil Studies*, 2012), and 'The Figure of the Prostitute in the Works of G. Nagarajan and Dandapani Jeyakantan' (*Mattruveli*, 2010).